South Dakota

T. D. Griffith
Photography by Paul Horsted

COMPASS AMERICAN GUIDES
An Imprint of Fodor's Travel Publications, Inc.

South Dakota
Second Edition

Copyright © 1998 Fodor's Travel Publications, Inc.
Maps Copyright © 1998 Fodor's Travel Publications, Inc.

LIBRARY OF CONGRESS CATALOGING-IN-PUBLICATION DATA
   Griffith, Tom. 1958-
   South Dakota/ T.D. Griffith: photography by Paul Horsted.—2nd ed.
      p.   cm. —(Compass American Guides)
      Includes bibliographical references and index
      ISBN 1-878867-47-4
      I. Title.   II. Series: Compass American guides (series)
   F649.3.G74 1998   97-38560
   917.8304'33—dc21   CIP

Editors: Kit Duane, Julia Dillon,   Designers: Christopher Burt,
   Deke Castleman, Jessica Fisher   Candace Compton-Pappas
Managing Editor: Kit Duane   Map Design: Eureka Cartography and Mark
Photo Editor: Christopher Burt   Stroud, Moon Street Photography
First published in 1994 by Compass American Guides,
5332 College Avenue, Suite 201, Oakland, CA 94618
Production House: Twin Age Ltd., Hong Kong   Printed in China
10 9 8 7 6 5 4 3 2 1

Photographs by Paul Horsted are © 1994, 1998 Paul Horsted, All Rights Reserved.

The Publisher gratefully acknowledges the following institutions and individuals for the use of their photographs and/or illustrations on the following pages: **Center for Western Studies at Augustana College,** pp. 21, 29, 41, 45, 48, 51, 54, 178, 179, 191, 202, 214, 233, 271, 282; **National Museum of American Art, Smithsonian Institution, Gift of Mrs. Joseph Harrison, Jr.,** pp. 23, 34, 35, 38-39; **Library of Congress,** pp. 24-25, 49, 55, 206; **South Dakota State Historical Society, Pierre,** pp. 26, 31, 36, 42, 43, 46, 47, 57, 63, 67, 74, 76, 81, 83, 95, 110, 123, 124, 139, 146, 147, 154, 163, 238, 240, 241, 255, 285; **Adams Museum, Deadwood,** pp. 53, 209; **Underwood Photo Archives,** p. 59; **Denver Public Library,** p. 88; **Adelheid Howe,** p. 94; **South Dakota Art Museum, Brookings,** p. 105; **Georgia State University Foundation, Pullen Library,** p. 115; **National Archives,** p. 144; **Paul Jones,** pp. 145, 184, 188, 208, 269; **Buffalo Bill Historical Center, Cody, WY,** pp. 156, 204; **Marquette University Archives, Milwaukee,** pp. 162, 164, 183; **National Park Service,** p. 216. We also wish to thank the following individuals for their contributions to this book: **Ruth Johnston** for her buffalo recipe; **Rex Alan Smith** for his expert reading; **Werner L. Janney** for proofreading; **Claudia Nicholson** and **Marvene Riis** of the South Dakota State Historical Society in Pierre; **Harry Thompson** from the Center for Western Studies; **Candace Compton-Pappas** for illustrations.

   Thanks also to the **South Dakota Department of Tourism** for permission to use those images by Paul Horsted which reside in their collection.

*For Charles and Patricia, who taught me
that any road is negotiable at the proper speed.*

C O N T E N T S

Literary Extracts

Topical Essays

Maps

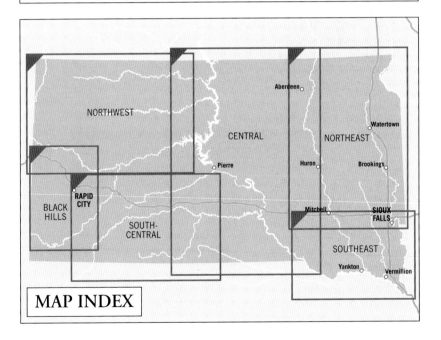

MAP INDEX

FACTS ABOUT SOUTH DAKOTA

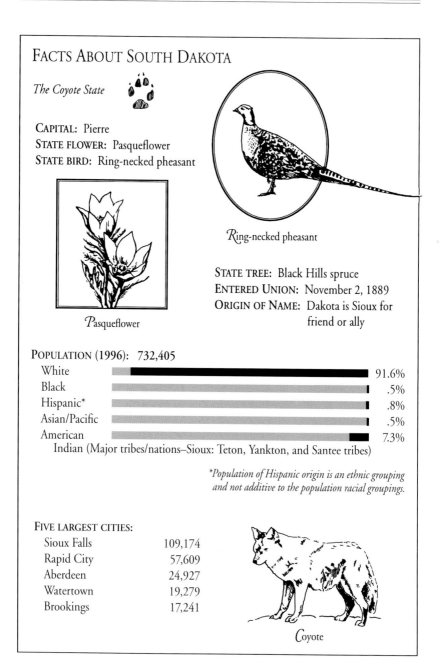

The Coyote State

CAPITAL: Pierre
STATE FLOWER: Pasqueflower
STATE BIRD: Ring-necked pheasant

*R*ing-necked pheasant

*P*asqueflower

STATE TREE: Black Hills spruce
ENTERED UNION: November 2, 1889
ORIGIN OF NAME: Dakota is Sioux for friend or ally

POPULATION (1996): 732,405

White	91.6%
Black	.5%
Hispanic*	.8%
Asian/Pacific	.5%
American Indian (Major tribes/nations–Sioux: Teton, Yankton, and Santee tribes)	7.3%

*Population of Hispanic origin is an ethnic grouping and not additive to the population racial groupings.

FIVE LARGEST CITIES:

Sioux Falls	109,174
Rapid City	57,609
Aberdeen	24,927
Watertown	19,279
Brookings	17,241

*C*oyote

*B*lack Hills spruce

ECONOMY:
Principal industries:
  agriculture, services, manufacturing
Principal manufactured goods:
  food and kindred products, machinery,
  electric and electronic equipment
Chief crops (1995):
  corn, oats, wheat, sunflowers, soybeans,
  sorghum
Per capita income (1996): $21,516
Tourism (1996): Travelers' impact $1.25 bil.

GEOGRAPHY:
Size: 77,116 sq. miles (197,417 sq. km)
Highest point: 7,242 feet (2,202 m) at Harney Peak,
                                 Pennington County
Lowest point: 966 feet (294 m) at Big Stone Lake,
                                 Roberts County

CLIMATE:
Highest temperature recorded: 120°F (49°C) at Gannvalley on
                                 July 5, 1936
Lowest temperature recorded: -58°F (-50°C) at Mcintosh on
                                 February 16, 1936

Wettest place:
29.99" (76.2 cm) annual rainfall at
  Deadwood in Lawrence County

Driest place:
12.29" (31.2 cm) annual rainfall at
  Ludlow in Harding County

FAMOUS SOUTH DAKOTANS:
Sparky Anderson ◆ Oscar Howe ◆ "Calamity Jane" ◆ Cheryl Ladd
Crazy Horse ◆ Al Neuharth ◆ Dr. Ernest O. Lawrence
George McGovern ◆ Sitting Bull ◆ Mary Hart ◆ Billy Mills

SOUTH DAKOTA

0 10 20 30 40 50
miles

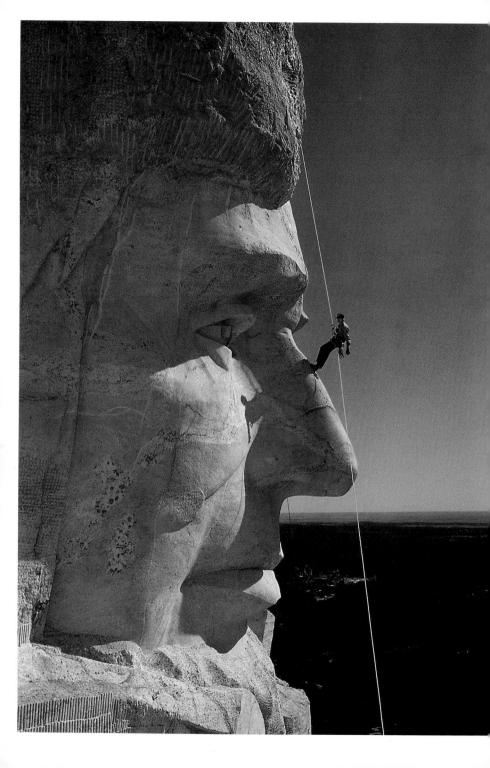

ACKNOWLEDGMENTS

THERE IS NOT ROOM ENOUGH on these pages to thank the South Dakotans—friends and strangers—who lent me support, and sometimes directions, during the months of traveling and writing. In a state where you're a newcomer unless your grandparents are buried in the local cemetery, I was welcomed and assisted time and again. Of my many helpers, several stand out: Jim Kuehn, former editor of the *Rapid City Journal;* Rex Alan Smith, a wonderful writer and friend; Sheri Sponder, a research librarian with her hands on the pulse of South Dakota; historians Keith and Bonita Cochran; and Larry Atkinson, whose good nature is cherished and admired. Others helped as well, whether in tracking down leads or pointing me in the direction of the next great South Dakota vignette: Bonnie Krueger, Deb Fowler, Paul Putz, Gordon Garnos, Jerry Olson, Terry Reetz, Susan Edwards, Dee Dee Rapp, Kristen Brost, Robb DeWall, Jim Popovich, Bill Honerkamp, and the entire staffs of the South Dakota Department of Tourism, the Rapid City Public Library, the South Dakota Heritage Center, and the Adams Museum of Deadwood. Commendations are due my editors, Kit Duane and Julia Dillon, and my publishers, Chris Burt and Tobias Steed, for patience unbecoming their profession. It is also certain that this book would not have been fit for public consumption without the support of friends David and Nancy Bertocchi, Karl and Louie Lalonde, and photographer Paul Horsted, whose brilliant eye and camera have focused on the heart of this great state. And finally, my loving wife Nyla, whose gentle nudging is reflected in the copyright date, as well as in every page.

(left) National Park Service worker Karl Bachman climbs down the face of Abe Lincoln during an inspection of cracks at Mount Rushmore.

INTRODUCTION

WANDER THROUGH SOUTH DAKOTA today and you'll explore a land which has been home to great Indian warriors, French fur traders, prairie settlers, and gold prospectors. Today, vast regions of the state remain sparsely settled, its towns often no more than meeting places for farmhands or cowpokes. Buffalo are rare now, the once-wild rivers have been tamed, and much of the state's native grassland has been replaced by crops, yet quiet South Dakota still sheepishly claims the title "America's Outback."

Driving across their state, South Dakotans can see almost too much sky, more than a hundred miles to the horizon. This landscape offers some lovely surprises—millions of acres of rugged badlands, river breaks, fertile farmland, and an emerald oasis known as the Black Hills. To truly see South Dakota, travelers must get off the interstates, the well-worn ribbons of concrete known as I-90—the 380-mile (612-km)-long roadway bisecting the state east to west—and I-29, which stretches 245 miles (394 km) north to south in extreme eastern South Dakota, and wander through small towns and visit numerous parklands and lakes.

The people who live here are proud of their heritage and of the livings they carve from the prairies and plains. If South Dakota has hosted some of the most colorful characters of the Old West—Sitting Bull, Calamity Jane, and Wild Bill Hickok—the state has also been home to some of the nation's most industrious and generous people. More South Dakotans are employed in agriculture than any other occupation. Nearly half South Dakota's residents live on the state's 35,000 farms, and farms and ranches cover about nine-tenths of the state. Most farmers and ranchers are also hospitable to a fault—on the back roads, they'll wave at you from their battered pickup trucks (and will know you're from out of town if you don't wave back). Each fall, rural South Dakotans welcome urban neighbors and tourists at fairs and festivals celebrating the state's heritage. At colorful powwows and buffalo roundups, South Dakotans recall their ancestors—the Sioux warriors, sodbusters, and frontiersman whose pride and tenacity are trademarks of the folks you'll meet there today.

(left) Prairie in full spring bloom in Custer State Park.

(following pages) The Badlands seem magical on starry moonlit nights.

H I S T O R Y

SOUTH DAKOTA WAS, OF COURSE, for millions of years undefined by the rectangle that marks it off as the fortieth state of the Union. Its prehistory witnessed shifting climatic zones, changes in the course of the Missouri River that divides it, and the evolution of its flora and fauna. To the east of the Missouri were lowland prairies, to the west the arid sweep of the continent's dry, high plains region. Within and above the prairies evolved a complex natural life we're only now beginning to appreciate, but most evident were its great herds of buffalo and millions of migratory birds that nested in lakes and waterways, as they flew south from Alaska and north from the warm Caribbean.

Into this vast sweep of land came gradually the first humans, those pre-historic people we now define rather academically as "Paleo-Indians"—hunters whose ancestors had followed game across the land bridge of the Bering Sea from Asia, and eventually, over centuries, migrated south into the American continent. By the time European explorers arrived in the area, South Dakota was peopled by the Arikara (or Ree), Cheyenne, and Sioux Indians, whose descendants inhabit South Dakota still. Magnificent horsemen, fearless warriors, they were the proud possessors of an independent life and a world they found abundant.

After the early 1600s, history as we know it began to accelerate. Explorers sent by the great European powers came to claim territory and look for commercial opportunities. Twenty-seven years after he wrote the Declaration of Independence, Thomas Jefferson, as President of the fledgling United States of America, sent American explorers Lewis and Clark to map this region in 1803. By the end of the nineteenth century, thousands of Europe's poor and America's pioneers were moving into the region, with perspectives and dreams of their own, and their ambitions clashed with those of the Sioux, Cheyenne, and Arikara. As immigrants built fences, settled towns, and often prospered, both Indian culture and the great herds of buffalo were confined and crushed.

In the twentieth century, South Dakota's history moved on with the rest of the nation's, as its citizens watched the end of the Gilded Age, suffered through the dustbowl, the Depression, and two world wars. In the volatile 1960s and '70s, the Sioux, now living on reservations, began to gather strength and fight for cultural renewal, and today they remain one of the most powerful and well-known of all

(opposite) A photograph of an unidentified Sioux tribal leader from the extensive archives at the Center for Western Studies at Augustana College in Sioux Falls.

America's tribes. In the late twentieth century South Dakota has emerged as a place holding fast to many of the best values imbedded in the American psyche as well as adding its spark to the nation's entrepreneurial energy.

■ EARLY INDIAN ERA

Anthropologists now estimate that up to four great migrations of four very different groups of people crossed the land bridge from Asia over a period of 30,000 years and covered the North American continent. The first clear indications we have of a human presence in South Dakota are the remains of a "Paleo-Indian" who hunted in the prairies over 9,000 years ago, and was found buried with skinning knives and finely crafted spear points. This small, five-foot five-inch (1.6-m tall) hunter probably led buffalo "surrounds," in which the animals were prodded to stampede, then steered over the edge of a butte. That Indians were using buffalo hide to make tepees 2,500 years ago is evident from carbon-dated tepee rings from that era that can still be seen in Custer State Park. More recent Plains Villager sites dating back 1,000 years have been discovered along the Missouri and other South Dakota rivers. These people were both hunters and gardeners—planting maize, crafting earthenware ceramics, and constructing large earth-lodge towns surrounded by ditches and dirt walls to fend off enemies. Those inhabiting the fertile land near the Missouri river used bison scapulae hoes to plant maize and other plants; those further west relied more heavily on bison hunting. Artifacts which belonged to the semi-nomadic Mound Builders and date about A.D. 500-800 have been uncovered in the northeastern part of the state. These people took great care in burying their dead: the body was often wrapped, and the departed's most precious possessions—fine spears, flints, tools, and hide pouches—were buried alongside in large earthen mounds.

During the millennia, Indian tribal groups ebbed and flowed across and up and down the North American continent. In most cases, tribes settled their conflicts peacefully. When warfare could not be avoided, most Plains Indians fought in ritualized battles and small ambushes, killing few people. But in A.D. 1325, near present-day Crow Creek, 500 Arikara men, women, and children were massacred in one of the most ruthless examples of pre-Columbian tribal violence in the archaeological record. Most likely feeling the pinch of increasing population and the concomitant depletion of natural resources, the attackers stormed the village, burning it and mutilating the dead. The remains were discoverd and excavated on an archaeological dig by the University of South Dakota in 1978.

By 1500, the Arikara (or Ree) Indians were inhabiting the state. The Sioux (or Lakota) Indians began migrating from the Mille Lacs region of Minnesota into South Dakota in the 1700s, in turn driving the Arikara north and west. For a good 150 years the Sioux reigned supreme in the Dakotas. Organized into three major tribes (Teton, Yankton, and Santee), smaller bands, and clans or "tiyospaye," they followed strict rules of behavior that provided for the well-being of the community and the care of children. As horsemen and hunters they were unparalleled, as warriors fearless and ruthless.

Though fighting for land among themselves, by the seventeenth century many tribes were also being pressured from the east by European settlers. The British settlers who came to Jamestown in 1607, two hundred and fifty years before pioneers moved in force into South Dakota, recorded seeing the Sioux and buffalo in

"Prairie Meadows Burning" by frontier artist George Catlin.
(National Museum of American Art, Smithsonian Institution)

(following pages) A stunning photograph by John Grabill of a
Brule Indian village in 1891. (Library of Congress)

the Shenandoah Valley. During those centuries, the Sioux and many other groups forged their way west, battling for living and hunting space. They would eventually be pushed aside, defeated by the superior numbers and arms of white settlers. With their demise a wild, uncompromising culture—marked by buffalo hunts and trance-inducing Sun Dances—began to flicker and fade.

■ EXPLORERS AND TRADERS

In the seventeenth and eighteenth centuries, the French sent explorers and Jesuits to plant their feet firmly on bleak bits of land and, surrounded by curious Indians who didn't understand French, claim territory in the name of their king. It was in this spirit that, in 1743, Francois and Joseph La Verendrye claimed the region near present-day Fort Pierre in central South Dakota for Louis XV, a monarch almost 5,000 miles (8,130 km) away who wore white wigs and satin pants, and was as famous for his indolence as for his mistresses. The La Verendryes left behind a metal plate attesting to their claim, which presumably everyone else ignored.

Thirty-two years later, in 1775, French Canadian mountain man Pierre Dorion came up the Missouri River from St. Louis, stopped near Yankton, and married into the Yankton Sioux tribe. In the 1790s Jacques d'Eglise and Joseph Garreau,

The La Verendrye Plate, originally buried in 1743, was discovered by children playing on a hillside outside of Pierre in 1913. (South Dakota State Historical Society, Pierre)

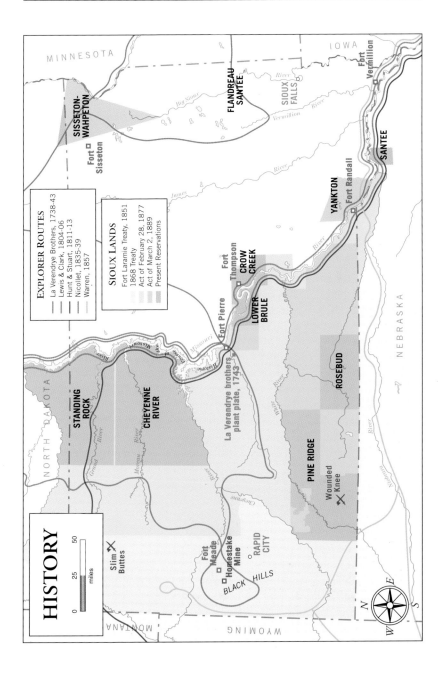

HISTORY

0   25   50
miles

Slim Buttes ✗

EXPLORER ROUTES
La Verendrye Brothers, 1738-43
Lewis & Clark, 1804-06
Hunt & Stuart, 1811-13
Nicollet, 1835-39
Warren, 1857

SIOUX LANDS
Fort Laramie Treaty, 1851
1868 Treaty
Act of February 28, 1877
Act of March 2, 1889
Present Reservations

MINNESOTA

IOWA

SISSETON-WAHPETON

Fort Sisseton

FLANDREAU SANTEE

SIOUX FALLS

River

Fort Vermillion

SANTEE

Big Sioux

River

Vermillion River

James

River

YANKTON

Fort Randall

Fort Thompson

CROW CREEK

LOWER BRULE

Fort Pierre

La Verendrye brothers plant plate, 1743

River

ROSEBUD

River

NEBRASKA

Missouri

River

STANDING ROCK

CHEYENNE RIVER

Grand River

Moreau River

Bad River

White River

PINE RIDGE

Wounded Knee ✗

NORTH DAKOTA

Belle Fourche

Cheyenne River

Fort Meade ✗

Homestake Mine

RAPID CITY

BLACK HILLS

Niobrara

River

MONTANA

WYOMING

N
W   E
S

SIOUX NATION

Sioux Indians comprise the second most populous language family north of Mexico (the largest being the Algonquian) and take their name from the largest and best-known confederacy of that group, the Sioux (or Lakota). Their name is an abbreviation of "Nadowessioux," a French corruption of "Nadowe-is-iw"—Ojibwa for "snake," or "enemy." The Sioux in western South Dakota refer to themselves as "Lakota," or "an alliance of friends;" those in the east call themselves "Dakota."

Before their contact with non-Indians, the Sioux occupied much of the land extending from the Mississippi north from the Arkansas River, and west almost to the Rocky Mountains. Those in Arkansas were first encountered by Spanish explorer Hernando de Soto in 1541. The Dakota—the Sioux tribe now in eastern South Dakota—lived on the east side of the Mississippi between the Wisconsin River and Mille Lacs; the Winnebago and other northern Sioux tribes lived in Canada, toward Lake Winnipeg, and their lives were recorded by Jesuit missionaries in the 1640s and 1650s. Another group of Sioux lived in the South, occupying parts of Virginia, Mississippi, and the Carolinas; colonial Virginians recorded Sioux living in the Shenandoah Valley early in the seventeenth century.

In the first half of the eighteenth century, the Ojibwa Indians, who'd been supplied by the French with guns, forced the Dakota Sioux out of present-day Minnesota, pushing them onto the South Dakota plains. They weren't the only group that were forced to move: the Chiwere Sioux tribes split from the Winnebago and also moved toward the Missouri River; and the Siouan Mandan and Hidatsa tribes were pushed from the upper Missouri by the migrating Dakota. Yet by the end of the eighteenth century, the Sioux were at the height of their power, living on a vast tract of land covering about 80 million acres, the center of which lies in present-day South Dakota.

These many inter-related Sioux tribes did have some things in common. They were divided into bands, then into still smaller groups called "tiyospaye," an extended family whose members lived together. Children, elders, and the sick were cared for by the entire tiyospaye, and decisions were left to the older, respected members. Most of the southern tribes of the western Sioux and almost all of the eastern tribes raised corn, but the Lakota and the Crow—those inhabiting the Great Plains—depended on buffalo and other game. Eastern tribes inhabited bark and mat wigwams, while those on the Great Plains built earth lodges and buffalo hide tepees. The Sioux kept dogs for food and to carry babies and tepees as the tribe moved. Through their trade with the tribes of the Southwest, the Sioux acquired horses, and rode them in pursuit of buffalo and in warfare. The Sioux tribes had no written language. However, among the western tribes, history and heritage were preserved through storytellers and "winter counts"—drawings arranged in a spiral on an animal hide, one drawing for each winter. A single hide might have drawings covering 50 years or more.

Over 70,000 Sioux live in South Dakota today. The three major tribes are the **Teton,** including the Oglala, Minneconjou, Brule ("Burned Thigh"), Hunkpapa, Sihasapa, Oohenonpas (or Two Kettle), and Itazipchos; the **Yankton,** comprising the Yankton and Yanktonai; and the **Santee,** made up of the Sisseton, Wahpeton, Wahpekute, and Mdewakanton. There are nine Sioux tribal governments in the state, six with reservation boundaries and three without. The six with reservation boundaries are the Cheyenne River, Crow Creek, Lower Brule, Pine Ridge, Rosebud, and Standing Rock; the three without are the Flandreau Santee, Sisseton-Wahpeton, and the Yankton. Indians on these reservations hold public ceremonies or powwows, offering non-Indians a glimpse into their lives. (See "Festivals and Events" in "PRACTICAL INFORMATION.")

—Julia Dillon

An unidentified Sioux woman poses in full costume. (Center for Western Studies)

French Canadians in the employ of the Spanish (who were established in the Southwest and California, and off and on in Louisiana), went into Dakota territory to trade furs. Their insolence offended both the Arikara and the Sioux, and in 1794 the Spanish Missouri Company sent out an expedition, under the leadership of former schoolteacher Jean Baptiste Truteau, with orders to stop d'Eglise and Garreau from representing them in the territory. Truteau safely entered Indian territory, spending the winter of 1795 near the future site of Fort Randall. The company passed a year with the Arikara until the Sioux attacked the tribe in May 1796. The white men, not yet considered a threat to Indians, were let go.

By 1803, South Dakota was part of an area claimed by the French that Americans referred to as the Louisiana Territory. Thomas Jefferson, in order to protect America's western flank and its trade on the Missouri and Mississippi rivers, offered to buy the vast wilderness for three cents an acre from France. Napoleon, needing money to finance his campaigns in Europe, agreed, and the United States was soon the owner of a 828,000-square-mile swath west of the Mississippi extending from New Orleans in the south to the Rocky Mountains and Canada. To map this new land and open it up to Americans, Jefferson asked Congress to authorize an expedition headed by Lewis and Clark. Before they undertook his journey Jefferson sent them the diary of Truteau's experience nearly 10 years prior.

■ LEWIS AND CLARK

In 1804, Meriwether Lewis, personal secretary to President Jefferson, set out to explore and map a route through the western wilderness to the Pacific Ocean. Together with his long-time friend, William Clark, he was directed to follow the Missouri River to its headwaters, hop the supposedly short divide to the Columbia River, and observe the growing British presence in the Pacific Northwest. The pair was also charged with introducing native people west of St. Louis to the concept of American government. The Corps of Discovery included 29 additional men, all of whom could contribute to the success of the expedition. Some were excellent hunters, and one played the fiddle. Another was Clark's personal servant, York, whose physical bulk, great strength, and black skin unfailingly impressed those who saw him.

MEETING THE SIOUX

30th of August, 1804

*T*he fog was so thick that we could not see the Indian camp on the opposite side, but it cleared off about eight o'clock. We prepared a speech, and some presents, and then sent for the chiefs and warriors, whom we received, at twelve o'clock, under a large oak tree, near to which the flag of the United States was flying. Captain Lewis delivered a speech, with the usual advice and counsel for their future conduct. We then acknowledged their chiefs, by giving to the grand chief a flag, a medal, a certificate, with a string of wampum; to which we added a chief's coat; that is, a richly laced uniform of the United States artillery corps, and a cocked hat and red feather. One second chief and three inferior ones were made or recognized by medals, and a suitable present of tobacco, and articles of clothing. We then smoked the pipe of peace, and the chiefs retired to a bower, formed of bushes, by their young men, where they divided among each other the presents, and smoked and eat, and held a council on the answer which they were to make us to-morrow. The young people exercised their bows and arrows in shooting at marks for beads, which we distributed to the best marksmen; and in the evening the whole party danced until a late hour, and in the course of their amusement we threw among them some knives, tobacco, bells, tape, and binding, with which they were much pleased. Their musical instruments were the drum, and a sort of little bag made of buffalo hide, dressed white, with small shot or pebbles in it, and a bunch of hair tied to it. This produces a sort of rattling music, with which the party was annoyed by four musicians during the council this morning.

—The Journals of the Expedition
of Lewis and Clark, 1804

From the collection of the Cultural Heritage Center, South Dakota Historical Society in Pierre.

Between Vermillion and Yankton, the explorers met their first Sioux, and gained a Sioux interpreter—Pierre Dorion, the same French Canadian who'd come to the area more than 30 years earlier and married into the Yankton tribe. Lewis and Clark passed fairly peaceably through South Dakota. There was one stand-off with the Teton Sioux, a belligerent tribe that by this time had pushed most of the Arikara into western South Dakota. Warned that the Tetons were known to rob traders, Lewis and Clark ordered the corps to be armed and ready to fight. The explorers and the tribe entered into negotiations lasting a few days. With the help of whiskey and a show of bluster—the explorers ordered their men to draw their swords when a besotted Teton got rowdy—Lewis and Clark managed to pass on through without violent incident.

Farther up the Missouri, the party was joined by French trader Toussaint Charbonneau and his 15-year-old wife Sacagewea, a Shoshone who'd been captured by the Blackfeet, sold as a slave to the Hidatsa Sioux, and won by the Frenchman in a gambling match. Sacagewea accompanied the expedition all the way to the Pacific.

When Lewis and Clark returned east in 1806, their diary was avidly read. Lewis had a knack for recording elegant, detailed observations. William Clark's passages were more earthy. Both were rife with misspellings. Their personalities were as different as their writing styles. Lewis, scholarly and refined, was prone to depressions. During the trip, whenever he fell under a dark cloud, he stopped writing and his partner continued. Clark was personable, having a good rapport with the Indians and a knack for doctoring. When Lewis was feeling good, Clark was a slack diarist, usually just copying Lewis's meticulous notes.

Spanish explorer and entrepreneur Manuel Lisa paid close attention to Lewis and Clark's reports before leaving in 1807 for the upper Missouri valley to trade with the Indians. By 1809, Lisa had organized the fur trade between the St. Louis Fur Company and the Indians along the entire length of the Missouri River, thereby opening the way for frontier forts, pioneer settlements, and inevitable confrontations between Indians and whites. Lisa eventually served the U.S. government as sub-agent to the upper Missouri Indians from 1814 to 1817—under William Clark, then superintendent of Indian Affairs in St. Louis.

■ MOUNTAIN MEN AND ARTISTS

Another fur company to make its mark on trade in South Dakota was the Rocky Mountain Fur Company, which organized trading parties in 1822 and 1823. The core of that group contains many of South Dakota's—and the Wild West's—most familiar names: James Clyman, Jedediah Smith, Thomas Fitzpatrick, Jim Bridger, Hugh Glass, Edward Rose, David Jackson, and William Sublette. Thanks to their discovery, exploration, and publicizing of Yellowstone, Jackson Hole, Salt Lake, and more, these men encouraged travel to the West—with South Dakota and the Missouri River en route.

By the early 1830s, most of the mountain men had gone west of the Dakota region, and steamboats were paddling up and down the region's rivers. The *Yellowstone*, the first steamboat on the Missouri River, reached Fort Tecumseh (later known as Fort Pierre) in 1831. Years earlier, men such as Henry Brackenridge, who published a journal of his 1811 journey with Manuel Lisa, traveled on the Missouri by keelboat. In his journal he commented, "The beauty of the scenery, this evening, exceeds any thing I ever beheld—The sky as clear as in a Chinese painting, the country delightful . . ."

The steamboat made river travel faster and easier, and the territory began attracting more settlers, as well as other temporary visitors who came to paint, write, or study rather than fight or trap. Among these visitors was George Catlin, who spent his days on the *Yellowstone* taking notes and making somewhat romanticized sketches of the Indians and landscapes he saw. Catlin's appreciation for the beauty of the West and his admiration for the Indians were reflected in his writing and art. He described his sorrow at the tragedy of the lives he saw disappearing before him—one entire Dakota-area tribe, the Mandans, was wiped out from smallpox contracted from fur traders.

Another traveling artist was the Swiss Karl Bodmer, who accompanied Maximilian, prince of Wied, and illustrated Maximilian's thorough and informative book, *Travels in the Interior of North America*. Maximilian himself had served as a general in the Prussian army in the Napoleonic Wars; both he and Duke Paul Wilhelm, who recorded his travels in the Dakota region in the latter 1820s, numbered among the Europeans who sought a New World tour to broaden their education, much as their counterparts in the eastern United States took the grand tour of Europe to further theirs.

"Little Bear, A Hunkpapa Brave" by George Catlin, perhaps the frontier's pre-eminent artist. *(National Museum of American Art, Smithsonian Institution)*

In 1843, one of America's quintessential nineteenth-century "characters," John James Audubon, journeyed up the Missouri River. Born in Haiti to a slave trader, Audubon was brought up in France, and smuggled himself into the United States to avoid being drafted into Napoleon's army. Once in the United States he set about failing at most things he undertook, but he did like to wander, and became skilled at drawing pictures of the many birds he shot and stuffed on his travels. When he arrived in South Dakota, he described a bleaker landscape than his earlier fellow travelers. In responding to Brackenridge's descriptions of natural beauty, Audubon wrote that he saw "no 'carpeted prairies,' no 'velvety distant landscape.'" And of Catlin Audubon commented that the earlier artist must have seen different natives entirely to paint such ideal scenes.

In the same year that the *Yellowstone* paddled to Fort Tecumseh, the first permanent white settlement in South Dakota was established at Fort Pierre Chouteau in central South Dakota, near present-day Pierre. An increasing number of trading and military posts were providing security and comfort to whites. In the years that followed, conflict with the Sioux escalated, and most fur-trading posts were turned over to the military.

"Fort Pierre, Mouth of the Teton River 1200 miles above St. Louis." Mr. Catlin over-estimated the distance between Fort Pierre and St. Louis when he titled this view near the fort in 1832. (National Museum of American Art, Smithsonian Institution)

■ SODBUSTERS AND PIONEERS

Like a wave on a prairie ocean, immigrants to the American frontier kept pushing westward in search of unbroken ground and a lease on the future. Most of those who came into South Dakota in the mid-nineteenth century followed the route of trappers and traders, heading west out of St. Louis and north through Nebraska via the Missouri River. They settled first in the southeastern corner of the state, in Vermillion, Yankton, and Sioux Falls, fanning out and building their homesteads along waterways: the Big Sioux, Vermillion, James, and Choteau rivers. Their vision for a new life included farms and houses, and to their eyes the land they first encountered was empty.

In 1862, the U.S. Congress passed the Homestead Act and sold 160 acres of unsettled land (for about 18 dollars in parts of the Dakota Territory) to men and women willing to meet a few government requirements. Once a pioneer had paced off 160 acres as his claim, the government compelled him to complete several steps to "prove up"—or hold onto—his claim. The first order of business was to

Mrs. Gustav Hanson of Hartford, just north of Sioux Falls, poses with children and neighbors before a typical prairie sod house. The lack of timber and extreme winter cold made it necessary to use sod strips like bricks for construction and insulation. (South Dakota Historical Society, Pierre)

construct a dwelling. Due to a lack of building materials, early dwellings were most often tarpaper shacks, dugouts carved from swells in the land, or sod shanties. "Sodbusters" cut long strips of three-inch (7.6-cm)-deep sod with a spade and then sliced the strips into manageable lengths. These were stacked like bricks into four walls, with openings for a window and a door. If the settler was lucky, trees growing on banks of a nearby stream or creek would provide enough wood to construct a crudely framed roof strong enough to support more sod. The completed sod shanty was windproof, fireproof, and structurally sound, but it often failed to keep out rain.

Though few of these original structures can be found today, they once littered the landscape. The large number that were built, only to be summarily abandoned, provided mute testimony to the struggles of trying to make a life on a vast, treeless prairie, broiling hot in the summer, freezing cold in the winter, and for the most part, arid.

The deep, impacted prairie grasses rendered planting the first crops extremely difficult. No matter how sharp their blades, plows could rarely churn up earth so entangled with tough roots. After chopping at the earth with an ax, many settlers simply dropped seeds into the crevices, then waited in their little "soddies" for the grain to grow. If the first crop was spared by drought, hail, grasshoppers, and fire, a homesteader might have enough money by the end of the summer to buy seed to plant a few additional acres. With luck, the cultivated acreage would increase each year, allowing the family to grow a vegetable garden, buy a milk cow, purchase lumber for a real house, and get shoes for the children. The success of these pioneer families often relied as much on their own ability to endure in the face of solitude and misfortune as it did on the weather.

■ BROKEN TREATIES

Like other hunter-gatherer cultures, the Great Plains Sioux needed to control a wide swath of territory to sustain the animals they hunted. Their traditions, legends, art, and folklore revolved around a roaming and hunting life, and when they observed whites on their lands, the last thing they wanted was to emulate them by settling down and growing corn. Rather, they fought off settlers as they would an encroaching Indian tribe, and they considered a farming or ranching life to be one

(following pages) "Eagle Dance" by George Catlin circa 1845–48.
(National Museum of American Art, Smithsonian Institution)

without spirit or soul. These differences engendered an endless series of skirmishes, massacres, and battles, as whites and Indians fought, and made treaties, broke them, and fought again. Control of either side by a central authority proved difficult. Whites, hungry for land, individualistic, and intrepid, kept pouring into any "empty" space they could find, indifferent to treaty boundaries. And although one Indian chief might sign a treaty, the tribes themselves were divided into fiercely independent groups that more or less did what they pleased. When these small self-directing groups were out hunting on the prairie and found yet another group of whites trying to plant crops in Indian hunting grounds, they saw blood.

The Laramie Treaty of 1851 attempted to deal with the problem by allotting the Sioux 60 million acres and establishing tribal borders. The U.S. government recognized the sovereignty of the Indian tribes and, in recognition of the fact that their hunting grounds were being infringed upon, promised an annuity to each tribe. In return the Indians agreed to allow the government to construct roads and military posts within their territory, and they guaranteed restitution should any U.S. citizen be wronged. They also promised to keep the peace among themselves—a futile gesture, since the Sioux tribes were not centrally governed, rendering such self-policing impossible. In addition, the U.S. Senate did not approve the annuity terms of the treaty, committing themselves only to compensate the Indians for losses of property and buffalo for the next 10 years. By 1856, the U.S. government had sent the topographical engineer Lt. G.K. Warren through Nebraska into Sioux territory to explore land near the Black Hills.

During the late 1850s, the first land speculators arrived. One large group from St. Paul, Minnesota, settled in the Sioux Falls area, while the other large group, hailing from Iowa (usually Sioux City), settled in Yankton. Although much of the land just west of these towns belonged to Indians, the speculators envisioned settlers—perhaps even a railroad—on that land. In 1858, the organizer of Sioux City's Upper Missouri Land Company, Capt. J. B. S. Todd, a cousin of Mary Todd Lincoln, took part in the negotiation of a treaty with the Yankton Sioux for the purchase of 14 million acres between the Big Sioux and Missouri rivers for 12 cents an acre.

Following the Yankton Treaty of 1858, Norwegians began to establish claims near the Vermillion and James rivers, forerunners of thousands of Norwegians who would eventually settle in the state. Irish immigrants began arriving in 1860, and the region had attracted enough residents in 1861 for Congress to organize it under U.S. law. Part of Dakota Territory, it was administered along with present-day North Dakota, Wyoming, and Montana. Yankton, a small settlement in extreme southeastern South Dakota, was designated territorial capital. With the passing of the Homestead Act of 1862, by which settlers could purchase 160-acre parcels of land for $18 each, the territory's population continued to grow.

Following the Minnesota Uprising in 1862—when Sioux tribes in that state violently protested a government order confining them to small reservations—and a series of skirmishes and raids that left hundreds of settlers and Dakota Indians (the Sioux tribe in Minnesota and eastern Dakota Territory) dead, the government made a last attempt to pacify the Indians while continuing to allow westward expansion.

The 1868 Fort Laramie Treaty established the Great Sioux Reservation, which included the Black Hills, as permanent home of the Sioux Nation and preserved Powder River and Bighorn Country as "unceded Indian territory." It granted the tribes rights to all land in Dakota Territory west of the Missouri River to the Bighorns of western Wyoming. The treaty nonetheless limited the land the Sioux felt entitled to roam and inhabit, and the American officials were hard-pressed to coax Oglala Sioux chief Red-Cloud—one of the most powerful Sioux leaders—into signing. Finally, treaty negotiator Major Dye persuaded Red Cloud to sign by informing him that the U.S. government would withhold ammunition from the Sioux if he didn't sign.

Chief Red Cloud of the Oglala Sioux.
(Center for Western Studies)

In addition to establishing the reservation, the Treaty of 1868 assigned the Sioux tribes to a number of agencies, which would distribute yearly allotments of food, clothes, and money to the Indians. (These agencies would later become instruments of U.S. governmental control over the tribes.) Also, under the terms of the treaty, the American army was to defend the Great Sioux Reservation against white settlement. But continued reports of gold in the Black Hills and unrelenting pressure from a flood of immigrants helped changed the government's collective mind, and soon compromised its honor.

■ GOLD RUSH

Back in 1848, when Father Pierre-Jean (Peter John) De Smet visited the Black Hills on South Dakota's southwestern border, an Indian chief presented the priest with a bag of glimmering powder. Recognizing it as gold and already fearing for Indian rights in the area, De Smet quickly responded, "Put it away and show it to nobody." Unfortunately, during the two decades following the Homestead Act,

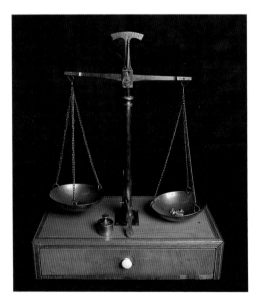

A gold scale used in the Black Hills during the late nineteenth century. (South Dakota State Historical Society, Pierre)

*Indian scout
helmet. (South
Dakota State
Historical Society,
Pierre. Photo by
Paul Jones)*

the secret got out of the bag. Hordes of whites came to the sacred Paha Sapa (Black Hills), a beautiful wilderness of pine-clad cliffs and mountain meadows.

In the early 1870s, the Northern Pacific Railroad began laying track through the Powder River country west of the Black Hills. Though angered by the obvious violation of their treaty, the Sioux did not go to war. In 1873, the legislature of the Dakota Territory asked Congress to provide soldiers to drive "hostile" Indians—those who rebelled against reservation confinement—from the Black Hills, which, the Dakota legislature asserted, served as their retreat. On July 2, 1874, a charismatic leader with flowing yellow hair, Lt. Col. George Armstrong Custer, was sent with ten cavalry and two infantry companies on the first white expedition into the Black Hills. Although ostensibly sent to gather information about the region, Custer widened his purpose looking for the gold he'd heard rumors about. Much to his surprise, Custer met with few Indians, and so he had plenty of time to admire the landscape and write dispatches to his commanding officers in Bismarck. Then in one such dispatch, Custer casually mentioned that gold seemed to be everywhere in the Black Hills. A Chicago newspaper picked up the word that the "Custer Expedition" had confirmed the presence of gold in the sacred land of the Sioux. The paper ran the news, and the gold rush was on.

Meanwhile, the War Department, attempting to protect the Black Hills, called a meeting with all of the region's major tribes—the ten Sioux tribes plus the Arapaho and the Northern Cheyenne—at which government negotiators encouraged the tribes to sell off their land for money that would be needed when the buffalo died off. No decision could be reached. In late 1875, the Commissioner of Indian Affairs issued an order to the Sioux that all bands not already reporting to the reservation agencies to which they had been assigned must do so by January 31, 1876. Those Indians who didn't return would be considered "hostile" and would be sent back to their agencies by force if necessary.

The commissioner's order, intended to quell attacks on settlers, soldiers, and peaceful Indian tribes, was ill conceived and poorly timed. It made no allowance for smaller groups absent from their tribe: even a few dozen hunters attempting to supplement the government's meager rations with wild game were considered hostile. The order reached some agencies only days before the deadline and it failed to take into account the realities of travel in the middle of winter on the northern Great Plains. Indeed, due to severe weather, the army had stopped its operations on the Plains in late November. Yet Indian warriors, women, and children—not nearly as well clothed or well fed—were expected to travel many miles across wind-swept plains during the coldest month of the year.

In March, Gen. George Crook took the field against the hostiles, and Lt. Col. George A. Custer commanded one of the forces sent. The Indian response was led by the Hunkpapa Sioux leader Sitting Bull, who summoned Sioux, Cheyenne, and even some Arapaho warriors to his camp in Montana Territory. Crook's troops were forced to retreat in a battle on June 17, and the Indian chiefs moved their encampment into the valley of the Little Bighorn River in what is now southeastern Montana. There Sitting Bull performed the Sun Dance, entering into a trance and receiving a vision in which soldiers fell from the sky like grasshoppers. Custer and his men spotted the Indian camp on June 25, 1876, and he elected to divide his forces and attack. One group was assigned to Capt. Frederick Benteen and the other to Maj. Marcus Reno. Custer took his own troops and led the charge onto the battlefield of Little Bighorn. Custer and his command, however, had severely underestimated the strength of their adversary. After being pinned down by some of the 4,000 warriors in the camp, Benteen and Reno could only watch as smoke filtering over the plains signaled the annihilation of Custer and over 200 soldiers.

The Indian victory was short-lived. After scattering to the winds, homesickness, starvation, and cavalry pursuit eventually led most of the Lakota back to the agencies of the Great Sioux Reservation. By August 1876, Congress even began punishing the peaceful agency Sioux for the acts of their hostile brethren by cutting off their food and rations until they agreed to cede the Black Hills and allow passage through the rest of their land.

President Ulysses S. Grant appointed the Manypenny Commission—with its "sell or starve" agenda—to meet with the Sioux. Ironically, the commission was made up of prominent friends of the Indians, who believed that if the Sioux relinquished their land, the Indian nation might thrive, perhaps joining white civilization or forging a more "modern" way of life. In despair, some leaders of the tribe signed an agreement that fall and the Black Hills were lost to the Lakota. Congress moved quickly and ratified the agreement February 28, 1877, unleashing another great gold rush.

Soldiers marching across the state during the Indian campaigns of the 1880s.
(Center for Western Studies)

■ SIOUX RESISTANCE

As miners and "mule skinners" (muleteers, or mule drivers) flocked to the Black Hills and established gold mining camps in the summer of 1876, three bands of the Lakota remained at large. The bands of Sitting Bull and Gall had fled to the Canadian wilderness while Crazy Horse and his people remained in the Bighorn Mountains. After pressure from other Indian leaders, Crazy Horse and his band of about 1,100 men, women, and children surrendered to authorities at the Red Cloud Agency—near Fort Robinson in present-day Nebraska—on May 6, 1877.

■ CRAZY HORSE

Later that summer, knowing that the Sitting Bull and Gall bands roamed free, Crazy Horse became restless and began planning to escape the agency. When his mood became known, army officials decided to arrest him rather than allow the Dakota leader to influence others and lead a mass exodus. In early September, troops were sent to the village of Crazy Horse and found it had broken up the previous night. Most of the band was quickly returned to the agency, but Crazy Horse had fled on his own. However, he too was soon in the custody of the military, which escorted him to Fort Robinson. When Crazy Horse was taken to a guardhouse and learned he would be confined, a struggle ensued and the great Sioux leader received a fatal wound from a soldier's bayonet. He died at midnight on September 5, 1877.

Sioux horse effigy. (South Dakota State Historical Society, Pierre. Photo by Paul Jones)

■ S I T T I N G   B U L L

Sitting Bull, whose strong "medicine" foretold of falling bluecoats and Custer's Last Stand, would also die at the hands of authorities, albeit after spending years in the presence of whites and even traveling to Europe in Buffalo Bill's Wild West Show.

Five years after the Indian victory over Custer's Seventh Cavalry at Little Bighorn, Sitting Bull remained in Canada with a remnant of his people. After numerous visits by commissions from the United States, the Canadian government finally wearied of its uninvited guests and ordered Sitting Bull to leave. The great medicine man of the Hunkpapa Sioux surrendered and was escorted to Fort Buford (on the Missouri in present-day western North Dakota) and finally to Fort Randall in the same territory. After two years of confinement, Sitting Bull was sent to the Standing Rock Agency near Fort Yates, North Dakota.

Nine years later, in the fall of 1890, warriors in Sitting Bull's camp became swept up in the spiritual fervor spreading through America's Indian tribes—in a sense the only recourse left to them in an increasingly bitter and impoverished life—the practice of "Ghost Dances." Ghost Dances were rites taught by Wovoka, a Paiute holy man known as Jack

Indian chief bonnet. A feather was added for each successful coup. (South Dakota State Historical Society, Pierre. Photo by Paul Jones)

Wilson to the Nevada family that had adopted him. According to Wovoka, if the Indians prayed and danced long and sincerely enough, all dead Indian warriors would return and the white men would disappear. Although Sitting Bull himself did not believe in the teachings, he did nothing to discourage his people from participating. Nearby whites, who found the dances mysterious and threatening, began to advocate military action.

On the morning of December 15, 1890, thirty-nine Indian policeman and four special agents under the command of Shave Head and Bull Head appeared in Sitting Bull's camp and pulled him from his bed. As he was being led from his home, his son taunted him for being taken captive so easily. Two shots were fired from a crowd of Indians who had gathered to watch the arrest. In the melee that followed Shave Head, Bull Head, three other policeman and eight Indians were killed, as was Sitting Bull.

■ GALL

A war chief of the Hunkpapa Sioux, Gall led the third band of renegades who refused to subject themselves to reservation living. But, in the fall of 1880 and after staying with Sitting Bull in Canada for nearly five years, Gall chastised Sitting

A rare photo of a Ghost Dance performed by Sioux on the Rosebud Reservation in the fall of 1890. In the next few months, the Ghost Dance frightened American settlers and officials enough to provoke further violent repression of the Sioux. (Center for Western Studies)

Bull, labeled him a coward and a fraud for not openly confronting the U.S. government, and returned to the United States. Scarcely into the new year, he too surrendered with some 300 of his followers. Gall settled on a farm on the Standing Rock Reservation, ultimately became a friend of the whites, and was influential in inducing the Indians to accept the government's plans to educate their children. Gall died several years later at his home on Oak Creek in South Dakota.

The great chief Sitting Bull in 1884. (Library of Congress)

MASSACRE AT WOUNDED KNEE

*M*eanwhile, the tension in the square became something larger—a feeling of peril that was ominous and growing. The Indians felt it. They remembered that this was the Seventh Cavalry. At the Battle on the Greasy Grass (Little Big Horn) it had suffered the bloodiest defeat ever given white soldiers by Indians. It had lost Long Hair Custer and two hundred sixty-four men, whereas the Indians had lost only a handful. There were some who claimed that the Seventh had been thirsting for revenge every since. Their sense of danger was quickened even more by Yellow Bird as he continued to dance among them chanting, "Don't be frightened—let your hearts be strong to meet what is before you—the Great Holy is with you—your ghost shirts will keep the bullets from you." Nerves tightened like drying bowstrings, and there was a feeling in the air like the cold wind that runs ahead of a thunderstorm.

The young troopers were as nervous as the Indians. They were green and unseasoned, and the greatest military danger most of them had experienced so far was learning to ride a horse. Now, suddenly, they were facing the Sioux. They knew from their dime novels that the Sioux were treacherous, butchering savages. On top of that there was a fierce-looking old man wearing a painted and feathered nightshirt hopping around out there, chanting and blowing a whistle and throwing dirt at them. Their palms moistened and their fingers curled around the triggers of their old Remingtons.

The officers smelled danger, too. Lieutenant Mann recalled, "I had a peculiar feeling come over me—some presentiment of trouble." He passed the word quietly through K Troop, "Be ready. There is going to be trouble."

Colonel Forsyth called to Philip Wells, who was trying to persuade the influential Horned Cloud to quiet the medicine man and the young Indians, "You'd better get out of here. It's looking dangerous."

"Just a minute, Colonel," replied Wells, "I'm trying to get this fellow to quiet them.' Even as he spoke, however, Wells saw a powerful young warrior stalking toward him from behind. Turning, Wells cautiously began to back out of the square.

Meanwhile, Black Coyote (or Hosi Yanka) had torn a strip of paper from an old brown bag and had moved off to the side. Holding his beloved rifle in the crook of his arm, he was trying to roll a big cigarette in the paper. As he did so, two sergeants who were after his gun slipped up from behind and seized him. There was a quick, fierce scuffle. The gun pointed skyward and fired. Then all in the same instant Yellow Bird threw a cloud of dust into the air, and half a dozen young Indians threw off their blankets and aimed their Winchesters at K Troop.

Lieutenant Robinson yelled, "Look out! They are going to fire!"

Varnum looked up from the search line and cried, "By God! They have broken!"

Philip Wells whirled around to find his Indian stalker lunging at him with a knife.

Lieutenant Mann remembered thinking, "The pity of it! What can they be thinking of!"

A split second later the Indian volley ripped into K troop, and Mann heard himself screaming, "Fire! Fire on them!"

Instantly, both B and K Troops fired volleys into the Indians, and the square exploded into a roar of gunfire and disappeared under swirling clouds of yellow-gray powder smoke.

"There was an awful roar." (Dog Chief)

"It sounded much like the tearing of canvas." (Rough Feather)

"Everything was smoking from then on." (Peter Stand)

"The smoke was so dense I couldn't see anything." (White Lance)

"People were lying all about where formerly they were all sitting or standing." (Richard Afraid-of-Hawk)

Philip Wells partially deflected his attacker's knife—it sliced through the end of his nose, which dangled over his mouth, held on by only two strips of skin.

Captain Wallace was running to rejoin K Troop when the second Indian volley tore away the top of his skull.

Big Foot struggled to sit up, caught a bullet in his head, and fell back beside the body of Horned Cloud. Seeing her father fall, Big Foot's daughter ran screaming toward him, was shot in the back, and fell dead across him.

—Rex Alan Smith, *Moon of Popping Trees*, 1975

Chief Big Foot lies mortally wounded on the battlefield at Wounded Knee. (Center for Western Studies)

■ SETTLERS MOVE ONTO RESERVATIONS

The 1880s saw the beginning of the reservation period in earnest. The bison were on the brink of extinction from the many settlers and soldiers who hunted them and the ranchers who used the grassland for cattle-grazing, and with them was eradicated the way of life of the Plains Indian. The original inhabitants of this changing environment were forced to rely on the political whims of the federal government for rations of food and clothing.

From 1882 to 1889, several government commissions attempted to persuade the Dakota to give up more of the tribal lands. The "Great Dakota Boom" and its accompanying influx of Bohemians, Germans, Swedes, Finns, Poles, and Swiss made land scarce and confrontation likely. Finally, on March 2, 1889, the Sioux relented, gave up nearly half of the Great Sioux Reservation, and agreed to allow it to be divided into six smaller ones. In later years the reservations would be reduced even further in size. Through the Dawes General Allotment Act, land not allotted to the Indians was designated as surplus and open for white settlement. South Dakota entered its first year of statehood in 1889 with open ground, settlers sweeping the state, hammers pounding, and white civilization closing the door on the Sioux.

In addition, with no buffalo to hunt, drought stalking their attempts at farming, and rations of flour, corn, and beans reduced below treaty obligations, the late 1880s were a time of considerable hunger for the Sioux. As with other Indian tribes throughout the West, the Lakota sought solace in the Ghost Dance teachings of Wovoka. To the whites who feared an Indian uprising and further bloodshed, the Ghost Dance movement was known as the Messiah Craze, alarming Indian agents and army troops. After first contributing to the death of Sitting Bull, the Ghost Dance religion resulted in a far more terrible experience at a place called Wounded Knee, where 200 Indians were massacred by the Seventh Cavalry.

■ DAKOTA FEVER

Despite feeble attempts by the federal government to enforce provisions of its treaty with the Lakota and keep whites from entering the Black Hills, settlers by the hundreds stormed the Paha Sapa. In their steep canyons and lush meadows, placer miners began building sluices and shacks, gambling for gold against defensive Indian attack and an army scolding. Deadwood, known as one of the wildest and the wickedest mining camps in the American West, sprang to life after Custer's confirmation of gold. Seven months after the news of gold was out, the population of the gulch swelled from a few ramshackle huts to more than 7,000 uninvited residents.

The settlement of the Black Hills led to a stampede on the remaining frontier in Dakota Territory. As western South Dakota grew, so did the needs of miners and businessmen: supplies, equipment, food, and an efficient way of delivering them. Until 1878, farming settlements were generally restricted to extreme southeastern South Dakota. Only a few settlers had drifted into the rich river valleys of the James, Vermillion, and Big Sioux, leaving the vast expanse of prairie in central and northern South Dakota virtually uninhabited.

But in that unbroken prairie, immigrants, Civil War veterans, and the sons and daughters of earlier homesteaders caught "Dakota fever." Railroad officials saw dollar signs—not only did settlers need transportation to their plots, but with plots so isolated, they would certainly require a means of shipping crops and livestock to market or to their fellow settlers in the Black Hills. Together, railroad tycoons,

The rough-and-tumble main street of Deadwood circa 1880s. (Adams Museum, Deadwood)

An allotment crew ready to divide land on Pine Ridge Reservation. (Center for Western Studies)

riverboat captains, and real estate agents promoted Dakota Territory's rich river valleys and open plains to eager immigrants.

As fears of Indian uprisings diminished, and farming and commerce swept the state, railroads extended their lines west from Minnesota. Residents of Vermillion and Yankton took advantage of an increasing number of steamboats plying the Missouri River, laden with supplies for settlers and miners. Cattle ranchers drove their herds from Texas, eastern Colorado, western Nebraska, and Wyoming onto the virgin grasslands west of the Missouri River and north of the Black Hills. Early settlers lobbied for county seats and railroad stops. When railroaders ignored some requests, whole communities packed up and rebuilt their settlements next to the line. Today, southeastern South Dakota, indeed the entire state, is dotted with townsites abandoned as soon as the settlers saw that access to transportation would be limited.

The "Great Dakota Boom," one of the last massive land rushes in the United States, witnessed thousands of immigrants pour into Dakota Territory. From 1870 to 1880, the population of the southeastern area of the state rose from about 10,000 to 82,000. By 1885, a quarter million inhabitants were engaged in farming, trades, and business, or vying for the marginal tracts of land that remained open under the Homestead Act.

But the region's population increase by no means indicates that life in the Dakota Territory was easy. Major blizzards occurred in 1873, 1880–81, and 1888. Plagues of grasshoppers destroyed crops in 1864–65, 1873–74, 1876, and 1936. Drought fried the fields in 1889, 1894, 1910–1911, and during the dust storms of 1933 and 1934. As if that wasn't enough, disease was never far away: in 1869–1870, the early years of the the Dakota Boom, settlers had to be concerned with consumption, freezing, fever, and pneumonia, the most common causes of death that year. Other frequently cited causes of death included croupe, dropsy, acute diarrhea, cancer, diphtheria, gunshot wounds, cholera, lung fever, bronchitis, and fits. Ten years later, the causes of death were even more varied: gravel, worms, alcoholism, heart disease, sunstroke, and teething; and getting struck by lightning, kicked by a horse, murdered, gored, scalded, struck by a falling body, killed by Indians, and "shot sparking another man's wife." And then there were the economic depressions, the worst being the Great Depression of the 1930s which left thousands of marginal farms and small-town merchants destitute.

Despite the dangers of disease and violence, and the setbacks borne by insects, drought, blizzards, and depressions, the settlers who stuck it out left behind strong, healthy and determined descendants, qualities which have become time

Wind erosion in the mid-1930s virtually blew away South Dakota's topsoil, ruining most farmers in the state. (Library of Congress)

The State Capitol building in Pierre.

honored in South Dakota. This was not a world in which laboring from dawn to dark was found remarkable, or the activities of leisure time (with the exception of hunting and fishing) a major topic of discussion. Residents continued to toil in grasshopper-infested fields and on parched prairie; leaders continued to extend rail lines and commerce, dam rivers, and make even its most inhospitable places habitable.

■ STATEHOOD

As the territory's population rose despite hardship, so did its residents' voices clamoring for statehood. The voices were most numerous in the south, where the population was almost twice that of the north. The settlers of southern Dakota wanted admission of separate southern and northern Dakotas as much as they desired statehood itself, for they believed the southern region, with its greater resources and higher population, should benefit from its own wealth. Those in the north, fearing that Congress might not think the northern territory's numbers high enough, believed that a "one-state" drive was their only hope.

In 1885, Dakota governor Gilbert Pierce, a two-state advocate, called a second constitutional convention (the first one, called in 1883, had failed to acquire statehood). In the 1885 southern Dakota election to approve the constitution, voters elected a state government, approved the constitution, and named Huron the new state capital. That same week, Indiana senator Benjamin Harrison introduced the bill admitting North and South Dakota to statehood. The two-state proposal met with much political debate, as both the Democratic Congress and President Cleveland realized that admission of the largely Republican territory as two states would mean four Republican senators, rather than two. After a few years of obstacles—rejection of the Harrison bill by the House Committee on Territories, the appointment of a new one-state territorial governor, Congressional endorsement of a northern Dakota one-state plan, and the Northern Pacific Railroad preference for any one-state plan—the constitutional convention met again.

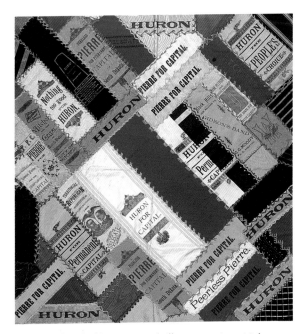

A political ribbon crazy quilt illustrates various cities' efforts to be chosen state capital. (South Dakota State Historical Society, Pierre)

By 1889, the tide had turned, perhaps because it became clear to the politicians that public sentiment favored the admission of the Dakota Territory as two states; it also favored the admission of Montana and Washington. Benjamin Harrison was even elected to the Presidency, though Cleveland himself signed the bill before leaving office. The boundary with North Dakota was drawn, and on November 2, 1889, South Dakota became the nation's fortieth state. The city of Pierre was nominated for "temporary" capital because it was the most central town in the state, and it defeated five other contenders, largely because competition among the others—Mitchell, Huron, Chamberlain, Watertown, and Sioux Falls—was so heated that the tiny central South Dakota town slipped through unnoticed.

■ SOUTH DAKOTA TODAY

Since World War II, hydro-electric projects, control of the Missouri River, farm mechanization, industrial expansion, and massive memorials carved from the ageless granite of its mountains have signaled a new prosperity for South Dakota. Today's powerlines, interstates, and convenience stores reveal vast changes in lifestyle from those endured by South Dakota's early pioneers. But its landscape has changed little since Crazy Horse, Sitting Bull, and other Sioux leaders traversed it with their nomadic bands centuries ago.

It took a mountain carving known as Mount Rushmore, built 1927–1941 in the Black Hills, to attract international attention to South Dakota. More than six million tourists visit the state each year, generating a billion dollars worth of economic activity and employing one out of every dozen workers in South Dakota.

With more than 35,000 farms and three quarters of a million people, South Dakota's population is nevertheless smaller than the cities of Minneapolis, Minnesota, and Denver, Colorado. Its largest city, Sioux Falls, boasts a population of 110,000, and the next largest, Rapid City, only half that. South Dakota is a place where the state bird, the imported Chinese ring-necked pheasant, still outnumbers the taller, two-legged residents who attempt to shoot it out of the sky each fall. As a matter of record, people also are outnumbered by deer, walleye, trout, corncobs, cattle, and ponderosa pine.

First National Bank of Brookings circa 1920s. On Roosevelt's "Bank Holiday" in 1933, the Nystrom Bank in Wall was the only bank in America not to close: apparently nobody notified the owner about the President's proclamation. (Underwood Photo Archives)

THE SOUTHEAST

A FEW YEARS AGO, a South Dakota newspaper editor was visiting Los Angeles when, feeling a bit weary of city life, he sought the comforting confines of a taxicab. As his tension lessened, the editor struck up the obligatory banter with the cabbie who, with a firm grasp of the obvious, guessed that his passenger was from out-of-state.

"Where ya from?" the cabbie asked.

"South Dakota," the editor answered, then waited for some form of recognition. Following a lengthy pause, and a couple of nervous glances in the rearview mirror, the cabbie said, "Isn't that one of those square states?"

Well, not quite square. But *almost* as square as nearby North Dakota, Wyoming, Colorado, and perhaps Kansas. What throws South Dakota off the list of straight-line states are a few rivers on which surveyors conveniently relied to draw the state's borders. The location of Lake Traverse and Big Stone Lake in extreme northeastern South Dakota allowed Minnesota to take a geographical bite out of that region, but the path of the Missouri River along the state's southeasterly edge recouped some land from Nebraska.

As the Missouri reaches its confluence with the Big Sioux River, it forms a "toe" that extends to the southeast from South Dakota's lower right border. Surrounded by Nebraska on the west and Iowa on the east is a mini-peninsula. A legion of North Sioux City and other I-29 residents here can enter three states in a matter of minutes, but because they are cradled in the arms of two rivers and between the lines on a map, they call South Dakota home.

■ HISTORY

Long before steam engines, asphalt roadways, and concrete runways, wild rivers were the major means of transportation in the southeastern corner of South Dakota. On these rivers—the Big Sioux, Vermillion, James, and Choteau—Arikara and later Sioux Indians fished and gathered food. In 1804, explorers Lewis and Clark traveled through the area, and commented in their journals on the treachery of the Missouri River, as well as its beauty. Most of South Dakota's first adventurers and fur trappers followed the Missouri up into the state, as did the pioneers who

THE SOUTHEAST

arrived after 1862 when the Dakota Territory was opened to homesteaders. In the early 1860s, the only part of the state settled was a strip along the Missouri extending from present-day Sioux City, Iowa (just over today's South Dakota border), up into Yankton. By 1870 the region had expanded to include the area extending from the mouth of the James east to the Big Sioux River as far north as Sioux Falls. On this treeless prairie, sodbusters built their homes with sod strips and chopped at the grass-clogged earth with an ax before planting seeds.

Today, the fertile soil of South Dakota's eastern half is home to the majority of the state's farms. In the southeast, the towns of Yankton, Vermillion, and Sioux Falls are the anchors of economic and cultural life. Outside of these areas you encounter rambling farmsteads, feedlots, vast cornfields, and river valleys. Dust clouds and plumes of diesel smoke rising from tractors and combines working the flat fields announce spring planting and fall harvest. In winter, the landscape is a barren, snow-packed tundra. From early November until mid-March, most rural residents huddle in their houses, hang out at the local cafe, attend 4-H Club meetings, or root for a basketball team in a packed high-school gymnasium.

Most years, when an adequate but not excessive amount of sun shines and rain falls, it's a comfortable existence. At other times, when dark clouds cover the plains like a wet blanket for weeks at a time, or when the sun bleaches the soil and paints a brown tint all the way to the horizon, it's not as easy. Each of those years, good times and bad, success and struggle, can be found on the faces of old-time residents of this region, in their determined smiles and the weathered creases around their eyes.

■ VERMILLION

Vermillion, a few miles west of I-29 on State Highway 50, is located on a Missouri River bluff and named for the red clay on which it was built. With a population of 10,000, it has an unpretentious small-town atmosphere. It's clean, maybe even scrub-brushed, and because the University of South Dakota is here, Vermillion.is pleasantly collegiate.

The earliest settlement in the area was Fort Vermillion, established by the American Fur Company in 1835. The town itself originally was founded on the banks of the Missouri and Vermillion rivers a mile south, but a major flood hit the valley in 1881 and swept away most of the existing structures. Following the flood, houses were built higher up, on surrounding bluffs that overlooked the original townsite. Today, Neoclassical and Queen Anne influences abound in the residential architecture, and examples of Italianate and Mediterranean styles stand among homely bungalow houses.

The well-manicured campus of the **University of South Dakota** was founded in 1862, when the territorial legislature selected Vermillion as home to Dakota Territory's first university—but failed to provide funding. Civic-minded residents, led by pioneer banker and politician Darwin Inman, took matters in their own hands and raised the funds to underwrite the institution. Its architecture is dominated by the Neoclassical style of the **Old Main** building and the handsome Georgian Revival style of the **Inman House,** which serves as the alumni center. On campus, as well, are the state's only medical and law schools.

A walk around the campus and surrounding neighborhoods yields the usual mix of academics, athletes, and aesthetes among the student body of approximately 7,000. Alumni of this University, all devoted to their mascot, the coyote, like nothing better than to look down their noses at the other South Dakota institutions of higher learning. The "Cow College" (South Dakota State) at Brookings, where the

Randolph Street in downtown Vermillion, circa 1870.
(South Dakota State Historical Society, Pierre)

noble jackrabbit serves as mascot, often is their favorite target. One of the less refined habits of USD students during winter basketball contests between the two schools is to throw dead, frozen jackrabbits on the hardwood floor—a great way to ignite a hometown crowd. Some of the same USD students have recently discovered that if they let the furry critters thaw out under their seats until halftime, they don't bounce. In the early 1980s jackrabbit hurling suffered its greatest setback when some South Dakota State students threw a well-preserved but equally inanimate coyote to the floor of the gym. It didn't bounce either.

The University campus boasts several fine museums. The **W. H. Over State Museum** at 1110 Ratigen, features exhibits of natural history and heritage through the work of its namesake, who was South Dakota's most distinguished naturalist. The museum's **Clark Memorial Collection** provides an extensive array of pre-reservation and early reservation Lakota art and artifacts, as well as pioneer artifacts, firearms, and historic photographs and costumes. For information call (605) 677-5228.

The **Austin-Whittemore House** at 15 Austin Avenue was built in 1882 and, resting on a riverside bluff overlooking Vermillion, serves as headquarters for the

The Shrine to Music Museum in Vermillion contains an eclectic collection of musical instruments.

Clay County Historical Society Museum. Filled with Victorian displays and settings, it is perhaps the finest example of Italian villa-style architecture in the state, and is worth a visit.

The most unusual museum in the community is the **Shrine to Music Museum** at USD (Clark and Yale streets). Widely acknowledged as one of the finest institutions of its kind in the world, the Shrine to Music Museum is home to more than 6,000 rare antique musical instruments presented in seven galleries. Its renowned collections include ivory lutes from Elizabethan times, Civil War band instruments, hand-painted Persian drums, and instruments by the Italian masters. Specially featured are a spectacular trumpet mask from the South Pacific, an eighteenth-century Swiss organ, and one of only two Antonio Stradivari guitars known to have survived. For more information call (605) 677-5306.

■ SPIRIT MOUND

Seven miles (11 km) north of Vermillion, visible from Route 19, Spirit Mound rises above the surrounding prairie, a bald, brown mound interrupting the flat horizon. On a hot and gusty August day in 1804, Meriwether Lewis and his dog Seaman, William Clark, and members of their expedition walked to the mound, which an Oto Indian had told them was inhabited by feisty midget-sized warriors. In their journals, the explorers noted that they observed a flock of swallows feeding on insects on the lee side of the mound and were afforded a splendid view of the surrounding grasslands from the mound's apex. They did not report sightings of pygmy warriors.

■ YANKTON

On U.S. 29, less than 30 miles (48 km) upriver from Vermillion along the tree-lined banks of the Missouri River, Yankton, the Mother City of South Dakota, claims a heritage steeped in riverboat and railroad investment schemes, frontier development, and just a hint of lingering dissatisfaction over not being selected the state capital in 1889. The sleepy burg recalls its days as a riverboat boom town on lazy summer evenings, when residents hear the steady chugging of the *Far West* paddle-wheeler, its deck lined with travelers looking out across the still waters.

A passenger on this scaled-down version of the original *Far West* could easily wonder whether riverboat travel was once more exciting than this. It surely must have been. A century ago, before dams slowed the current and deeper water and dredges virtually eliminated the danger of sandbars, settlers must have questioned the next bend, the security of their worldly possessions, and the coming of tomorrow. But today, riding a paddle-wheeler doesn't differ much from taking a stagecoach or being caught in the left lane of a traffic jam. It's a slow journey and you can't get off. Perfect for the faint of heart.

Named for the Yankton Sioux tribe that once dominated the area, the community has devolved from its heyday as capital of the Dakota Territory in the 1860s, to a college town (Yankton College) with grain elevators. Its central business district gives the appearance of a town somebody started but didn't finish. Stores and service stations accommodate families and fishermen, all stocking up for a weekend of camping, boating, and other out-of-the-office—or more commonly, out-of-the-cornfield—pleasures. Its homes are filled with retired farmers and a few young families—the rest are making a living on the farms outside of town. It's a friendly, old-fashioned place with Extension Clubs, clean streets, manicured lawns, and Fourth of July parades. Its replica of the old capitol building and its stately historic homes and museums document a history molded by Indians, explorers, settlers, riverboat captains, and railroad tycoons. Some of the town's 13,000 residents still claim kinship to the well-paid steamboat captains and pioneer passengers who first settled the area.

The most bustling town in the region in the nineteenth century, Yankton was a favorite stop for travelers, traders, and soldiers. When Lt. Col. George Armstrong Custer was headed west in 1873, he camped with his Seventh Cavalry at Yankton. According to the *Yankton Daily Press and Dakotan* (founded in 1861 and still published today), the U.S. Army took more than 20 years to settle its debts with local merchants after Custer's visit.

■ HISTORIC DISTRICT

Wander around Yankton's historic district, as many of its citizens like to do on humid summer nights, and imagine the time when riverboats were king and Yankton was the commercial center of the Dakota Territory. Roughly laid out along Fifth and Sixth streets between Mulberry and Cedar, and along Douglas, Capital, and Pine streets, its 152 buildings reflect a variety of styles, including Queen Anne and Italianate residences and Gothic churches.

The **Charles Gurney Hotel** at Third and Capital, at one time the courthouse, was the site of the second trial of desperado Jack McCall for the murder of Wild Bill Hickok. McCall had earlier been acquitted by a vigilante court in Deadwood, and left for Nebraska, where he made the mistake of bragging about Hickok's murder. He was caught and turned over to the Yankton authorities, where residents gladly hanged him and buried him in an unmarked grave. (See "BLACK HILLS" chapter for more about Wild Bill Hickok.) The Charles Gurney Hotel was also the scene of perhaps the first murder of a territorial official, when a local banker fatally shot South Dakota's first territorial secretary.

A block away at Fourth and Capital stands the Neoclassical Carnegie Library, which still retains most of its original 1902 features, including ornate woodwork and leaded windows. Nearby is the **Cramer-Kenyon Heritage Home** and its memorial gardens at 509 Pine Street, an interesting stop for those with a botanical bent or a passion for furnishings from the 1870s and '80s. The **Yankton College Conservatory** (1883), and the **African Methodist Episcopal Church** (1885) at 508 Cedar Street (built by former slaves and the oldest black church in Dakota

Yankton waterfront during a major flood in 1881.
(South Dakota State Historical Society, Pierre)

Territory) are worthwhile historic stops. The **Excelsior Mill** at Second and Capital was built in 1872, when milling locally grown wheat was one of Yankton's major industries. Constructed of soft yellow sandstone and Sioux quartzite, the building now houses **Gurney Seed and Nursery,** in business since 1894, which distributes a variety of seeds around the world. The **Dakota Territorial Museum,** located at 610 Summit Street, contains Sioux artifacts, steamboat memorabilia, and period furnishings and clothing. It also exhibits the musical instruments and papers of Felix Vinatieri, the Italian-born musician who immigrated to the Dakota Territory and was asked by Lt. Col. Custer to join the Seventh Cavalry as bandmaster. Vinatieri enlisted, served as chief musician, but missed the fabled Last Stand when Custer ordered the band left behind. Call (605) 665-3898 for more information.

■ **B U B B L E   M A C H I N E**

In 1928, WNAX Radio went on the air in Yankton and helped jump-start the long career of a middle-American phenomenon. Lawrence Welk, a young accordionist from Strasburg, North Dakota, had just run out of cash in Yankton. A long way from anywhere, and with no dance hall dates in sight, Welk and his band sought to replenish their reserves by coaxing some broadcast time out of WNAX. After the station manager fed the band, he put them on the air. Listener reaction, particularly from the Norwegian and German farmhouses scattered through the countryside, was immediate and positive. Despite the low pay, Welk accepted the manager's offer for a regular spot and stayed for nine years. Eventually, Welk and his band went on to perform in one of television's most popular family programs.

Today, reruns of the "Lawrence Welk Show" echo the folksy, fox-trotting tone of much of South Dakota, in places cable television hasn't penetrated, where residents are as out of touch with the world of fashion and musical trends as they are in touch with their neighbors, the latest town scandal, and Friday's final high-school basketball score. It's a slow-paced world, and it's not for everyone. Nonetheless, people in this region seem to revel in it. Ask rural South Dakotans why they choose to live here, and they're as inclined to wonder why you asked as they are to answer the question.

■ LEWIS AND CLARK RECREATION AREA

What Yankton and its environs lack in sophistication is more than made up for in their natural beauty and waterways, some found in the **Lewis and Clark Recreation Area**, five miles west of town on State Highway 52. The 22-mile-long, (35-km) Lewis and Clark Lake can be, in any season, either tranquil or challenging. At times, its silence is interrupted by little more than the occasional call of a meadowlark, while at other times, its tree-lined bluffs resound with the drone of powerboats and are whipped by the same relentless prairie winds that drove hundreds of homesteaders crazy.

The lakeshore of Lewis and Clark alternates between rolling golf courses, campgrounds, cabin sites, beaches, and marinas. More than 40,000 people per week visit Lewis and Clark, the majority between May and September when getting near the water for water-skiing, sailing, or reclining in a chaise lounge becomes a necessity. The lake isn't known for its fishing. Weekenders with a penchant for flashy speedboats and a pocketbook for 14-foot (4-m), benched-seat fishing boats find this an ideal spot to look around for used watercraft, especially in late fall, when arctic blasts and the fiscal realities of winter lead to a run on "For Sale" signs at the local hardware store. For those without a boat, the setting may be a little obnoxious. But for those with the right speedboat, in summer, when the marina

Awesome thunderstorms rake South Dakota every spring and summer; in springtime, tornadoes develop in the eastern part of the state.

slips are packed and beer sales peak, Lewis and Clark Lake is a roaring, wave-crashing vacation spot. For help in planning a visit call (605) 668-3435; for camping reservations, 665-9030; and for accommodations, 665-2680.

■ YANKTON RESERVATION

About 40 miles (64 km) west of Yankton on State Highway 50 stands the Yankton Reservation, a 36,561-acre reserve established in 1853. The southern boundary of the reservation is formed by the Missouri River, a portion of which has been impounded by **Fort Randall Dam.** At the base of the massive earthen dam stands the **Fort Randall Historic Site,** which commemorates a military outpost established in 1856 to keep peace between the white settlers and the Sioux. Its roster of visitors included Philip Sheridan, William Tecumseh Sherman, George Custer, and Sioux leader Sitting Bull, who was held prisoner at the fort for two years before being allowed to return to Standing Rock Reservation. The only structure still standing at the site is the **Fort Randall Chapel,** a white-chalk rock structure constructed in 1875. For information call (605) 487-7844.

■ RURAL LIFE ALONG THE HIGHWAYS

One of the best ways to see the countryside of the southeast is to follow **U.S. 81,** which extends due north from Yankton, roughly retracing the path of the state's first homesteaders. Three miles (5 km) out of town, the multi-lane highway returns to two-lane blacktop that passes cornfields and silos and a small town every 12 to 15 miles (20 to 25 km).

In each community, the accents of long-time residents announce the lineage of the town's founders. The Germans, Czechs, and Norwegians who first settled southeastern South Dakota tended to band with their own kind to establish towns in the early years. In doing so, most found comfort in facing the trials of everyday life and weather that was alternately colder and hotter than their homelands. More than a century later, the nondescript one- and two-story buildings on each main street belie the locals' enthusiasm for their ancestry. Despite being fourth-generation Americans, most of these folks still spend a weekend every few months celebrating their heritage at a festival or street fair, eating bratwurst or lefse.

HUSBAND AND WIFE ON THE PRAIRIE

That summer Per Hansa was transported, was carried farther and ever farther away on the wings of a wondrous fairy tale—a romance in which he was both prince and king, the sole possessor of countless treasures . . .

These days he was never at rest, except when fatigue had overcome him and sleep had taken him away from toil and care. But this was seldom, however; he found his tasks too interesting to be a burden; nothing tired him, out here. Ever more beautiful grew the tale; ever more dazzlingly shone the sunlight over the fairy castle.

How could he steal the time to rest, these days? Was he not owner of a hundred and sixty acres of the best land in the world? Wasn't his title to it becoming more firmly established with every day that passed and every new-broken furrow that turned? He gazed at his estate and laughed happily, as if at some pleasant and amusing spectacle . . . . Such soil!

❖ ❖ ❖

Beret [Hansa] had now formed the habit of constantly watching the prairie; out in the open, she would fix her eyes on one point of the sky line—and then, before she knew it, her gaze would have swung around the whole compass; but it was ever, ever the same . . . . Life it held not; a magic ring lay on the horizon, extending upward into the sky; within this circle no living form could enter; it was like the chain inclosing the king's garden, that prevented it from bearing fruit . . . . How could human beings continue to live here while that magic ring encompassed them? And those who were strong enough to break through were only being enticed still farther to their destruction! . . .

They had been here four months now; to her it seemed like so many generations; in all this time they had seen no strangers except the Indians—nor would they be likely to see any others. . . . People had never dwelt here, people would never come; never could they find home in this vast, wind-swept void . . . . Yes, *they* were the only ones who had been bewitched into straying out here! . . . Thus it was with the erring sons of men; they were lost before they knew it; they went astray without being aware; only others could see them as they were. Some were saved, and returned from their wanderings, changed into different people; others never came back! . . .

At these times, a hopeless depression would take hold of her; she would look around at the circle of the sky line; although it lay so far distant, it seemed threatening to draw in and choke her . . . .

—Ole Edvart Rölvaag, *Giants in the Earth,* 1927

Along the direct route between Sioux City and Sioux Falls on I-29, towns are sometimes few and far between, so pit stops are a necessity. For motorists entering the state at its southeastern edge, where billboards bark orders to stop at every interchange, **Edgar's Ol' Fashion Soda Fountain** in the Pioneer Drug at Elk Point, just over the southeast border—60 miles (96 km) south of Sioux Falls on I-29 and 26 miles (42 km) south of Vermillion—is a worthwhile stop. The restored turn-of-the-century soda fountain boasts original wooden booths, counter stools, and root beer floats, sodas, and banana splits that'll make you forget about checking the gas gauge.

A side trip from I-29 is **Newton Hills State Park.** Located at the southern tip of the Coteau des Prairies (Hill of the Prairies), Newton Hills is arguably eastern South Dakota's most idyllic park. Located 11 miles (18 km) east of I-29 a little south of Canton on State Highway 11, its rich soil was rescued from the plow and now supports an abundance of plant and animal life. Grassy knolls and wooded ravines harbor deer, marmot, fox, wild turkey, and more than two hundred species of birds. Both the park's **Woodland Trail** (a National Recreation Trail) and the

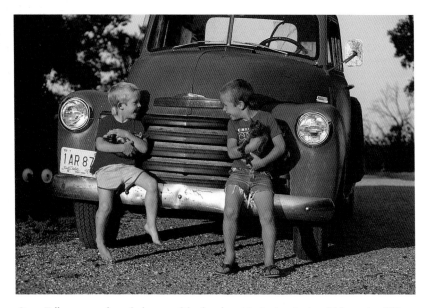

Sioux Falls was recently ranked as one of the three best cities in America in which to raise children.

A cold winter moon looms over a lonely farmstead.

Coteau Trail provide three-quarter-mile-long (1.2-km) escapes into unsettled South Dakota. You'll share the park with hikers, campers, horseback riders, skiers, birders, and photographers.

Liberally scattered throughout this landscape are hundreds of ponds and lakes, which range in size from three to 15,000 acres. Hidden from major roadways, they are worth seeking out, as anglers can find walleye, bullhead, perch, northern pike, crappie, and largemouth bass, as well as rainbow trout, catfish, and bluegills.

■ HUTTERITE COMMUNITIES

At the junction of Wolf Creek and the James River, north of Yankton on U.S. 81 and west on U.S. 18 near Olivet, the **Wolf Creek Colony** has maintained a fruitful existence as the second oldest Hutterite community in the state. Wolf Creek Industries, its most recent business venture, now takes orders for furniture and

Quilt making was an essential home industry in the Hutterite community of Bon Homme when this photo of a quilting bee was taken in the late 1890s. (South Dakota State Historical Society, Pierre)

lumber, often supplying newly established colonies with necessary building materials for new churches, schools, and houses. But its staple remains agriculture, and the colony raises 120 milk cows, 450 pigs, 1,000 beef cattle, 16,000 chickens, and 50,000 turkeys annually.

The Hutterite sect originated in Moravia and Tirol in 1533 as a branch of the Anabaptists, taking its name from Jacob Hutter before he was martyred in 1536. Between 1872 and 1879, one hundred Hutterite families left Russia to establish new colonies in Dakota Territory. Persecuted during World War I, most Hutterites fled to Canada. Gradually, in the 75 years since, Hutterites have returned to South Dakota, replenished their stock, expanded the number of colonies, and dramatically increased their land holdings. Once reportedly numbering less than 100 worldwide, today more than 30,000 Hutterites live predominantly in South Dakota and Canada. Thirty-five colonies currently exist in the state, while 40 can be found elsewhere in the U.S. and another 200 are operational in Canada.

Preferring a plain and simple life, with little outside intervention and no exposure to radio or television, Hutterites quietly go about their business of farming and furniture making. Theirs is a life of worship and hard work centered around family and tradition. Men work the fields and maintain equipment; women wash, cook, and tend the gardens, as if little has changed around them and they live at the center of a pure and completely understandable world.

In their simple lives, the Hutterites resemble the Amish, the conservative Christian agricultural communities of western Pennsylvania and parts of the Midwest. But unlike the Amish, Hutterites do not reject technology. Their farms feature the latest in agricultural equipment and computers, each used to create greater efficiency and more profit for the colonies. Hutterites are inclined to expand operations, purchase property, create new colonies as membership increases, and establish manufacturing businesses to diversify their holdings and provide new jobs as technology overtakes agriculture in employment prospects. Nonetheless, farming remains the cornerstone of most colonies, particularly those in southeastern South Dakota.

Their success in communal living has fostered envy from neighboring farmers concerned over the amount of property owned by Hutterites. That concern, which flares every decade or so, has even led to proposed legislation to restrict land acquisitions by Hutterites. Fortunately for the Hutterites, South Dakotans have always favored individual liberty over state regulation, and such bills die a quick and meaningfully silent death in legislative committee.

■ SIOUX FALLS

In 1856, the Western Town Site Company claimed a strip of land near the falls of the **Big Sioux River,** began enticing settlers, and started constructing the territory's newest community. In 1862, violence overflowing from the Minnesota Uprising to the east became more tangible when a father and son, haying on the outskirts of town, were killed by Indians. That act sent the entire town scampering for Yankton two days later, and the claim was all but abandoned. Following the Civil War, pioneer homesteaders returned to the area, only to find the deteriorating and charred remnants of their village, which had been destroyed by Santee Indian raiders.

With protection from the U.S. Cavalry, the rebuilding of Sioux Falls began in the late 1860s, and by 1873 the town claimed 573 residents. From a sweat-stained start as a trade center for agricultural products and fur pelts, Sioux Falls slowly evolved into a major trade and distribution hub. With the arrival of the railroad in 1886, the water and power available from the falls of the Big Sioux, and growing stockyard and exchange activities, the city became the leading commercial center in South Dakota by 1890. In the 1890s, South Dakota's relatively lax divorce

Sioux Falls' Main Street, early 1900s. (South Dakota State Historical Society, Pierre)

(right) The Old County Courthouse and Museum in downtown Sioux Falls.

laws kept attorneys, hoteliers, and merchants busy catering to a colorful collection of people sitting out the required six months in Sioux Falls to obtain their divorces. It wasn't until 1908 that religious leaders were able to rally their forces and have the residency requirement lengthened.

■ SIOUX FALLS TODAY

The only city in the state with more than 100,000 residents, Sioux Falls is located at the junction of interstates 29 and 90. In addition to industry and commerce, Sioux Falls can rightly lay claim to being the cultural capital of the state as well. Private and college-affiliated art galleries abound in Sioux Falls, as do museums, a symphony orchestra, playhouses, and dance companies. Theaters, sporting events, and 62 park areas encompassing 1,600 acres of land—including an exceptional greenway through town—make Sioux Falls the most cosmopolitan community in the state. The mature city also claims pricey boutiques, world-class health-care facilities, five golf courses, amusement parks, a respectable zoo, and more than 150 restaurants, including **Minerva's** at 301 South Phillips Avenue, probably the finest—and dearest—cuisine in Sioux Falls.

Despite its continued efforts to be the state's cultural capital, Sioux Falls still smacks of its agricultural origins. At church suppers and square dances, rodeos and neighborhood taverns, life goes on much the same as it has for decades. Sioux Falls is still the place that farmers go when they get all slicked up, locate their cleanest baseball cap, and head to town on business or pleasure.

Sioux Falls has accomplished what most ag-based economies have not over the past 20 years by attracting new industry and providing new jobs. Unlike many midsize Midwestern towns, this one is growing at a steady clip. Sioux Falls owes much of its success to a blend of about 5,000 businesses involved in manufacturing, banking, medical services, transportation, communications, and wholesale and retail trade. Citibank and the John Morrell meatpacking company, both with major operations in Sioux Falls, are among the state's leading employers.

The *New York Times* reported in 1991, "With business proliferating as fast and thick as the black-eyed Susans, tiger lilies, and prairie roses in nearby fields, Sioux Falls is becoming equally renowned as a major regional retail center, a rapidly growing medical center . . . and a transportation and wholesale distribution hub." About the same time, *Newsweek* magazine said Sioux Falls was the best place to live in the United States because of its exceptionally low crime rate, lack of pollution, low-cost housing, abundance of jobs, and laid-back lifestyle. For South Dakotans, who battled downturns in the agriculture, mining, and timber industries in the 1980s and '90s, Sioux Falls' success is a matter of pride.

The downside to Sioux Falls' development is that the city is suffering some growing pains. Modern office buildings are constructed in the muddy remains of fields that held rows of corn just last year. Streets are becoming congested, and an increasing number of strip malls, chain restaurants, discount stores, and parking lots have begun to overpower the town's quaintness and intimacy.

■ H I S T O R I C   D I S T R I C T

In the early days of Sioux Falls, prosperous businessmen constructed grand Queen Anne-style homes, several of which still stand today. The depression of the 1890s stalled further construction on so grand a scale, but families and preservationists continue to maintain several of the classic structures in the **St. Joseph's Cathedral Historic District,** located between Fourth and Tenth streets and bordered by Prairie and Spring streets.

One of the most interesting historical homes is that of South Dakota's first full-term U.S. senator—Richard F. Pettigrew. The senator purchased the 1889 Queen Anne-style house in 1911. An avid traveler, Pettigrew collected artifacts from around the world. Then, upon his death in 1926, he donated the house and its contents to the people of Sioux Falls. Historians speculate that Pettigrew made the donation to ensure some measure of immortality, which may not have been assured based on his political career. During two six-year terms in the Senate, Pettigrew was a Democrat, a Republican, a Populist, and finally a Socialist before South Dakota voters began to regard him as an eccentric radical and removed him from office. His personal and professional career was equally turbulent. Described as a mover and shaker in his early career, Pettigrew amassed a multi-million-dollar fortune and claimed ownership in more than a dozen Sioux Falls area businesses. When the Panic of 1893 hit the financial world, Pettigrew's investments faltered and he was forced to close or sell off the majority of his holdings.

The restored **Pettigrew Home & Museum** on the corner of Eighth and Duluth offers a glimpse into the senator's political, personal, and business life, as well as an insightful tour of exhibits that explore the natural and cultural history of Sioux Falls and Minnehaha County. The displays feature many Native American objects, and the home's research library contains Pettigrew's personal papers and a 5,000-volume library.

WIND AND DUST SPELL DISASTER

One November morning in 1933, the weather bureau in Huron, South Dakota, reported "a disturbance moving rapidly southeastward" over Canada. They didn't predict that the next day, a clear, crisp Sunday morning in Sioux Falls, the seemingly harmless air mass of moderate winds would become a huge dust storm.

Midwestern windstorms generally fall into three categories: tornadoes or whirlwind storms; cyclones or shift-wind storms; and—most unusual of the three—straightwind storms. Straightwind storms are formed when a low-pressure point or cyclone meets a high-pressure point or anticyclone, and, as the barometric pressures of the two systems equalize, gale forces erupt. It was the latter sort of storm, coming after years of drought, that was to initiate the disastrous period that came to be known as the Dust Bowl.

That Sunday morning of November 12, the wind picked up as the sun rose, and quickly reached 35 mph (56 kph). As its speed increased, the wind became a black cloud carrying seeds, sprouts, and topsoil as well as tumbleweed, gravel, and small rocks. Within a few hours the cloud grew to 9,000 feet (2,743 m). As the cyclone moved southeast, so did the windstorm, and by the time the storm reached Sioux Falls, the turbulent mass of dirt and dust—now moving at 60 mph (96 kph)—was 100 miles (160 km) wide. By 11:00 A.M., the city, reported the Sioux Falls *Argus Leader,* was "plunged into darkness."

The storm carried cacophonous noise, and the wind "howled throughout the day, snapping off telephone poles and trees, smashing windows, and grounding fences." The storm continued on through Iowa, pulling bricks off chimneys. One woman's roof was lifted from her house, then carried and deposited across the street, completely intact. The storm then swept through Minnesota, Nebraska, Missouri, and Illinois.

Around 3:00 P.M. that Sunday, the wind died down, and as the dust hovering in the air settled, the city of Sioux Falls began to emerge from darkness. Sunday night the temperature dropped from 50 degrees to 18 degrees F (10° to -8° C). When Midwesterners awoke Monday morning, their world, inside and out, was covered in dust, gravel, and grime.

If Sioux Falls was badly damaged—caved-in storefronts, destroyed displays—the rural areas suffered much greater loss. The *Argus Leader* stated: "The wind exposed the roots so that winter killing is inevitable even where the grain was not completely blown from the ground. ... It is estimated that farmers, already hard hit by economic and climatic conditions, will not be able to receive seed back from their fields." The worst news, however, was yet to come. The drought that had already turned the soil to dust continued relentlessly. Broken-down soil took on the consistency of ash, and small gusts swept up clouds of dust. Estimates are that 300 million tons of topsoil blew away from the Great Plains during this era.

The U.S. Soil Conservation Service was established in 1935 to develop techniques to slow soil erosion. Agronomists suggested contour plowing, strip cropping, and other techniques in a near-futile attempt to make the land productive, but not until 1939 did normal amounts of rain fall. By then, 100 million acres of farm land had become desert, and 3.5 million people had lost their livelihoods. Only after years of good rain fell and millions of government dollars were spent did the shifting sands become productive land once again.

—Julia Dillon

A massive dust storm (sometimes called a "black blizzard" in the Dust Bowl)
bears down on the town of Gregory in the spring of 1934.
(South Dakota State Historical Society)

The restored **Old Courthouse Museum** at the corner of Sixth and Main offers some of the same reflections on local history as the Pettigrew Home, but adds to its interpretation with a series of special activities throughout the year. In spring, the Almost Forgotten Crafts program reanimates sheep shearing, tin smithing, weaving, and other pioneer skills through a series of demonstrations. A fall buffalo feed is capped with regional talent performing Native American and ethnic dancing as well as traditional crafts, and in September the Tribal Arts Festival attracts fine native artists from around the nation and visitors from around the world.

Filled with historic grandeur, the Old Courthouse is embellished with 16 murals of varying sizes created by artist Ole Running in 1915. Most of the murals early Sioux Falls scenes. Between the second and third floors, staircase murals represent scenes of what are believed to be Running's native Norway. A particularly interesting dream-like painting portrays a lush forest with an elk. Above the trees a waterfall flows and even above that, high on a mountaintop, sits a lonely castle.

The building, constructed in 1890 of Sioux quartzite, also houses the **Minnehaha County Historical Society** and the **Sioux Valley Genealogical Society Library**. Both museums are listed as National Historic Landmarks and each continues to collect objects for the purpose of preserving, exhibiting and interpreting the history of the "Sioux land" region.

As far from the ocean as possible on the North American continent, amid a vast sea of prairie, rests a memorial to a ship and the men who sailed her. The **USS South Dakota Memorial Museum**, Twelfth and Kiwanis, honors the battleship which bore the name of the state and the 42 men who died serving on her.

The most highly decorated battleship of World War II, the USS *South Dakota* fought in every major battle in the Pacific between 1942 and 1945, and earned 13 battle stars and two U.S. Navy unit commendations. Today, a video and numerous photographs show the ship in combat actions, while historical items on display tell of a different, and less peaceful, era.

■ WESTERN AND INDIAN ART

Before the price of Western and Native American art began to skyrocket in the 1980s, Sioux Falls was already home to a host of galleries featuring such work. Today, several of those same galleries and a few more feed the appetites of art collectors and sidewalk gawkers. You won't see many local residents writing checks in these overpriced salons.

Most of this gallery art is for tourists, for the Easterners and West Coasters who will happily pay thousands of dollars for "Indian art" sometimes made by artisans with no Native American blood, and sometimes by Chinese in Taiwan. Rest assured though, that when this art is actually made by an Indian, a white man often makes the majority of the money from its sale. That's the way it is in South Dakota, and that's the way it's been with few exceptions for a hundred years.

On the other hand, discriminating tourists and serious collectors who peruse the galleries can recognize the finest of authentic Indian art. They appreciate the exquisite detail in the pieces created by Indian men and women most often living a lonely existence on one of South Dakota's bleak reservations. There, in a dimly lit cabin or a government-built house, is where true Indian art is created, and in that there is little glory. Only, sometimes, money.

Although it is impossible to provide a comprehensive list of galleries here, several Sioux Falls galleries distinguish themselves not only with rich displays of art depicting early-day South Dakota, but by combining that artwork with contemporary pieces by local, state, national, and international artists. (For more Sioux Falls galleries, see pp. 285–286 in "PRACTICAL INFORMATION.")

A pair of Sioux tepee-bags. Dogs often carried tepees in these across the prairies and plains.
(South Dakota State Historical Society, Pierre)

The **Jim Savage Western Art/Gift Gallery and Historical Center** at 3301 East 26th Street provides a unique blend of old, traditional, and modern Western art and collectibles, as well as numerous antiques, pottery, handmade jewelry, and clothing. Named for the late master wood sculptor, the historical center houses many of Savage's original works, including his sculpture of White Bull, created with more than 2,000 inlaid wooden pieces. The sculpture proves that Savage was not only a master of art but of patience as well.

The **Prairie Star,** located downtown amid a number of lesser galleries, features the best in South Dakota-made art. It boasts one of the state's premiere selections of handmade Native American artistry, including beadwork, drums, star quilts, rattles, quilled and horsehair work, and dance sticks. The jewelry of Lakota silversmith **Reed Haskell** is a bonus for the visitor. Haskell's award-winning work, which includes finely detailed bolo ties and belt buckles, is stunning and unequaled in the state.

■ AUGUSTANA COLLEGE

The Center for Western Studies at Augustana College, at 2111 South Summit Avenue, already has proven its dedication to preserving and interpreting the history and cultures of the northern prairie and plains through displays of historic photographs and manuscripts, Sioux Indian artifacts, Norwegian rosemaled furniture, and prairie art. Its gift shop has a fine selection of books, original artwork, jewelry, and bronzes. For information call (605) 336-4007.

Also at Augustana College is a reminder of Sioux Falls' own ambivalent cultural attitudes—the statue of Moses. In 1976, full-scale bronze castings of Michelangelo's *Moses* and *David*—each a monumental work—were donated to the city by Thomas Fawick, a wealthy philanthropist. As far from Florence, Italy, as they could be, Sioux Falls civic leaders truly believed the sculptures would bring a sense of culture, prosperity, and pride to the city.

At the time of the acquisition, judged by many to be among the most significant in the city's cultural history, supporters faced the Midwestern sensibilities of a group of well-heeled but modest local residents. As city fathers debated the final site of the striking but unclothed David, residents of a nearby highrise scolded community leaders for their plans to make them face David and all his full-frontal glory on a daily basis. After considerable debate, city fathers relented. David now gazes over a viaduct and a dreary railroad yard, his back turned meekly toward the highrise apartments and their occupants. Meanwhile, the robed Moses continues to stand on the campus of Augustana College.

■ S H E R M A N   P A R K

Located on a 32-acre site at the corner of Sixteenth and Kiwanis, Sherman Park is home to the Great Plains Zoo and the Delbridge Museum of Natural History. Each gives residents and visitors a place to go when they tire of fast-food, dusty roads, and strip malls.

Siberian tigers, black-footed penguins, grizzly bears, and birds of prey stalk visitors at the **Great Plains Zoo,** where exhibits approximate the natural habitat of a variety of species from five continents. Modeled after the San Diego Zoo, but scaled back by several hundred acres, visitors to Sioux Falls' zoo can experience the rugged expanse of a North American plain, the wild recesses of an African veldt, and the serenity of the Australian Outback, with attractions that include a children's zoo, penguin pool, primate building, birds of prey island, and bear dens.

Delbridge Museum of Natural History displays an unusually large collection of mounted game animals from around the globe. An African elephant, a rhinoceros, giraffe, giant panda, and thousands of other animals are each displayed in a natural, albeit indoor, setting. Its African water hole, Nile riverbank, and "restless Earth displays" are of particular interest.

The collection, among the largest known in the world, was assembled by one Henry Brockhouse, an unlikely candidate for the task. For years Brockhouse, who hunted big game in the far reaches of the globe, displayed his trophies at the back of the unkempt and dusty hardware store he owned in north Sioux Falls. Each day, curious kids with parents in tow would wind their way through packed aisles, past curtain rods and hammers, power tools, and widgets, to view Brockhouse's fearsome assemblage of dead animals. When Brockhouse died, his collection was purchased by C. J. Delbridge, who donated it to the city with the stipulation that it build the appropriate facility to house it. The museum opened in 1985.

■ M A L L S

As the regional retail hub for southeastern South Dakota, southwestern Minnesota, northeastern Nebraska, and northwestern Iowa, Sioux Falls has become a community filled with the same chain stores and asphalt parking pads of a thousand communities in the United States. Its more boosterish residents, eager to discount the magnetic appeal of Mount Rushmore in the western part of the state, are quick to note that Sioux Falls' massive **Empire Mall** is visited by four times as many people as the mountain memorial each year. In fact, the mall's only distinguishing characteristic is its size; it's interchangeable with any other mall in the country. There are three other malls and a myriad of specialty shops, bookstores, and galleries that make Sioux Falls South Dakota's only true shopping center.

■ NORTH TO GARRETSON

The area north of Sioux Falls is part of a region of vast farmlands that extend from Wisconsin through southern Minnesota and onto the seemingly endless prairies of central South Dakota. The eastern half of the state produces nearly a quarter billion bushels of corn each year, ranking South Dakota ninth in the United States for corn production. In addition to corn, in 1991 South Dakota produced 38.5 million bushels of oats (first in the United States); 96.2 million bushels of wheat (sixth); 17.9 million bushels of barley (sixth); 1.2 million bushels of rye (second);

Despite variations in the national economy, Sioux Falls continues to grow and prosper.

13 million bushels of sorghum (eighth); 58.3 million bushels of soybeans (ninth); 550.9 million pounds of sunflower seeds (second); and 8 million tons of hay (fifth).

A few miles north of I-90 on State Highway 11 lie the town of Garretson, population 924, and nearby **Devil's Gulch, Split Rock Park, and Palisades State Park.** The area's unique red-quartzite rock formations and creek-carved canyon walls are all accessible to the average hiker. Its fame stems from America's penchant for elevating its outlaws to hero status, and Garretson's touch of glory came at a shaded footbridge over a hidden canyon known as Devil's Gulch. By 1876, **Jesse James** and his brother, Frank, had led their gang on a 15-year, $300,000 spree that speckled the Plains with bank heists and strong-armed robberies. But after a decade and a half of losing family fortunes and a few town residents to errant bullets, settlers decided that they didn't have to take it anymore.

In the fall of 1876, the James Gang rode into Northfield, Minnesota, intent on relieving local townsfolk of their stored-up currency. The villagers, heavily armed and deeply irritated, elected to foil the robbery. They killed two gang members in a Main Street shoot-out, then formed a posse to dispose of the rest of the renegades in similar fashion.

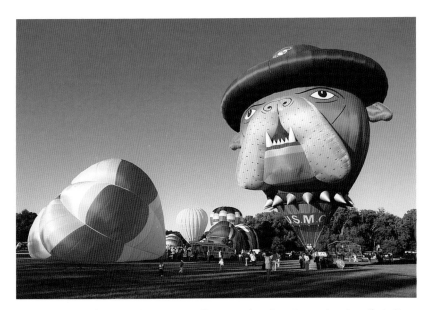

Annual balloon rallies take place in towns all over South Dakota. Pictured at this rally in Sioux Falls is a Marine "bulldog" balloon from the Soukup & Thomas International Airship & Balloon Museum in Mitchell.

With his wounded brother in tow, Jesse split from the rest of the gang to avoid the posse. The two brothers headed for the lawless sanctuary of Dakota Territory, only to discover that the posse had pursued them, rather than the other outlaws. Just north of Garretson, the James brothers went separate ways and attempted to outrun the law-enforcers on horseback. Frank scurried down the west side of Split Rock River and Jesse took the east side, not knowing that a deep, impassable chasm known as Devil's Gulch lay ahead.

As Jesse James reined in his horse and cursed his luck, he stared across a canyon 20 feet across and 50 feet deep (6 m by 15 m). The hoof beats of the posse were getting louder and the shots from carbines were echoing off the canyon walls when Jesse retraced his steps to get a running start. Then, with a whooping battle cry, Jesse dug his spurs into his horse's flanks and together they leaped the ravine, leaving the posse to mill about in disbelief on the other side.

After reuniting and holing up in a cave near present-day Palisades State Park for a few days, the James brothers headed into Nebraska. Unable to establish a new gang because of their notoriety from the Northfield fiasco, the brothers attempted the straight life. Jesse was shot and killed by Robert Ford six years later for $10,000 in

bounty money. Soon after, Frank turned himself in and was found not guilty of assorted crimes by a sympathetic jury. He held a variety of jobs until he died peacefully in 1915.

Jesse James (left) with brother, Frank. (Denver Public Library, Western History Dept.)

In late June each year, a **Jesse James Roundup Day** is held at Split Rock Park in Garretson. Activities include a Dutch oven cookoff, craft fair, chuck wagon feed, and a theater production commemorating the exploits of one of the most famous outlaws ever to set foot in South Dakota. For information, call (605) 428-3674.

■ MITCHELL AND VICINITY

About an hour west of Sioux Falls on I-90, Mitchell, a quaint Midwestern town of 14,000, has a tradition of attracting the unusual, the notable, and the road-weary. The steeple of its massive brick Catholic church is visible from 20 miles (32 km) away on the interstate. Its downtown is filled with old-time jewelers, law offices, and bars, all tucked inside three- and four-story storefronts. Most of the major chains have relocated to the strip malls on the town's northerly edge, leaving the tourists to roam the downtown streets. Nearby residential neighborhoods are quiet and shaded by hundred-year-old cottonwoods. On summer nights, thousands of locusts hide in those trees, sounding a loud and pulsating chorus. In winter, those same neighborhoods are still and bare.

Mitchell is home to the world's only **Corn Palace**, or as old-timers term it, the world's biggest bird-feeder. The first Corn Palace was built in 1892 to celebrate the area's fertile farmland and to promote settlement. The success of the "Corn Belt Exposition," held each autumn in the whimsical corn-encrusted building, prompted the construction of new, larger structures in 1905, when it was officially christened "the Corn Palace," and again in 1937, when its Moorish-inspired minarets, turrets, and kiosks were added.

The present palace is decorated with 3,000 bushels of corn, grain, and native grasses and, odd as it is, that's what pulls camera-toting motorists off I-90 and into downtown Mitchell each summer. The building hosted virtually every touring Big Band in the 1930s, '40s and '50s, and top-name performers such as Bob Hope and Andy Williams. And, after seeing it, there can be some certainty that several stars had harsh words for their booking agents.

When American bandmaster and composer John Philip Sousa was invited to "Play the Palace" for the thirteenth annual festival in 1904, he quickly telegraphed his South Dakota admirers with the four-word retort, "What is Corn Palace?"

(following pages) Mitchell's famous Corn Palace is covered with grain, native grasses, and thousands of ears of corn, fashioned to create colorful illustrations.

Apparently that question was answered satisfactorily, because Sousa and his band arrived at the city's train depot that fall. Even then, the world-touring bandmaster remained skeptical and unbudging in the seat of his Pullman car until concert organizers brought him $7,000 in cash. Sousa and his band then played a twelve-concert series.

Each year, before crowds gather for country western concerts and the carnival atmosphere surrounding **Corn Palace Week** in mid-September, crews strip the decorative murals from the building and apply a new decor. It's precise work which carries a price tag of about $35,000. Throughout the summer, workers apply new corn murals to the wooden panels of the exterior facade. Instructions are printed on roofing paper and attached to the panels. Varying types and colors of corn are cut and applied to the panels according to the artist's specifications. When completed, the murals depict life on the prairie through mosaics of windmills, grazing cattle, and horse-drawn plows.

The corn mosaics on the Corn Palace in Mitchell are changed every year.

Exterior panels are changed and adapted to a new theme each year, but the Palace's permanent interior panels remain the most exceptional work. Six of the interior panels, including a mural depicting the area's bountiful pheasant hunting, were designed between 1948 and 1971 by Oscar Howe, a Yanktonai Sioux painter whose geometrically abstract designs earned him critical acclaim and worldwide recognition.

The **Oscar Howe Art Center,** located about three blocks from the Corn Palace at 119 West Third, provides an in-depth look at the artist's work. Howe studied at the Sante Fe School, served as Artist Laureate of South Dakota, and taught at the University of South Dakota until his death in 1983. His work reveals a dedicated painter whose vision combines stories of Indian life and spirituality with a modern influence, all in vivid color. Howe's powerful paintings, effectively displayed in this center (listed as a National Historic Site), provide a testament to the artist's life-long ambition to inspire fellowship between Native Americans and whites.

Still more of Howe's work can be found at the **Friends of the Middle Border Museum** at 1311 South Duff. The original 1886 home of Louis Beckwith, co-founder of the Corn Palace, has been restored and serves as the focal point for a large collection of art, Native American exhibits, horse-drawn vehicles, early farm implements, and antique autos. The museum's **Case Art Gallery** contains sculptures, original prints, and paintings by artists such as Gutzon Borglum, Harvey Dunn, James Earle Fraser, and Childe Hassam.

Once travelers have visited the Corn Palace, many check out the 4,000 dolls displayed in a new castle called the **Enchanted Doll Museum** directly across the street. And as doll museums go, the collection of antique and modern dolls displayed in fairy tale settings is worth a stop for the collector, or for girls between four and eleven. Tomboys, however, have been known to fidget. Among the newest additions to the community is the **Soukup & Thomas International Balloon & Airship Museum,** whose name is full of hot air. Mitchell also is home to **Dakota Wesleyan University,** a small (570 students) liberal arts school on the city's south side.

Those who venture north of town to the shores of Lake Mitchell will discover the state's lone National Archaeological Landmark. The **Mitchell Prehistoric Indian Village,** a town site dating back to about 900 B.C., offers a rare glimpse into the lives of prehistoric peoples who vanished from the northern Great Plains in the

thirteenth century, possibly as the result of an extended drought. Continuing research at the site, which also is designated a National Historic Landmark, has revealed a place where as many as 1,000 semi-nomadic hunters and gardeners stalked buffalo, built lodges, raised vegetables, and protected one another from hostile bands of warriors. The village also offers a relaxing walk over a swinging bridge, through a hunter's lodge, museum, and visitors center. Guided tours are available May through October.

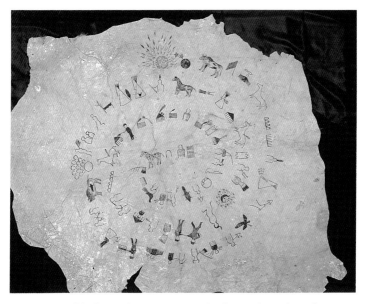

Winter counts, like this one by Lone Dog, served as historical records. Each winter, a pictograph representing the year's events was added to a buffalo skin. (South Dakota State Historical Society, Pierre)

(left) "Ghost Dance" by Indian artist Oscar Howe. (Courtesy of Adelheid Howe) Howe once said of his own work: "It has always been my version of Indian traditions—to make it individualistic in my own way—but every part comes from Indian and not White culture. I have been labeled wrongfully a Cubist. The basic design is 'Tahokmu' (spiderweb). From an all-Indian background I developed my own style."

THE NORTHEAST

IN THE NORTHEASTERN REGION OF THE STATE, the gently rolling hills and prairie potholes are interspersed with lakes, several state parks and recreation areas, and two national wildlife refuges. Drained by the valleys of the Big Sioux and James rivers, then sliced across the top by the curves of the Bois de Sioux River, Big Stone Lake, and the Minnesota River, the northeast has many terrains. In the eastern reaches of the region, near the Minnesota border, tree-lined lakes lie between gentle hills which drop into shallow ravines with thickets and wildflowers. Closer to the Missouri in the western part of this quarter, the land is drier, and cattle ranches are more common than farms.

The lakes in this region were formed when glaciers from the last Ice Age slowly receded across northeastern South Dakota 11,000 years ago, scouring and gouging the earth, leaving behind miles of prairie speckled with more than 120 lakes. Glaciers also left deposits of debris, sand, soil, gravel and rock—up to 400 feet (120 m) deep over the bedrock in spots—forming the rough, arrowhead-shaped range of hills that blankets the eastern ridge of the state. These **Coteau des Prairies** (Hills of the Prairie) were home to several succeeding Indian cultures. Burial mounds, shards of pottery, and hand tools are evidence of the Woodland People who lived in the region about A.D. 1200.

Sioux Indians made their way here by traveling west from the woodlands of present-day Minnesota. They found the Paha Tanka (Great Hills) of northeastern South Dakota teeming with elk, buffalo, deer and antelope. Rugged, timber-covered hills and ravines afforded easily defended campsites and an abundance of fish-filled lakes, wild fruits and vegetables, and fuel. The Sioux inhabited this region for about a century before the first white men—French fur traders exploring the western frontier—discovered its bounty.

■ JOSEPH NICOLLET

In 1838, the U.S. Secretary of War engaged a French-born mathematician and astronomer, Joseph Nicollet, to survey the area. In producing his "mother map,"

THE NORTHEAST

Nicollet also became fascinated with the gentle grandeur of eastern South Dakota, its broad prairiescapes, lush river valleys, grasslands, and wildflowers:

> *May* I not be permitted in this place to introduce a few reflections on the magical influence of the prairies? . . . Their sight never wearies . . . to ascend one of its undulations, moving from wave to wave over alternate swells and depression; and finally to reach the vast interminable low prairie, that extends itself in front, be it for hours, days, or weeks, one never tires. . . . It is then they should be visited; and I pity the man whose soul could remain unmoved under such a scene of excitement.

Nicollet realized that by mapping this region he was setting in motion a chain of events that would destroy the lives and livelihoods of the American Indian, and had profoundly mixed feelings about what he was doing: "Then it was I bade a last adieu to the unconstrained liberty of the (Indians), who, it requires no great foresight to anticipate, will soon have to yield to the restraints of civilization."

Nicollet's map was published four years after his journey ended and in the same year as his death. Although his maps have been proven highly accurate by modern-day aerial surveying, Nicollet received little attention until his journals were translated from French to English and published in 1976. Today, the Frenchman's efforts are memorialized by a rather incongruous 75-foot (23-m)-tall tower, a gift from a handful of Sisseton senior citizens. The tower and interpretive center are located near Sisseton at I-29 and State Highway 10.

■ SETTLEMENT

As Indian tribes were forced westward by treaties and U.S. cavalry troops, European immigrants followed, encouraged by railroad promoters and land agents, who hoped to attract new settlers, establish new towns, and increase commerce. Promising a paradise of blue sky and soft soil to any bundle-laden immigrant just off the boat, land agents would cajole, ingratiate, bribe, and otherwise use any means at their disposal to talk pioneers into heading for the townsite that they represented. And with increasing rail access, larger waves of settlers came.

Merchants followed and constructed stores and liveries. Newspaper editors brought presses and printed land notices, newsy bits, deeds, and drivel. Bankers built vaults. Connecting all these tiny towns—delivering supplies and departing with cattle, crops, and cash—was the railroad. So important was rail service in the

SETTLING A NEW CLAIM ON THE SOD

*I*t was a marvellous adventure. By noon we were up amid the rounded grassy hills of the Sisseton Reservation where only the coyote ranged and the Sioux made residence.

Here we caught our first glimpse of the James River valley, which seemed to us at the moment as illimitable as the ocean and as level as a floor, and then pitching and tossing over the rough track, with our cars leaping and twisting like a herd of frightened buffaloes, we charged down the western slope, down into a level land of ripened grass, where blackbirds chattered in the willows and prairie chickens called from the tall rushes which grew beside the sluggish streams.

Aberdeen was the end of the line, and when we came into it that night it seemed a near neighbor to Sitting Bull and the bison. And so, indeed, it was, for a buffalo bull had been hunted across this site less than a year before.

It was twelve miles from here to where my father had set his stakes for his new home, hence I must have stayed all night in some small hotel, but that experience has also faded from my mind. I remember only my walk across the dead-level plain next day. For the first time I set foot upon a landscape without a tree to break its sere expanse—and I was at once intensely interested in a long flock of gulls, apparently rolling along the sod, busily gathering their morning meal of frosted locusts. The ones left behind kept flying over the ones in front so that a ceaseless change of leadership took place.

There was beauty in this plain, delicate beauty and a weird charm, despite its lack of undulation. Its lonely unplowed sweep gave me the satisfying sensation of being at last among the men who held the outposts,—sentinels for the marching millions who were approaching from the east. For two hours I walked, seeing Aberdeen fade to a series of wavering, grotesque notches on the southern horizon line, while to the north an equally irregular and insubstantial line of shadows gradually took on weight and color until it became the village in which my father was at this very moment busy in founding his new home.

My experienced eyes saw the deep, rich soil, and my youthful imagination looking into the future, supplied the trees and vines and flowers which were to make this land a garden.

I was converted. I had no doubts. It seemed at the moment that my father had acted wisely in leaving his Iowa farm in order to claim his share of Uncle Sam's rapidly-lessening unclaimed land.

—Hamlin Garland, *A Son of the Middle Border*, 1917

last half of the nineteenth century that people who'd established communities before rail service arrived dismantled whole towns and reassembled them next to the railroad line. Those communities stubborn enough not to move are all ghost towns today.

■ MADISON

Founded in 1875, the town of Madison stands northwest of Sioux Falls at the intersection of I-81 and State Highway 34. The small town is home to Dakota State College, originally founded in 1881 as the state's first normal school. On campus at North Eighth Street is the Smith-Zimmerman State Museum, with its displays of farm implements and household items dating from settlement of the area following the Homestead Act of 1862. Call (605) 256-5308 for more information.

Just a few miles west of **Madison** on State Highway 34, the little **Prairie Village** marks the early settler's way of life all summer. From Memorial Day to Labor Day, life is as it was, and fortunately, for all but the faint of heart, is carried on only as a memory in a few places such as this. A sod house squats on one corner of this living museum and the opera house where Lawrence Welk got his start sits just

Rural life along State Highway 34.

past the livery stable. Authentically restored all the way down to the 1893 steam carousel and its hand-carved wooden horses, Prairie Village is a bit of a movie set, but kind of a kick. The people of Madison, by the way, are modern and friendly and less inclined to leave you feeling pinched for your dollars than their counterparts manning the host of attractions along the interstates. On the last full weekend in August, the looms and farm tractors are in full gear for the **Prairie Village Steam Threshing Jamboree,** a festival with demonstrations of horse-powered feed grinding, antique tractor plowing, grain threshing, rug weaving, quilting, and spinning.

Other towns in the northeast host festivals commemorating their sodbusting founding fathers and mothers at festivals and party weekends. In June, **Webster** hosts the **Sodbuster Fest.** In **Miller,** residents go to the **Old Settlers Picnic,** and in **Lonetree, Sodbusting Days.** Many sodbusting communities were formed by immigrant groups such as Germans, Norwegians, Swedes, and Czechs who built their churches and supported their own ecclesiastical schools and hospitals. Some northeastern South Dakotans remember these ethnic roots, as in **Eureka** (on State Highway 10 in the extreme northwestern part of the region), where each September residents hold a **German Schmeckfest.** Costumes and dances are authentic, beer flows freely, and wursts are the best pick of the day.

Old-time fiddlers do their thing at the South Dakota State Fair.

■ FLANDREAU AND VICINITY

South Dakota has joined the latest American gold rush: gambling. After years of pari-mutuel betting on dogs and ponies, the state legalized video lottery machines, and in 1989 voters approved limited stakes gambling in Deadwood to raise the necessary funds to preserve its Wild West character. But it took Congressional action to bring games of chance to the Indian reservations, and South Dakota responded enthusiastically.

The **Royal River Casino,** located at **Flandreau** off I-29, is 26 miles (41.6 km) north of Sioux Falls. Despite the fact that the casino building lacks both the Wild West flavor and Victorian architecture of those found in Deadwood or the pizzazz of the mega-casinos of Las Vegas and Atlantic City, the proximity of the Royal River to Sioux Falls allows it to attract thousands of visitors each week who are lured by blackjack tables, poker games, and the incessant ringing of 235 slot machines.

As with other Indian casinos in the state, and indeed the nation, this Santee Sioux tribe-owned hotspot has brought new economic prosperity to a reservation once plagued by joblessness and despair. Visitors to Flandreau today will find a revived community of 2,300 residents that was first settled in 1869 by 25 Christian Santee Sioux families. The reservation is also the site of a school widely attended by Indian children. Visitors may question the marriage of reservations and gaming as if something had been lost, some soul or mystique. But in South Dakota, whose reservations have traditionally been among the poorest areas in America, there is a new outlook, a new mood, and it shows on the faces of those who live there.

The **Moody County Museum Complex** displays antiques and collectibles from the area's pioneer past, and the county courthouse and community center offer numerous murals of the Indians and homesteaders who have traveled through the 120-year-old history of the community. Flandreau has several historic houses of worship, including the **First Presbyterian Church,** the oldest continuously operating church in South Dakota.

Flandreau's location on the Big Sioux River is scenic and uncrowded and each year, on the third weekend in July, residents celebrate their heritage in authentic costumes and traditional ceremonies at the **Santee Sioux Powwow.** For more information, call (605) 997-3871.

■ BROOKINGS

Twenty-three miles (36.8 km) north of Flandreau and 49 miles (78.4 km) north of Sioux Falls on I-29 stands another community named for a settler and known for its tree-lined boulevards and university campus. In the 1940s, Brookings was a sleepy town of 6,000 residents whose future was tied to South Dakota State University, which in turn depended on the largesse of the ag-dominated state legislature. Then a few thousand education-hungry servicemen returned home following World War II, and the town took off. Even though its population has remained constant at just over 16,000 in recent decades, Brookings is home to more quality artwork and museums than its past, population, or location would suggest.

Born in Woolwich, Maine, **Wilmot W. Brookings** earned his degree from Bowdoin College, then became one of South Dakota's pioneers in August 1857. In February 1858, acting as manager of a land company, Brookings set out on horseback from present-day Sioux Falls to establish a town at Yankton. Fifty miles later, a severe blizzard struck and the temperature plummeted to -30° F (-34° C). Already in danger of frostbite and death, Brookings compounded his problems by falling from his horse and landing in the Split Rock River. Wet and unprotected, Brookings realized his only hope for survival rested in a return trip to Sioux Falls in darkness. His feet were frozen when he finally reached the settlement. Under the most primitive of conditions and with only a butcher knife, a small saw, and no anesthetics, Dr. J. L. Phillip performed the first amputation in the history of what is now South Dakota.

Even with both legs gone below the knee, Brookings cast his lot with the Dakota pioneers and, because of his education, soon became a leading force in the territory. In a half-century of service to the state, Brookings was among the first members of the Squatter Legislature, was named governor of Dakota Territory, served as associate justice, published the *Sioux Falls Leader,* organized a railroad, served as a member of the state constitutional convention, and worked variously as promoter, owner, and director of six major banks and companies in the state.

■ SOUTH DAKOTA STATE UNIVERSITY

Today, the city that bears Brookings' name is quaint and would be resoundingly quiet if it weren't for the more than 8,500 students who attend South Dakota

State University, the state's largest educational institution. Founded in 1881, the university, with its botanical gardens, museums, and cultural and social organizations, is the focal point of the town. With programs in 200 majors, minors, and options, SDSU offers more than 2,500 courses annually, as well as bachelor's, master's, and doctoral degrees. Because of its beautiful setting and strong academic program, the university is popular and attracts a high percentage of out-of-state students. In 1992, more than a third of its students came from 43 states and 30 foreign countries.

South Dakota State's chief rival is the University of South Dakota at Vermillion. Brookings students like to say that the highest point in South Dakota is Harney Peak (7,242 feet or 2,202 m), and that the lowest point is at Vermillion, especially where the USD football team plays. So much for collegiate wit.

The **South Dakota Art Museum** on the SDSU campus houses works by two of South Dakota's finest artists. One is Harvey Dunn, the son of sodbusters and a painter who produced a vivid, though sometimes overly romantic, account of the good moments in the life of a prairie homesteader. In those paintings, viewers find little of the sod houses and tarpaper shacks, the fierce winters and dry summers, and the ceaseless, tedious labor which filled life on the South Dakota frontier. Classic, romantic, and beautiful, the paintings seem to illustrate the all-is-right-with-the-world version of life which Laura Ingalls Wilder described in her series of pioneer adventure books.

The second important artist represented in the museum is Oscar Howe, a Sioux Indian whose work derives from traditional Indian painting techniques but also reveals influences of twentieth-century European movements. Born on the Crow Creek Reservation in 1915, Howe recorded the life, history, and legends of his people, the Yanktonai Sioux. His vision was powerful and mystical, modern, colorful, and commanding, and his life and work have served as an important model for other aspiring Indians.

In addition to the collections of Dunn and Howe, the museum offers the work of contemporary South Dakota artists and handiwork of all the Sioux tribes, with examples of porcupine-quill embroidery, beadwork, eagle-feather headdresses, and intricately carved ceremonial pipes from the Crow, Dakota (eastern Sioux), Kiowa, Ojibwa (Chippewa), and Yakima tribes.

Delicate and refined work of a different tradition can be found in the museum's collection of **Marghab embroidery**, produced on the Portuguese islands of Madeira.

Given to the museum in the late 1970s by Emile and Vera Way Marghab, the collection is displayed in a custom-built room, with specially designed lighting and climate controls. Donor Vera Way was raised in South Dakota before she became a concert pianist and met and married Emile Marghab, a native of Cyprus. In Madeira, the two founded a linen company, the Casa Marghab, where Vera designed each of the company's offerings. When political unrest hit Portugal in 1978, Casa Marghab was closed and Vera selected the South Dakota State Museum for her complete collection of embroidered linens—1,918 pieces, including 282 designs. Vera herself later returned to Watertown, South Dakota. Collectors from around the world, including those at New York's Metropolitan Museum of Art, regard Marghab linens as the measure of excellence among such embroidered pieces.

Boosters of SDSU's **McCrory Gardens** bill it "as the prettiest 70 acres in South Dakota," and at summer's peak it's hard to argue the point. Featuring 14 formal theme gardens, including the newest Centennial Prairie Garden, the Children's Maze, and the Rock Garden, McCrory Gardens is a botanist's delight. In the adjacent **South Dakota Arboretum,** trees and shrubs are tested for tolerance to the state's uneven climate and varied soils.

Harvey Dunn's "The Prairie is My Garden" reveals the artist's romantic vision of prairie frontier life. The painting would make a perfect illustration for one of Laura Ingalls Wilder's idealized tales of settlers and sodbusting. (South Dakota Art Museum, Brookings)

Raising hardy plants is an appropriately calm activity in Brookings. Except perhaps on Friday nights when the frat houses and beer halls gear up for another party, it's rather subdued here—the Sunday morning church bells may be one of the noisiest events of the week.

■ OAKWOOD LAKES STATE PARK

Just north of Brookings, prairie potholes dot the landscape, marking one end of the northeast's chain of hundreds of clear blue lakes. Twice each year, these waters along the Central Flyway are visited by millions of ducks. Among these lakes are eight with 3,000 acres of water and surrounded by native hardwoods which comprise **Oakwood Lakes State Park,** 20 miles (32 km) northwest of Brookings on State Highway 30. Remnants of early habitation by the Woodland People—the Paleo-Indians who raised corn and beans in the Great Plains as long ago as 1000 B.C.—are found in 10 burial mounds within the park. Later, Sioux Indians called this area Tetankaha—"Home of the Great Summer Lodge." Also here is the cabin of the first white man to settle in the area, restored as a reminder of the rugged life of that era.

Fortifications built by soldiers following the Minnesota Uprising and later used as an Indian scout outpost for Fort Sisseton—a fort 93 miles (149 km) north (see "Sisseton")—are still visible in the park. Legend has it that an Indian princess was drowned in one of Oakwood's lakes by the warriors of her tribe after warning her soldier lover of an impending Indian attack.

■ DE SMET

Thirty miles (48 km) west of Oakwood State Park, near the shores of Mud Lake and Lakes Henry and Preston, is the hamlet of De Smet. De Smet traces its history to the coming of the railroad, and its name to a Jesuit missionary who spent his life among the Sioux Indians.

This town of 1,200 has a wonderfully renovated railroad depot and several paintings in a series by De Smet native Harvey Dunn. In his lifetime, Dunn painted more than 30 oils depicting pioneer life in South Dakota. In viewing several of those works now displayed at the **De Smet City Library,** it's difficult not to notice

Dunn's tendency to glamorize prairie life. His technique is refined and unfaltering, but his subjects are too content, too happy to portray accurately the ceaseless toil it took to conquer the land and the forces of nature. Dunn's paintings primarily capture the good things about homestead life—the occasional day of sunshine when the plow didn't break, the wind didn't blow, and the wildflowers were in full bloom.

Each year on the last weekend in June and the first two weekends in July, De Smet gives thanks to author Laura Ingalls Wilder. A resident of De Smet from the age of 12 until 27, Wilder immortalized prairie living in her series of pioneer adventure books, and described De Smet in one of them—*Little Town on the Prairie*. On these weekends, the town celebrates the pioneer way of life: actors recreate scenes from Wilder's books in an outdoor pageant and children can take free rides on a horse-drawn wagon. Visitors can ramble through the **Surveyors' Shanty** at 101 Olivet, the Ingalls' first home in De Smet, or the frame **Ingalls House** at 210 West Third Street that Pa Ingalls built in 1887, where many of his hand-crafted items are on display; call (605) 854-3181. Or they might stroll under the cottonwood trees planted by Mr. Ingalls that today tower over the little town.

Despite the bustle of tourists who retrace the life of Wilder and her family, the town remains relatively tranquil. Building facades and costumed attendants may reveal concessions to the tourist trade, but the residents of this town remain hospitable and genuinely friendly.

■ HURON

Had it not been for residents as persistent today as they were a century ago, Huron, located west of Brookings on U.S. 14, may have remained just another town along the rail. Surveyors for the Chicago & Northwestern Railroad first set up camp here in 1879. By the mid-1880s, Huron citizens tried to win the status of territorial capital (they succeeded) and, later, state capital (they failed) for their town. What they couldn't acquire in the commerce that hosting the state government would bring, they made up for with a strong agricultural economy. Today it serves as a regional hub for manufacturing, shopping, and health facilities.

Huron's **Campbell Park Historic District,** located between Fifth and Ninth streets S.W., preserves 89 turn-of-the-century structures, many of them modest but well-kept residences in Queen Anne and Colonial styles. A wonderful, flowing

(following pages) The sky rather than the land creates the striking scenery in eastern South Dakota.

A Different Kind of Prairie

*B*eyond the Big Sioux there were no more fields, no houses, no people in sight. There really was no road, only a dim wagon trail, and no railroad grade. Here and there Laura glimpsed a little wooden stake, almost hidden in the grasses. Pa said they were surveyors' stakes for the railroad grade that was not started yet.

Laura said to Mary, "This prairie is like an enormous meadow, stretching far away in every direction, to the very edge of the world."

The endless waves of flowery grasses under the cloudless sky gave her a queer feeling. She could not say how she felt. All of them in the wagon, and the wagon and team, and even Pa, seemed small.

All morning Pa drove steadily along the dim wagon track, and nothing changed. The farther they went into the west, the smaller they seemed, and the less they seemed to be going anywhere. The wind blew the grass always with the same endless rippling, the horses' feet and the wheels going over the grass made always the same sound. The jiggling of the board seat was always the same jiggling. Laura thought they might go on forever, yet always be in this same changeless place, that would not even know they were there . . . .Now they were in Dakota Territory going farther west. But this was different from all the other times, not only because there was no

Laura Ingalls Wilder, author of the "Little House on the Prairie"
series, poses for a family portrait. She is standing in the middle of
the back row. (South Dakota State Historical Society, Pierre)

cover on the wagon and no beds in it, but some other reason. Laura couldn't say how, but this prairie was different.

"Pa," she asked, "when you find the homestead, will it be like the one we had in Indian Territory?"

Pa thought before he answered. "No," he said finally. "This is different country. I can't tell you how, exactly, but this prairie is different. It feels different."

"That's likely enough," Ma said sensibly. "We're just west of Minnesota, and north of Indian Territory, so naturally the flowers and grasses are not the same."

But that was not what Pa and Laura meant. There was really almost no difference in the flowers and grasses. But there was something else here that was not anywhere else. It was an enormous stillness that made you feel still. And when you were still, you could feel great stillness coming closer.

All the little sounds of the blowing grasses and of the horses munching and whooshing in their feedbox at the back of the wagon, and even the sounds of eating and talking could not touch the enormous silence of this prairie.

—Laura Ingalls Wilder, *By the Shores of Silver Lake,* 1941

sculpture celebrates the contributions made by women to the state. Called "**Spirit of Dakota,**" it stands outside the **Crossroads Convention Center** in downtown Huron.

In 1904, Pierre may have been selected as the permanent state capital, but the same year Huron was chosen as the site for the annual state fair. Each August this town of 12,500 experiences a population explosion with the opening of the **South Dakota State Fair,** which takes place on the edge of town. The world's largest pheasant, tipping the scales at 22 tons (it's fiberglass), greets visitors along the highway as they arrive for grandstand entertainment, exhibits, carnivals, or the opportunity to see neighbors and discuss local politics. Four-H'ers show their best bulls, dairy cows, and calves for a week, then, following judging, watch their beloved animals sold at auction. Cowboys and cowgirls ride in rodeo performances, hoping to garner cash prizes offered in saddle bronc, bull riding, and barrel racing. In the exhibition halls, blue ribbons hang from the best-looking tomato, the most impressive squash, the loveliest flower arrangement, and the finest painting. Vendors hawk hot dogs and lemonade to fairgoers wandering around the midway carnival rides. The songs of country western stars fill the night, mingling with the musty smells emanating from the sale barns and beer tents.

■ HAYTI'S FARKLEBERRY FESTIVAL

Most of the early settlers of South Dakota learned to make do with what they had. There weren't many cries for public assistance (maybe because there was none to be had). Many of today's South Dakotans maintain the same make-do ethos. In fact, in one community on the shores of Lake Marsh, residents became so concerned with what they didn't have that they decided to invent something that no one else had. These were the 371 good-humored townspeople of Hayti (pronounced "HAY-tie"), 50 miles (80 km) northeast of Brookings on U.S. 81, who needed a gimmick to increase the community's commerce: Lake Marsh itself wasn't attracting any throngs of visitors, and even interest in the annual community celebration, called "Town & Country Days," was waning.

Enter Gordon Hanson, a Hayti native and teller of numerous "Ole and Lena" jokes. In 1986, the long-time South Dakota journalist discovered the mythical farkleberry, which any serious botanist would know claimed roots in its relative —the whortleberry. Thus was born Hayti's Fall Farkleberry Festival, which oddly enough was conducted in July.

For nearly a decade, the rest of South Dakota tried to separate farkle-fact from farkle-fiction. The event is no longer held in Hayti, but you can still get a smile by ordering farkleberry pie with your coffee. On the way out of town, don't miss the world's only farkleberry test plot. It'll be on your right.

■ WATERTOWN AREA

Almost 30 miles (48 km) north of Brookings on I-29 and just east on State Highway 22 is **Cochrane Lake,** one of the few spring-fed lakes in South Dakota, and a wonderful body of water that still retains the kind of clarity it did when glaciers created it some 11,000 years ago. The 400-acre lake features campsites, boating, and swimming in a picturesque setting of woods and water. More sailing and windsurfing is available further north, on lakes closer to Watertown.

About 20 miles (32 km) north of the Lake Cochrane Recreation Area lies Watertown, a center for regional commerce, near the shores of lakes Kampeska and Pelican. The founding of Watertown began in 1871, after the old Winona and St. Peter Railroad Company had completed a line from Minnesota to the east shores of Lake Kampeska, which proved an ideal site for a township. Originally called Kampeska, the town's more recent name is credited to two brothers whose native town was Watertown, New York.

Watertown was home to Dakota Territory's last governor and the state of South Dakota's first governor, Arthur Calvin Mellette. An attorney and editor from the East Coast who moved to Dakota Territory in 1879, Mellette was appointed territorial governor by President Benjamin Harrison, and in 1883 he built a red brick Italianate home in Watertown. Mellette was elected South Dakota's first governor by a wide margin in 1889. During his two terms in office, he tried to increase commodity prices paid to farmers and mitigate the effects of drought.

Following Mellette's term as governor, one of his best friends, the popular state treasurer W. W. Taylor, absconded with $367,000 of the state's money and left for an extended South American holiday. As one of Taylor's bondsmen, Mellette was liable for a portion of the loss. The former governor attempted to avoid scandal and restore confidence in state government by voluntarily surrendering to the state all of his family assets, including real estate and his home in Watertown. A short time later, a disillusioned Mellette moved his family to Kansas. He died there a year after leaving his beloved South Dakota.

The 1883 **Mellette House** at 421 Fifth Avenue Northwest, left in a state of decay for many years, has since been restored, thanks in large measure to concerned Watertown residents and donations of the original furnishings, family portraits, and heirlooms from the Mellette family. Visitors will find the house reconstructed and appointed as it was when it served as the cultural and political center of the region in the 1880s and '90s.

A good place to start a Watertown tour is at the new **Redlin Art Center,** near the intersection of I-29 and U.S. 212. The center, which opened in June 1997, features 92 original works by artist Terry Redlin, a widely collected painter of wildlife and Americana. The $10 million facility also houses a planetarium, private offices, and the visitor information center of the Glacial Lakes Association.

Visitors might also want to see the **Bramble Park Zoo** with its 400 mammals, reptiles, and birds from around the world. Gamblers can experience 24-hour action at the **Dakota Sioux Casino,** six miles (10 km) north of Watertown on Sioux Valley Road. Operated by the Sisseton-Wahpeton Sioux Tribe, the casino offers friendly blackjack ($100 limit), poker games, slot machines, live entertainment, and a restaurant and lounge.

■ LITTLE FELLOW OF CLARK

Perhaps because crime is low and news is scarce, South Dakotans tend to nurture legends. One such apocryphal story, the "Little Fellow," involved a young lad from Clark (west of Watertown on U.S. 212) and William F. "Big Bill" Chambers, a brakeman on the Chicago & North Western Railway (C&NW) in the 1880s and '90s. The boy was the son of either transient railroad cooks or poor homesteaders who lived in a shack along the tracks between Clark and Elrod, South Dakota.

Each morning, as the train passed near Clark, the 13- or 14-year-old boy would stand alongside the tracks, waving to all the railroad men on board. And the railroad men always waved back. But in 1888 the boy contracted smallpox, and died in August of that year.

After several weeks passed and the boy did not appear, the men noticed a small, bald mound on the prairie sod near the little boy's previous station. After inquiring, the crew learned that the boy had been buried in a plain wooden box near the railroad tracks—the spot the Little Fellow had requested—and the parents had disappeared. Beginning in 1889, Big Bill Chambers tended the grave every Decoration Day (Memorial Day) for 40 years. Today, the friendship of the "Little Fellow" and the rail crews is still honored at the annual Memorial Day celebration in Clark by a gathering of area residents, railroad buffs, and a local minister at the boy's gravesite five miles (8 km) east of Clark on U.S. 212.

■ WAUBAY NATIONAL WILDLIFE REFUGE

Tucked in a quiet area of the world midway between Watertown and Sisseton, surrounded by the waters of the Blue Dog, Hurricane, and Enemy Swims Lakes, lies Waubay National Wildlife Refuge. Waubay, appropriately named by the Sioux as "a nesting place for birds," contains 4,649 acres of prairie potholes separated by rolling hills and 700 acres of oak forest. Located on State Highway 12, 13 miles (21 km) west of I-29, Waubay attracts a variety of migratory waterfowl, including Canada geese, mallards, and blue-winged teal. Rare white pelicans and pairs of western grebes gather on its lakes and ponds as well. Other wildlife species have been attracted to the refuges since it was established in 1935. White-tailed deer are common in the upland areas, while Chinese ring-necked pheasants, gray partridges, and sharp-tailed grouse are abundant, but less commonly seen. In the coulees and timbered areas, beavers, muskrats, minks, raccoons, foxes, skunks and badgers make their dams and dens.

◾ HARTFORD BEACH

Century-old hardwood trees shade the confines of Hartford Beach State Park, 12 miles (19 km) north and two miles (3 km) west of Milbank on State Highway 15. On the shores of the 38-mile (61-km)-long **Big Stone Lake,** Hartford Beach is a 300-acre park with fishing, sailing, water-skiing, and skin diving. A number of hiking trails lead to the sites of early-day fur-trading posts, Indian villages, burial mounds, and overlooks with striking vistas. The park also manages a 100-acre wilderness island in Big Stone Lake. Those who are able to get there by boat and like old-fashioned camping (no running water) will find the island a quiet retreat from the RVs and busy campgrounds of Hartford Beach.

◾ FORT SISSETON

In the quarter-century preceding the Civil War, immigrants flocked to Minnesota, Iowa, and the Dakota Territory to build their settlements. Not surprisingly, this infuriated the people who already lived there. To make amends, the U.S. gov-ern-ment signed treaties with the Indians, agreeing to set aside certain lands for their use and pay them annuities in currency and supplies. Soon the self-sustaining Indian way of life vanished and the Indians were reduced to accepting handouts.

In 1862, Sioux chief Little Crow led a rebellion against settlers in eastern South Dakota and Minnesota. Subsequently, the U.S. government cracked down on "hostile" Indians and constructed a network of forts for the defense of soldiers and settlers. (Georgia State University Foundation, Pullen Library)

During the Civil War, the government ignored its treaty obligations. When months had passed with no disbursement of goods and cash to the numerous Sioux tribes, the bands began to starve. Their complaints were met with little sympathy and no response. One storekeeper remarked, "If they're hungry, let them eat grass."

On August 18, 1862, Little Crow, leader of the lower Sioux, declared war. Before his rebellion (which came to be known as the Minnesota Uprising, or Massacre) was quelled, 800 white men, women, and children were massacred in southern Minnesota, Dakota Territory, and northern Iowa. The deaths sent chills down the backs of settlers in the West, and Washington felt compelled not to meet its original treaty obligations, but to provide a show of force that would cost it far more than fulfilling earlier promises would have.

The policy shift resulted in the creation of the Military Department of the Northwest. Its mission was to combat roving bands of "hostile" Indians (those refusing to stay on specified lands) and to provide security to beleaguered settlers of the region. A network of forts was built to provide safe haven for soldiers and settlers and a supply chain for the growing army stationed in the West. In 1864, three companies of the Thirteenth Wisconsin Volunteers were dispatched to locate a site for a fort in northeastern South Dakota, a region which had seen conflict with Indians. Army officers agreed that the Coteau des Prairies region, with its rich supply of water, timbered valleys, fuel and clay, was an ideal area, and they set about to build **Fort Wadsworth** (now known as **Fort Sisseton**).

Following construction of its officers quarters, barracks, a hospital, stables, magazine, an oil house, and sawmill, Fort Sisseton became a center of activity for northern South Dakota and the army's newest stronghold on the frontier. Its officers authorized whites to trade with Indian tribes and provided agricultural supplies and seeds to friendly Indians.

White tablecloths, champagne, solid silver services, and military orchestras marked special occasions at the fort, especially during official visits from generals and dignitaries from the East. On one such occasion in the summer of 1865, General John N. Corse and his staff made their official inspection tour, arriving from Fort Snelling at St. Paul, Minnesota. According to Fort Sisseton researcher Karen Karie:

> *A* buffalo hunt was arranged for them by all the officers of the post. The party numbered nearly a hundred and was led by Gabriel Renville, the Indian scout, who conducted them to the vicinity of Buzzard's

Roost, where they encountered an immense herd of buffalo—25,000 to 30,000 strong . . . One of the general's aides, a young lieutenant, borrowed the finest and fastest horse and bragged that he would show the Indians how to hunt buffalo with his Colt revolvers . . . The young officer began the chase and in doing so, became so excited that he dropped one of his revolvers and shot his horse in the back of the head with the other, thus putting himself out of the hunt.

Fort Wadsworth was renamed Fort Sisseton for a local Indian tribe in August 1876 (after officials learned there was already a Fort Wadsworth in New York state). Although Fort Sisseton was the site of no major battles and bears no distinctive place of honor in the annals of military history, it served its purpose by discouraging hostilities between white settlers and the Sisseton and Wahpeton bands of the Sioux.

Thanks in large measure to reconstruction in the 1930s by the Works Progress Administration and its subsequent designation as a state park, Fort Sisseton remains one of the best preserved military posts in America. Located 10 miles (16 km) southwest of Lake City, the fort comprises 17 original and reconstructed structures. Its historical festival the first weekend each June brings back bluecoats, bugles, and bayonets for a nationally known and distinctive re-creation of pioneer life in the 1860s. Reminders of warring days—shooting matches, tomahawk throws, and cannon and cavalry demonstrations—are presented alongside festival standards—an arts and crafts fair, costume balls, and cook-outs.

While Fort Sisseton commemorates the frontier life of white soldiers and pioneers, a variety of museums and visitor centers in the area honor the handiwork of Native American artisans. The **Tekakwitha Fine Arts Center** (south of the town of Sisseton on the Agency Road a half-mile south of the Viking Motel) offers an impressive exhibit including the works of 37 Indian artists.

■ SISSETON AREA

Sica Hollow State Park, 15 miles (24 km) northeast of Sisseton off State Highway 10, has preserved the favored campsites of the Dakota bands which roamed the Great Plains. Although the species most important and sacred to the Dakota hunting parties—bison, wolf, and bear—have been pushed out by almost 150 years of settlement, the park still hosts great numbers of white-tail deer, wild turkeys, marmots, beavers, minks, raccoons, and songbirds.

BUY YOUR TICKETS VIA THE

CHICAGO, MILWAUKEE & ST. PAUL RY.

— TO —

THE NEXT BIG CITY,

SISSETON

Roberts County, State of South Dakota.

THE LARGEST LOCAL MARKET IN THE STATE.

THE NATURAL AND ONLY GATEWAY

TO A RICH AGRICULTURAL COUNTY.

A NATURAL ENTRANCE TO TWO GREAT STATES.

MEDICINAL SPRINGS RICH IN MINERALS.

ARTESIAN WATER AT 500 FEET.

The opportunity "THAT KNOCKS AT YOUR DOOR" will not ∴ be open long. ∴

PROGRESS, ENTERPRISE, ENERGY and PROSPERITY walk hand in hand THROUGH THE STREETS OF SISSETON.

PROPERTY that can now be purchased for from $50 to $1000 per lot will TREBLE and even QUADRUPLE in value within one to three years. ∴ ∴ ∴ ∴ ∴ ∴

1893.

The park re-awakens each spring with warm (and often wet) days and chilly evenings. By midsummer, the high humidity of eastern South Dakota accounts for hot, sweaty days and mild nights. September and October, when the park's 220-odd species of plant life display brilliant colors, are the best months to visit. A three-mile (5-km)-long road winds through ravines and along wooded hillsides, or, if you prefer hiking, walk the **Trail of Spirits**, a National Recreational Trail. Here, in spring and summer, sylvan wildflowers blanket the forest floor and woodland wildlife abounds.

Roy Lake State Park, along State Highway 10 between Sisseton and Britton, is remote and idyllic. On site are a state-owned resort (448-5498) on a 1,500-acre lake, campgrounds, picnic areas, cabins, concessions, and a footbridge to interpretive trails on Roy Island. Evidence of a prehistoric Indian village has been discovered on the shores of the lake. Archaeologists tied artifacts found at the site to those of the Great Oasis Culture, which occupied the region about A.D. 900–1300.

Today, three local beauties take part in an 1890s fashion contest and parade in the town of Bryant.

(left) An 1893 brochure promises the good life for those willing to relocate to "the next big city" of Sisseton.

■ BROWNS VALLEY MAN

On October 9, 1933, William Jensen was having gravel hauled from the munici-
pal gravel pit to the driveway of his grain elevator in Browns Valley, a small farming community on the South Dakota-Minnesota border about eight miles (13
km) southeast of Sisseton. As the dumptruck spread its load, Jensen discovered
several small bone fragments that appeared human. Further examination of the
gravel uncovered a small brown flint spearhead.

Jensen got in his car and hurried to the gravel pit, where he found a worker load-
ing a second wagon with gravel. Jensen sifted through the sediment, and his fingers
uncovered a grayish stone knife. Nearby, in a seven-foot (2.1-m)-high bank, he
found the front of a human skull, jawbones, teeth, and finally, the remaining undis-
turbed skeletal fragments of what would become known as the Browns Valley Man.

Jensen loaned the skeleton to the University of Minnesota for examination and
several scientific articles were published about the find. He later insisted that the
skeleton be returned to him, and in 1950 the amateur archaeologist, fearing the
theft of his greatest find, hid the remains in his fruit cellar. There the Browns Valley Man remained for the better part of four decades, sitting in a cardboard box,
locked in a dark, damp cellar.

In 1987, following the death of Jensen, the remains were rediscovered and sent to
the state archeologist at Hamline University in Minnesota. Carbon dating conducted in 1990 placed the age of the remains at 9,160 years old. As one of the "paleo-
Indians" who first inhabited North America, scientists contend, the Browns Valley
Man stood 5 feet, 5 inches tall, and was 25 to 35 years old at the time of his death.

Nine thousand years after he was buried with his skinning knives and finely
crafted spear points, and nearly 60 years after his chance rediscovery, scientists
confirmed that the Browns Valley Man was one of only a half-dozen sets of
human remains dating from the early habitation of the continent, and arguably
the oldest and most complete remains of a human ever found in the Western
Hemisphere.

■ ABERDEEN

The landscape of farmland and hills 100 miles (160 km) west of Sisseton is dotted
with myriad town sites and ghost towns, the majority of which were "sold" to
eager settlers by even more eager railroad promoters during the Great Dakota

Boom of 1878–1887. Pioneers who'd spent months or years building their prairie towns sometimes moved their whole communities—buildings, homes and all—onto the new railroad routes.

Aberdeen, with 25,000 residents, fared better than most. Located by the Milwaukee Railroad in a fertile valley of the James River in 1880, the scene is not vastly different from the Scottish Highlands community from which the town took its name. The town quickly became known as the "Hub City," due to the network of rail lines that extended from it like spokes on a wheel.

Because of its excellent rail facilities, Aberdeen became a wholesale and shipping center with large warehouses close to the tracks. The city expanded as the agricultural industry grew, and diversified into a manufacturing and service center. With increased trade and affluence, the community became a cultural center, offering "the best hotel accommodations between Minneapolis and the West Coast," and theaters which hosted entertainers and touring musicians, as well as political speakers, including Theodore Roosevelt, William Jennings Bryan, William McKinley, and later Franklin D. Roosevelt.

Aberdeen's 40 churches, representing 25 denominations, maintain the faith of the Scandinavian, German, Russian, and British immigrants who first settled the region. On the seamy side, a half-dozen strip bars, more than any other town in the state offers, testify to a raunchier side of the community. Although the city's residents voted a resounding "no" on state ballots authorizing expanded gambling in Deadwood and on South Dakota's Indian reservations in 1993, it's still probably harder to find a crisp dollar bill in Aberdeen than in any casino in the state.

Aberdeen also offers family-oriented entertainment. **Storybook Land,** a children's fantasy park at 2216 24th Avenue Northwest, features more than 50 larger-than-life exhibits such as Captain Hook's ship, as well as impressive gardens. The Yellow Brick Road and greeters dressed as Dorothy, the Scarecrow, the Tin Man, and the Cowardly Lion are an homage to former Aberdeen resident L. Frank Baum, the author of *The Wonderful Wizard of Oz.* Just outside the gates is **Wylie Park**, with over 200 acres of grassland, a variety of wildlife, picnic areas, and a swimming area. Animal compounds board bison, sika deer, elk, Barbados sheep, whitetail and white fallow deer, longhorn steers, goats, and ducks.

About 2,700 students attend **Northern State University** in Aberdeen. Founded in 1901, the Neoclassical buildings of the campus stand on 52 tree-shaded acres in the center of town.

Sand Lake National Wildlife Refuge is home to prairie chickens—as well as hundreds of species of wildlife and waterfowl.

The city's history is preserved and recounted in the city's **Dacotah Prairie Museum** at 21 South Main Street, which contains the **J. L. Zietlow Telephone Pioneer Museum,** and at **Centennial Village,** just north of town on Old U.S. 281 (open in summer). In addition, the **Aberdeen Highlands Historic District** features 17 impressive residences between 12th and 15th Avenues on Main Street.

■ SAND LAKE NATIONAL WILDLIFE REFUGE

Twenty-seven miles (43 km) northeast of Aberdeen (take U.S. 12 east to County Road 16, then 20 miles [32 km] north through the town of Columbia), Sand Lake features a 100-foot (30-m) tower similar to that at Waubay. Forty miles (64 km) of roads wind through Sand Lake's 21,451 acres, but the real story is off the road where hundreds of species of wildlife and waterfowl live in grasslands, forest, lake, and marsh. Except for howling prairie winds which whip through the tall grass and cattails like a comb through a child's hair, the refuge is exceptionally quiet. Even in the midst of summer, when the number of visitors to South Dakota may approach the number of full-time residents, you can hear only the honking of a few thousand ducks.

■ SAMUEL ORDWAY MEMORIAL PRAIRIE

Since settlement of the prairies, fences have hemmed in wildlife and overgrazing has damaged or eliminated many of the native grasses. Fast-moving grassfires that once rejuvenated the prairie by restoring nutrients and eliminating thickets and saplings have been all but eliminated.

Perceiving how man's interference was endangering the native grassland, the Nature Conservancy carved out the Samuel Ordway Prairie, a vast 7,600-acre tract of native grasses 50 miles (80 km) northwest of Aberdeen—nonetheless a relatively small haven for the prairie grasses which once characterized all of eastern South Dakota. Elevations here are measured in inches rather than feet, and even on a calm day it's so windy that even a seasoned cowboy strolling through will trade his Stetson for a baseball cap.

L. Frank Baum, author of "The Wonderful Wizard of Oz," may have been inspired by South Dakotan tornadoes rather than Kansan ones. This twister—the first ever photographed—swept past Howard, not too far from Baum's Aberdeen home on August 28, 1884. (South Dakota State Historical Society, Pierre)

CASHING IN HIS CHIPS

Al Neuharth founded USA Today *and was at one time chairman of Gannett. Now a multi-millionaire media mogul, he started out a poor country kid from South Dakota.*

I got my first job promotion when I was nine years old. Not a raise, but a big promotion.

I was promoted from harvesting cow chips by hand—that's manure to city folks—to herding cattle on horseback on the parched prairies of my grandfather's farm in South Dakota.

That was like going from garbage collector to grand marshal.

The pay was the same. No money. Just board and room for the summer.

It was 1933. Depth of the Depression and the Dust Bowl days.

My grandmother, Katharina, leaked the good news about my promotion. She came to pick me up in Grandpa's Model A Ford on my last day of school in the fourth grade.

Al Neuharth's humble South Dakota origins.
(South Dakota State Historical Society, Pierre)

"Allen, Grandpa's gonna give you the new job you want. You'll have your own horse to herd cattle. It's because you did such a good job picking up cow chips last summer," Grandma gushed. "But don't let on I told you . . . "

[Grandpa] was a gritty German who figured everyone should be treated alike and made to earn their way. I had been lobbying him all winter to give me a bigger job the next summer. But I lobbied Grandma to lobby for me, too. And that's what got me my promotion.

When we got to the farm and Grandpa made my new job official, he just said, "You did a good job with the cow chips last summer. Now, let's go pick out a horse so you can get to herding the cows."

My promotion as a kid taught me:

- If you have a lousy job, you're more likely to get promoted out of it if you buckle down and do your best, rather than be a wimp and do your worst.

- It works to cultivate friends in high places who will help get you promoted—even your grandmother.

—Al Neuharth, *Confessions of an S.O.B.*, 1989

C E N T R A L
S O U T H   D A K O T A

THE SWATH OF LAND which sandwiches the Missouri River from Chamberlain in the south to Mobridge in the north comprises central South Dakota. Its largest city, Pierre, is the state capital, chosen for no other good reason than its perfectly central location. On the eastern side of the Missouri is the rolling Midwest farmland, with small towns established by Civil War veterans and northern Europeans in the nineteenth century. On the western side lie the vast, dry grasslands typical of the Great American West, where spread two large Indian reservations, the Cheyenne River and the Standing Rock. Down the middle runs the Missouri, the great dividing line of the state. Mellowed by four earthen dams and pooled into giant reservoirs that have submerged more than 900 square miles of land, the river stretches 435 miles (700 km) through the heart of South Dakota. In central South Dakota are lakes Oahe and Sharpe, two of the so-called Great Lakes of South Dakota—the man-made monuments culled from the river, which are, incidentally, visible from space, according to native son and Space Shuttle astronaut Sam Gemar. The waters of the river and its lakes wash more than 3,000 miles (4,800 km) of shoreline and lap at the sites of frontier forts and the ruins of fur traders' outposts.

■ HISTORY ON THE MISSOURI

Although often commenting in their journals on the Missouri's beauty, explorers Lewis and Clark cursed its sandbars as surely as the men under them who bareknuckled boats and supplies upstream on their 1804 expedition. On good days, the expedition made 15 to 20 miles (24 to 32 km). The corps often stopped to investigate what lay behind the bluffs, to hunt, to collect berries, and to make measurements of wind, water, and temperature. Some of it must have been fun as well: when the explorers spotted their first prairie dog village, they attempted to dig to the bottom of one of the holes. When they gave up on that hole, they proceeded to pour five barrels of water into another hole without filling it. In their journals, the explorers in general found the surrounding prairies beautiful, teeming with

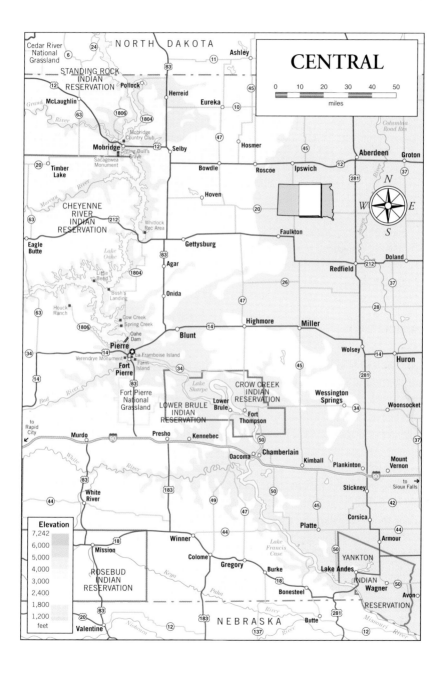

CENTRAL

0   10   20   30   40   50
miles

Cedar River National Grassland
STANDING ROCK INDIAN RESERVATION
Pollock
McLaughlin
Grand River
Mobridge Country Club
Mobridge
Sitting Bull's Grave
Sacagewea Monument
Timber Lake
CHEYENNE RIVER INDIAN RESERVATION
Moreau River
Eagle Butte
Lake Oahe
Little Bend
Bush's Landing
Houck Ranch
Cow Creek
Spring Creek
Oahe Dam
Pierre
Verendrye Monument
La Framboise Island
Farm Island
Fort Pierre
Fort Pierre National Grassland
Bad River
to Rapid City
Murdo
White River
Herreid
Eureka
Hosmer
Bowdle
Roscoe
Hoven
Faulkton
Gettysburg
Agar
Redfield
Onida
Highmore
Miller
Blunt
Wolsey
Huron
Fort Pierre
Lake Sharpe
Lower Brule
CROW CREEK INDIAN RESERVATION
Wessington Springs
Woonsocket
LOWER BRULE INDIAN RESERVATION
Fort Thompson
Presho
Kennebec
Oacoma
Chamberlain
Kimball
Plankinton
Mount Vernon
Stickney
to Sioux Falls
White River
Winner
Mission
Colome
Gregory
Burke
Lake Andes
Corsica
Platte
Armour
ROSEBUD INDIAN RESERVATION
Lake Francis Case
Keya
Paha
YANKTON INDIAN RESERVATION
Wagner
Avon
Valentine
Niobrara River
NEBRASKA
Butte
Bonesteel
Missouri River

NORTH DAKOTA
Ashley
Herreid
Eureka
Columbia Road Res.
Hosmer
Aberdeen
Groton
Ipswich
Doland
Whitlock Rec Area

Elevation
7,242
6,000
5,000
4,000
3,000
2,400
1,800
1,200
feet

PASSING THE MOUTH OF THE WHITE RIVER

15th of September, 1804

At the confluence of White river with the Missouri is an excellent position for a town; the land rising by three gradual ascents, and the neighbourhood furnishing more timber than is usual in this country.

After passing high dark bluffs on both sides, we reached the lower point of an island towards the south, at the distance of six miles. The island bears an abundance of grapes, and is covered with red cedar: it also contains a number of rabbits. At the end of this island, which is small, a narrow channel separates it from a large sand island, which we passed, and encamped, eight miles on the north, under a high point of land opposite a large creek to the south, on which we observe an unusual quantity of timber. The wind was from the northwest this afternoon, and high, the weather cold, and its dreariness increased by the howlings of a number of wolves around us.

— The Journals of the Expedition of Lewis and Clark, 1804

game and inviting further exploration. But, because of strong headwinds, nagging sandbars, and strong currents, the crew was often forced to use tow ropes and manhandle their boats and supplies in an upriver voyage through South Dakota.

The river was also a challenge to early settlers. South Dakotans like to claim that when early settlers first saw the Ol' Muddy they didn't know whether to drink it or plow it. And each spring, flooding forced nearby farmers to create dams with countless sandbags. In these early years of the Dakota Territory, the river also served to separate whites and Indians. Until, of course, white settlers crossed the river, intruding on Indian lands. Then, forts and frontier outposts were built at regular intervals along the muddy shore for the protection of traders and sodbusters.

No bridges crossed the river until the railroads arrived in the twentieth century. Between 1924 and 1926, the federal and state governments erected five highway bridges, opening western South Dakota to rapid expansion, increased tourism, and new interaction between the major population centers at the extreme edges of the state. Much of the land that Lewis and Clark viewed during their first two months in South Dakota was submerged between 1954 and 1966, when massive dams were built on the Missouri, backing up and widening the river.

■ EAST OF THE MISSOURI

Government officials, railroad promoters, newspaper editors, and land agents who came to the state in the mid-nineteenth century cast central South Dakota as prime farming land—"the sole remaining paradise in the western world." Germans, Norwegians, Irish, and a handful of Hutterites took the bait, claimed the land, and quickly found out how unsubstantiated the promoters' grandiose claims really were. Today, mile after mile, the wind blows down creek-cut coulees trodden only occasionally by cattle searching for forage and pheasants looking for a sheltered place to raise their young. Along the river, trees provide homes for eagles, osprey, and hawks which feed on field mice, rabbits, and other varmints that sneak through the ravines for a fresh drink of water each day. The only human inhabitants of this place, descendants of the homesteaders, reside in ranch houses sometimes set miles apart and most often hidden from the road by shelterbelts planted generations earlier. Rest assured, though, that they're home. Making a living on this land requires perseverance and a close relationship with the local banker.

In September 1804, explorers Lewis and Clark traveled this stretch of the Missouri River, near today's Chamberlain.

A journey through this region is as bland as travel gets—a 70-mile (112-km) sleepwalk through farmland and cow pastures interrupted by a scant half-dozen interchanges each signaling another farming community. Because of the straight-lined roadway and unchanging scenery, it's not unusual to see a South Dakotan with a paperback or a newspaper draped across the steering wheel as he races across the state. Almost as common are unplanned lane changes by motorhomes and semis whose drivers are drowsing at the wheel. Some say this monotony must be the reason they invented books on audio cassette.

Close to the Missouri, rangeland—rolling hillsides and sparsely wooded ravines, dotted with beef cattle—gradually appears. The small towns differ little from their counterparts in eastern South Dakota. Main Street businesses provide the essentials (real shopping is reserved for excursions to Mitchell and Sioux Falls), and town residents mingle with their rural neighbors in coffee klatches at the corner cafe. Wander in for a farmhand breakfast, and—whether or not you want to—you'll probably hear why the sheriff stopped at the Taylor's place Tuesday, who fell off the bar stool Saturday at the Dew Drop Inn, and whose "outfit" (pick-up) was parked behind the Seed-E Motel while his wife was visiting her mother in Yankton Friday night.

■ CHAMBERLAIN

As you crest the bluffs of the Missouri River above the town of Chamberlain on I-90, an unexpected panorama unfolds. It's best viewed from the state rest stop on the south side of the interstate, where walking trails lead out to the edge of the bluffs. In summer, visitors can stand on a knoll 300 feet (91 m) above the water and get their first whiff of wind cooled by the river, then filtered through dry prairie grasses. In spring, a subtle green tint clings to rolling hillsides gently sloping to the water's edge. By late summer and early fall, it's replaced by autumn golds and reds; the brittle grasses crackle underfoot. In winter, the same vantage point reveals an arctic tundra, scoured and reshaped daily by almost incessant frozen winds that whip the snow and send any semblance of powder scurrying for Nebraska.

On September 15, 1804, the Lewis and Clark Expedition passed the mouth of the **White River,** just south of Chamberlain, and paused the following day to let the crew rest and let the baggage dry out after three days of heavy rains. Along the bluffs

GRILLED MEDALLIONS OF BUFFALO WITH PEACH CHUTNEY

(Serves 6)

18 medallions of buffalo, 2 oz. each	1 1/2 tsp. of crushed bay leaf
1/2 cup of olive oil	juice of one small lemon
2 cloves of garlic, minced	1/4 tsp. freshly ground black pepper
1 T. of basil	salt to taste

Combine all ingredients except the buffalo in a food processor until mixed thoroughly. Pour mixture into a bowl and add medallions. Marinate for 4 hours.

PEACH CHUTNEY
(makes 4 cups; freezes well)

1 16 oz. can sliced peaches in heavy syrup	2 T. crystallized ginger, thinly sliced
1 cup white sugar	1 fresh lemon, thinly sliced with seeds
1 cup firmly packed brown sugar	removed, but peel remaining
1 28 oz. can diced tomatoes, drained	1 Scotch bonnet pepper, seeds
1 cup white vinegar	removed, chopped very fine
1/2 cup raisins	1/2 tsp. ground cloves
2 cloves garlic, finely chopped	1/2 tsp. ground cinnamon
1 1/2 large onions, thinly sliced	1 T. mustard seed
	dash of salt

Using an enameled pot, add syrup from peaches (set peaches aside), and add all other ingredients. Cook over high heat and bring mixture to a boil, stirring constantly. Continue to boil for about 1/2 hour, or until mixture thickens. Add peaches and return to boil. Allow to thicken, but do not allow peaches to break apart. Set aside to cool.

Remove medallions of buffalo from marinade. Grill medallions until rare or medium. Remove from grill, and top with chutney. Serve.

—Ruth Johnston, *The Buffalo Cookbook,* 1994

of the Missouri, the explorers' hunters killed buffalo, elk, deer, and pelicans. On September 17, after being confined to the boat for several weeks, Lewis set out on foot to explore the countryside along the river. The short, rich prairie grasses reminded him of a "beautiful bowling green" on which he spotted wolves and polecats, and circling above on the air currents, a number of hawks. The famed explorer, who would commit suicide only five years later, was altogether pleased by the scenery, and was impressed by a nearby buffalo herd which he estimated numbered 3,000.

The town of Chamberlain stretches out along the east bank of the Missouri. Named for Selah Chamberlain, director of the Milwaukee Railroad in 1880 at the time the town was founded, it's a ramshackle and random place with little to distinguish it from the hundred other South Dakota communities which were founded as steamboat stops and railroad sidings. Its southern city limits have been extended to the interstate, where small town entrepreneurs hope the visibility of a few fast food restaurants will pull motorists from the road.

The town's economic strength, though, continues to rest in the fertile soils of surrounding farmlands and visiting hunters and fishermen. Each fall, as the buds of winter wheat paint a deep green cast on the fields, sportsmen stalk pheasants, grouse, prairie chickens, turkeys, geese, and ducks, while big-game hunters bag antelope, mule deer, and whitetail deer. When combined with thousands of fishermen who frequent the 107-mile-long (171 km) Lake Francis Case, hunters, motorists, and area residents keep Chamberlain proper and its 2,300 residents busy filling coolers, pumping gas, and selling groceries.

Nonhunters—and you'll find few of them in South Dakota—enjoy *viewing* the state's wildlife. On nearly any drive off the main highways or any trek along a river bluff or through a wooded ravine, visitors can spot ring-necked pheasants, hawks, eagles, and a variety of waterfowl. Deer, antelope, and coyote are active in the early morning hours and at dusk in any season.

Chamberlain's **St. Joseph's Indian School** opened in 1927 as a school for Sioux Indian children. It provides general education courses, as well as studies in the Lakota language and culture, for approximately 200 students enrolled in grades one through eight. Originally founded with the intention of re-educating Indian children in Christian American culture and values, St. Joseph's and similar reservation schools were the products of progressive, liberal reformers who believed Indian

Central South Dakota offers numerous fishing opportunities.
Here Steve Nelson snags a walleye from Lake Oahe.

children should be encouraged to integrate with the rest of white America. Too often these schools succeeded only in creating a confusing, painful atmosphere for children unaccustomed to living away from their families. They were required to speak English, adhere to rigid time constraints, spend long periods indoors, and study Christian doctrine, often under the eye of overly severe nuns and priests.

Today, the school's **Akta Lakota Museum** provides a vivid look at a way of life that has vanished from the Great Plains. Across the river from Chamberlain—in its sister city, Oacoma—most travelers stop at **Al's Oasis**. This immense restaurant offers unexceptional food, including cuts of buffalo that it once tackily touted as being taken from the same herd that appeared in *Dances With Wolves.*

■ LOWER BRULE AND CROW CREEK

Turn off I-90 onto State Highway 50 to switch from four-lane interstate speed to a pace suitably slow to explore the interior of South Dakota. Twenty miles (32 km) north of Chamberlain on Highway 50 are two of the state's seven Indian reservations. The Lower Brule and Crow Creek reservations are separated only by the Missouri, the former tribe's land falling on the west, the latter on the east of the natural divide. In the heart of these reservations, the river makes a curious 24-mile (41-km) loop to form what is known as the Big Bend of present-day Lake Francis Case. When steamboats began to ply the river after 1831, passengers welcomed the bend as a chance to relieve some of the boredom of river travel. At one end of the loop, they would disembark, walk the mile and a half of prairie to the other end of the loop, then wait for the steamer to make its way around the river.

The two reservations are alike in appearance. Both hug the rolling river bluffs and extend outward onto the prairie about 125,000 acres. For a century there was little to do here but watch the sun rise and set. Today, as on so many of the nation's reservations, the sound of slot machine payoffs interrupts the monotony of prairie winds and slow-moving rivers. On the Lower Brule Reservation, legalized gambling provides numerous jobs for tribal members and revenues for tribal government. The **Golden Buffalo Casino** attracts a growing number of buses filled with the farm crowd from Iowa, Nebraska, Minnesota, and North Dakota, as well as in-state residents who would never consider a trip to Vegas or Atlantic City. But with the gaming hall close by and a friend or two to go with, a quick trip to the reservation becomes a perfectly acceptable form of entertainment. It's somehow fitting that these tribes can turn a profit from their white neighbors. The Indians say that life is a circle, and cash payments made from gambling revenues to each eligible member of the tribe gives some validity to the claim.

The Sioux celebrate their own heritage with powwows on both reservations each August. The **Lower Brule Fair and Powwow** is conducted at Lower Brule, (605) 473-5565; the **Crow Creek Powwow** is held at Fort Thompson, (605) 245-2221.

■ PIERRE

In 1743, two sons of French explorer Pierre Gaultier de Varennes, Sieur de La Verendrye, became the first whites known to venture into present-day South Dakota. After stumbling across the hostile, wind-blown prairie, the adventurers came upon the Missouri River and stopped to survey the view from one of the bluffs. There, above what is now Fort Pierre, the brothers left an inscribed lead plate which claimed the land for their king, Louis XV.

The plate stayed on that grassy bluff for 170 years, an undiscovered record of the first visit by whites to South Dakota. Then, in 1913, a group of children playing on the hillside accidentally unearthed the plate and placed it in the proper hands. Today the **La Verendrye Plate**, which remains in remarkably good condition despite its age, can be viewed at the South Dakota Cultural Heritage Center in the state capital, Pierre. State Highway 34 follows the Missouri to the northwest and roughly retraces the path of the La Verendrye brothers, early fur traders, and explorers Lewis and Clark. In nearly the exact geographic center of the state, that highway passes through Pierre.

Citizens of South Dakota will know you're an outsider almost as soon as you open your mouth—at least if you pronounce the capital's name as it's spelled. If you do, you'll draw a slightly condescending smile and a polite correction. The capital city of South Dakota is not pronounced like the name of the French explorer, but like the word "pier."

Pierre was chosen for the state capital by default more than anything else. Shortly after South Dakota acquired statehood in 1889, the choice of the capital city was put to a vote. Those backing Pierre as the best choice claimed that the community's location in South Dakota's geographic center would result in equal representation in the capital to all areas of the growing state. The argument may have made sense to some, but not to most. After several ballots, numerous bribes, and a lot of cajoling,

South Dakotans designated Pierre as the capital, but only because competition among Mitchell, Huron, Chamberlain, Sioux Falls, and Watertown was so fierce that no one could form a coalition to get the capital located anywhere else. Even then, South Dakotans didn't get a capitol building constructed until 1910.

Today, Pierre is off the beaten track. No interstate freeway passes through it, and it's serviced only by commuter airlines. It may well be America's most isolated state capital. For nine months of the year, it's even without legislators, a sleepy town of 13,000 residents who are content to perform their state and federal government jobs, stop at the store, and go home. During the remaining three months, which also happen to be the year's coldest, legislators gather for their annual session and transform the city into a hotbed of lobbying efforts, hospitality rooms, and partisan politics. A couple of hundred insurance agents, farmers, ranchers, businesspeople, homemakers, lobbyists, and lawyers debate the merits of naming a state fossil or changing South Dakota's appellation from "The Sunshine State" to "The Mount Rushmore State," as well as larger state issues.

Debate in Pierre often occurs between two very large "interest groups": those South Dakotans living on the west side of the Missouri, and those living to the east. Residents of the state refer to each other as either "East River" or "West River" folk—an important distinction to South Dakotans. Depending on your disposition and which side of the river you're on, your neighbors can be either too rough and regular, or conversely, too urban and liberal enough to belong in a suburb of Minneapolis. The denser population of the eastern half of the state means it dictates what happens in mundane daily matters such as school-funding formulas and mining regulation, and that sometimes sticks in the craw of West River residents who have their own opinions about education and employment.

Partisan and geographic politics aside, South Dakotans managed to build one of the most impressive capitol buildings in the country, even if they did model it after Montana's. For a state with a penchant for the practical, its grandeur, elegance, and expense were quite a statement. If, after 70-odd years of use, it had grown a bit shabby, a restoration completed in time for the state's centennial celebration in 1989 has left a beautifully restored original. The building has mosaic floors, marble staircases, stained-glass skylights, scagliola columns, and early nineteenth-century artwork. The capitol's exterior is made of Marquette sandstone and Indiana bedford limestone. The foundation is South Dakota boulder granite and the dome is solid copper.

The interior features Greek and Roman designs and stenciling, as well as several massive murals depicting the state's beginnings. In the rotunda are four fine bronze sculptures by Black Hills artist Dale Lamphere. The capitol grounds feature a man-made lake, several sculptures, an eternal flame, and the governor's official residence. The latest addition to the grounds is a powerful memorial to the late Governor George S. Mickelson and seven staff members and state leaders who all died in the fiery crash of a small plane in April 1993. The massive reproduction of sculptor Korczak Ziolkowski's *Fighting Stallions* was a gift from the people of South Dakota.

Every year on the day after Thanksgiving, a few dedicated South Dakotans arrive at the capitol armed with hundreds of handmade ornaments, ready to carry on the capitol Christmas tradition. Together, they set out to decorate nearly three dozen spruce, pine, and cedar trees that line the halls and adorn the rotunda. Each tree is decorated according to a different holiday theme. The results are dazzling: by the time state employees arrive Monday morning, the halls are bathed in a warm glow of holiday lights and color.

Looking up into the ornate dome of the capitol building in Pierre.

■ A R O U N D   T O W N

Nothing outside of the capitol grounds in Pierre appears to have been laid down with much thought or planning. As with so many South Dakota towns, inexpensive land is plentiful, and most people like to put some space between themselves and their neighbors. Residential and commercial districts sprawl. The layout of the downtown district seems random, and spans a mere four or five square blocks with a commercial strip extending past it for a mile in either direction. In summertime, petunias planted on virtually every boulevard in town add color to drab facades, but still fall short of providing any continuity to the place.

Nonetheless, there are some bright spots in Pierre. The new **South Dakota Cultural Heritage Center**—a modern building covered with native grasses—houses fine interpretive displays exploring the state's history. The museum's exhibits are less stuffy than one might expect, and together they effectively describe the settlement of South Dakota in context with the development of the rest of the nation. An advertisement that sought Catholic missionaries for Indian reservations in the state reminds visitors of what early settlement probably entailed:

> WE OFFER YOU: No salary; No recompense; No holiday; No pensions.
> But: Much hard work; A poor dwelling; Few consolations; Many
> disappointments; Frequent sickness; A violent or lonely death;
> An unknown grave.

Also worth a visit is the **Discovery Center and Aquarium** at 805 West Sioux Avenue. Its three giant aquariums hold native species of fish.

■ LAKE OAHE AND ITS DAM

In 1962, President John F. Kennedy traveled to Pierre to dedicate the **Oahe Dam.** Two decades later, the massive earth-rolled dam (ranked second largest in the world, for those who keep track) remains an outstanding example of what man can do with an unlimited budget, a couple of hundred dump trucks, and an overabundance of dirt. Located about seven miles (11 km) north of the city, the Lake Oahe Project was built and is maintained by the Army Corps of Engineers, which hasn't always been known for its ability to blend dams with the surrounding environment. This one is no exception, being visible from several miles away. Its power plant (tours are conducted daily in the summer months) houses seven of the

CASEY TIBBS, BRONCO BUSTER

1929-1990

America's greatest bronco buster was born in a log cabin on a remote family homestead 50 miles (80 km) northwest of Fort Pierre, near the banks of the Cheyenne River. He grew up breaking horses, and age of 14, started riding in South Dakota rodeos. A year later, Casey Tibbs was trailing bucking stock on the national circuit and by 19, had become the youngest man ever to win the world saddle bronc riding championship. In the '50s, he won a total of six saddle bronc riding crowns—a record still unmatched—plus two all-around cowboy championships, and one bareback riding championship.

Success in the rodeo arena brought him new opportunities, such as his syndicated newspaper column, "Let 'er Buck." He wrote, produced, and starred in several movies, and he worked regularly as a stunt man in television and film. Casey was feted on the television show "This Is Your Life," in 1958, the same year that he took a rodeo troop to perform at the World's Fair in Belgium. In 1973, he and his troop introduced rodeo to Japan.

On August 10, 1989, "C.T." was honored at the Pro-Rodeo Cowboy Hall of Fame in Colorado Springs at the dedication of a larger-than-life bronze statue of himself atop a bucking horse named "Necktie." During Casey's speech, the ailing star glanced at the imposing sculpture called *The Champ*, and said, "Thanks for making me look so good . . . Hell, I *was* good."

The life of Casey Tibbs is commemorated in displays at the National Buffalo Association headquarters in Fort Pierre and the South Dakota Heritage Center in Pierre. The Silver Spur Bar on Main Street, Fort Pierre, still turns on the light over his portrait each night, and, for the abstemious, another statue of C.T. stands two blocks away on U.S. 83.

Casey Tibbs.
(South Dakota State Historical Society, Pierre)

globe's largest generators and its water intakes occasionally create whirlpools on Lake Oahe. During the huge floods in the Midwest in the summer of 1993, South Dakota residents escaped relatively unscathed because of the dam at Lake Oahe.

As incongruous as this great lake seems with the surrounding prairie, it is now a fixture of South Dakota and backs up water well into North Dakota. Lake activities include fine sport fishing, pleasure boating for high-powered craft and leisurely houseboats, and (due to persistent prairie winds) some of the best freshwater wind-surfing east of the Columbia River Gorge in Oregon. Sailboat regattas color summer days on Lake Oahe, sleek sheets passing the anchored boats of walleye fishermen.

In the fall and winter, the lake's location on the **Central Flyway**, covering a vast north-south slice of the central United States, attracts millions of Canada geese and ducks, some of which end up on the holiday tables of hunters. Younger, lighter geese often use the Missouri as a rest stop in late October and early November before colder weather forces them as far south as Kansas. But, as many as 300,000 other Canada geese, most of which are older, larger, and less inclined to fly a couple thousand extra miles, make the Pierre area their home all winter, relying on open water and leftovers from the irrigated cornfields near the river to sustain them through the coldest months. Other birds, including mallard ducks,

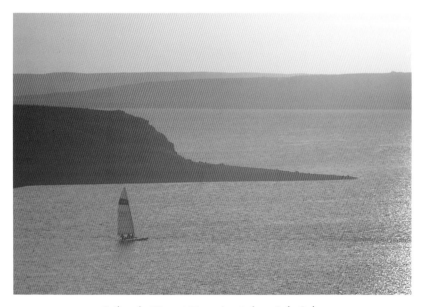

Sailing the Missouri River where it forms Lake Oahe.

Aerial view of Lake Oahe.

whooping cranes, and sandhill cranes, use the Missouri River as a stopping place during their annual spring and fall migrations, and eagles often can be found wintering in the giant cottonwoods below the Oahe Dam.

■ FISHING LAKE OAHE

In every season, and in almost every type of weather, fisherman can be found on the waters of Lake Oahe, staring into its depths, watching their rod tips, and occasionally glancing at the horizon, aware that sudden squalls can make this body of water treacherous. In general, they come for the walleye, which often grow to as much as 10 pounds (4.5 kg), as well as the chinook salmon (introduced in 1982), the trophy northern pike, and the solitude. Surrounding the Oahe are bluffs that are so round, so barren, and normally so brown that they appear as tan derby hats on the horizon. The isolation available on this lake has often been equated to "fishing on the moon."

Access areas are provided along the entire river, but most are found on its east side. West bank access is limited simply by a lack of roads near Oahe. Facilities are scarce and first-class resorts are nonexistent. Among the most popular marinas on Oahe are the Spring Creek/Cow Creek Area near Pierre, Bush's Landing near Little

Bend off State Highway 1804, and Whitlock's Area, near U.S. 212 south of Mobridge. Nearly everyone, including all of the successful fishermen on this stretch of river, uses boats, and the fishing vessels tend to be deep hulled due to high waves. Bank fishing is seldom fruitful. Inexperienced fishermen will find that hiring a guide, who most often comes with a boat, will increase their chances of success and enjoyment.

Guides, available for hire at marinas, through fishing publications, local brochures, bait shops, and even the bulletin board at area supermarkets, are inexpensive and they know the river that doesn't show up on the map. Because of the sheer size of Lake Oahe, their boats are often equipped with citizen's band radios in addition to the standard depth finders, beer coolers, and live bait wells. The radios are used to stay in touch with other guides and marinas to monitor the best fishing locations on a given day or hour.

Fishermen tend to be courteous and helpful, as long as they're not annoyed by greenhorns. Most have trailered their boats to the Missouri and at night you won't find them frying fish over an open campfire with a tent pitched in the background. If they're not staying at one of the area's low-priced motels, it's likely these fishermen are luxuriating in a well-stocked motorhome or fifth-wheel trailer, complete with a microwave, fridge, and queen-size bed. Still others will stay on their boats, which generally range from 16-foot (5-m) speedboats to 40-foot (12-m) cabin cruisers.

For a brief time during the spring, when large schools of smelt come into the shoreline shallows to spawn, the demographics of the fishermen change drastically. Because smelt "runs" occur at night, and only for a couple of weeks, they tend to attract beer-drinking partiers who revel in filling seine nets, dip nets, and anything else that will catch buckets of the five- or six-inch (13-15 cm) smelt. The limit is five gallons per person.

For the nonfisherman, **La Framboise Island** and **Farm Island,** both near Pierre, offer excellent hiking trails with views of the river, waterfowl, and wildlife. Parking is provided and both islands are handicapped accessible.

■ WEST ACROSS THE RIVER

Located across the bridge from Pierre, **Fort Pierre** claims 1,800 residents and a past firmly grounded in the origins of the state. The settlement was founded in

1832 by the American Fur Company. In 1839, the company sent Pierre Chouteau up the Missouri River to establish trade with the Indians. Chouteau piloted his steamboat, the *Yellowstone,* to the mouth of the Bad River and began trading with Indians from nine Sioux tribes. An average of 17,000 buffalo hides valued at three to four dollars each were traded each year, then shipped to eastern U.S. and European markets where they were made into hats and coats, until the government bought the fort in 1855 for use in quelling Indian attacks on white settlers. Even though nothing remains of the fort today and cows graze in the area of the original cottonwood stockade, the National Park Service designated the site as a National Historic Landmark in 1991.

A century ago, Fort Pierre was the cattle-shipping capital of South Dakota, when dusty Texas cattlemen drove their longhorns to Fort Pierre's stockyards for shipment by rail to eastern markets. The town of Fort Pierre still clings to its rough-hewn image: today, crowds at bars and restaurants sport a variety of apparel from cowboy hats and faded jeans to golf shirts and pinstripe suits, and rowdy crowds of weekend sportsmen mingle with the "suits" from the state capital. Prior to the capital city's issuance of several "on-sale" (drinking on site) liquor licenses in the early 1960s, Fort Pierre's **Silver Spur Bar** was the major social center in central South Dakota, reputably having the highest volume of on-sale liquor business in the state. Owner Irish O'Leary with typical wry humor bequeathed a large share of the Silver Spur to the local Catholic church in his will. When O'Leary died, the somewhat perplexed church fathers quickly and quietly resold the bar.

Today, Fort Pierre still attracts big bar crowds to the Silver Spur and the Hop-Scotch, the only bar in central South Dakota featuring nude dancers. Because Pierre is located in the Central Time Zone and Fort Pierre is in the Mountain Time Zone, at closing time serious tipplers often race across the Missouri River bridge for an extra hour of imbibing, particularly when the state legislature is in session. It's often quipped that you could call a quorum of the state legislature just before 2 A.M. at either place, and find the majority of the registered lobbyists and press in attendance as well.

Beyond those two establishments, the nucleus of Fort Pierre's business district is a bank, a taxidermist, and the **Chateau,** a down-home restaurant and bar on Main Street, where the barbecued steaks and onion rings make a trip across the river memorable.

■ WINNER

Fifty-five miles (88 km) west of the Missouri River on State Highway 44 is Winner, home to over 3,000 souls who have an uncommon habit of being nice. Like the residents of Mobridge and Watertown, Winnerites are a hearty lot of ranchers and small businessmen who tend to leave out-of-towners thinking they must have just dropped a $20 bill on the floor and failed to pick it up. There's nothing distinctive about the town other than the people, unless it's the large number of pheasants that live on its outskirts and make Winner a hunting headquarters during the fall season. Too small for a megamall or fast-food chain restaurants, Winner is one of those out-of-the-way places that still sports family-owned restaurants, bars, a drug store, barber shop, and service station. The local Elks Lodge is still the best place to meet the movers and shakers in town and they're likely to buy the first round just because you showed up.

Fort Pierre from an early sketch. (National Archives)

Part of the set for Dances With Wolves *near the Houck Ranch northwest of Pierre. (Paul Jones)*

■ NORTHWARD THROUGH THE PRAIRIE

When movie star Kevin Costner began searching America for buffalo herds and a landscape unchanged since the 1860s as the setting for an epic movie about the West, he discovered South Dakota and the **Houck Ranch** northwest of Pierre. With a herd of buffalo 3,000 strong and 53,000 acres of open plain and unscarred horizon, the ranch provided the ideal setting for *Dances With Wolves,* the story of a young Civil War officer assigned to the frontier and his first encounters with its Sioux Indian inhabitants.

To visit the ranch, travel 25 miles (40 km) northwest of Pierre on State Highway 1806. Unfortunately, you won't be able to saddle up and ride through the largest privately owned herd of bison in the world, but much of the perimeter of the ranch is accessible by car. A little imagination can transport a visitor back to the nineteenth century, when great herds of these snorting beasts roamed all of the Great Plains. North from Pierre, the landscape typifies central South Dakota. A windswept range populated with grasshoppers and the occasional herd of deer or buffalo unfolds for miles. The few ranchers who inhabit this region eke out a living on land that supports very little but sagebrush, cockleburs, and fence posts.

Northeast of Pierre on U.S. highways 14 and 83 are the small communities of **Blunt, Onida,** and **Agar,** which have a combined population of less than 1,200. Each one has seen better days. Residents are courteous and friendly, but the towns themselves are a little dreary.

The **Mentor Graham House** on State Highway 14 in Blunt gives a glimpse of that town's rather tepid heyday. Mentor Graham met young Abraham Lincoln in New Salem, Illinois, and convinced the country lawyer that he would have to study grammar and correct his backwoods speech if he wanted a future in politics. Lincoln studied grammar and surveying with Graham, and the two became fast friends. When Graham attended Lincoln's inauguration, the president spotted his old teacher in the crowd and invited him onto the dais. Graham and his son, Abraham Lincoln Graham (named for Lincoln long before he became famous), moved to Blunt shortly before the elder Graham died. Part of the house the Grahams lived in is open to the public today and displays some original furniture. The historic home stretches a connection to fame, but it is the highlight of Blunt.

Railroad under construction near Gettysburg. (South Dakota State Historical Society, Pierre)

■ GETTYSBURG

Five miles (8 km) east of U.S. 83 on U.S. 212 is Gettysburg, a town founded by Civil War veterans who joined immigrants in scrambling for some of the last land open for homesteading. Many of the area's early settlers jumped off the train at Pierre and headed north for open ground. Once there, they built their sod shanties and began breaking the ground and planting crops. Today, most of that marginal farmland has been returned to pasture and even so, much of it cannot support more than a few head of cattle. Gettysburg's 1,500 residents, huddled in an old town surrounded by rolling prairie hills, enjoy its tranquility and are undismayed by its remote location.

At the town's **Dakota Sunset Museum,** 207 West Commercial, artifacts from the numerous Mandan and Arikara campsites that once dotted the nearby prairies and river bluffs are displayed. The surface of Medicine Rock, a large flat boulder displayed in the museum, is carved with handprints, footprints, and bird and animal tracks, as if to signify all which had passed its way. Early Indians believed the rock to be sacred and left gifts of colored cloth, tobacco, beads, and herbs as offerings to the Great Spirit.

■ MOBRIDGE

About 50 miles (80 km) north-northwest of Gettysburg at U.S. 12 and State Highway 20 is Mobridge, standing on a sharply curved bank of the Missouri River and across from both the Standing Rock and Cheyenne River Indian reservations.

The first bridge traversing the Missouri River in South Dakota was built at Mobridge in 1906. The name of the town was derived from a telegraph operator's abbreviation of "Missouri Bridge." (South Dakota State Historical Society, Pierre)

In the summer of 1906, as Milwaukee Railroad crews labored to build a bridge across a horseshoe bend in the Missouri River, an unknown telegrapher sent word of their location as succinctly as possible. His abbreviated dots and dashes, intended to convey "Missouri Bridge," gave Mobridge its name.

Construction of the bridge allowed trains to start hauling hopeful homesteaders to the last of the open range. It's a wonder early settlers didn't head for greener pastures, because the weather is brutal, but a knot of tough-as-nails settlers stuck it out, and in that is the essence of Mobridge: you'd have to travel to extreme northwestern South Dakota to reach as isolated a community. Just the same, it is aboundingly clear that you'd be hard pressed to arrive in another South Dakota town as eager to greet you. Nowhere will you find such back-slapping, friendly folk. Or maybe they're just surprised that you came at all.

The town itself is not unlike a hundred others. Its storefronts have aged and there is little sign of improvements, save a recent $2 million upgrade to the 50-bed regional hospital, which also happens to be the town's major employer. But familiarity breeds comfort, a large part of Mobridge's charm. Walk into **Rick's Cafe** on

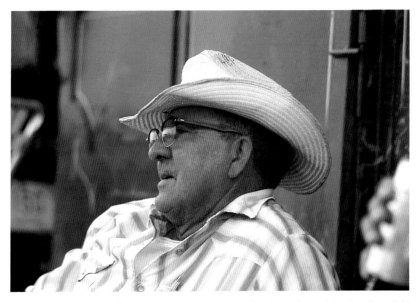

Bud Livermore (above) reflects on a stormy sunset sky over the plains of central South Dakota (left).

Main Street and local color surrounds you. Owner Rick Christman recently won the New York City Chili Cook-Off; the decor smacks of Rick's Cafe Américain in the 1942 classic *Casablanca*. Try the gourmet hamburgers and count the misspelled words on the handwritten signs tacked to the walls. For more refined fare and atmosphere, the **Wheel Restaurant** on West U.S. 12 fits the bill with great food as well as a panoramic view of Lake Oahe; call (605) 845-7474. Or try the **Captain's Table** at the Wrangler Motor Inn on U.S. 12 with its superb view of the river; call (605) 845-3641.

The **Scherr-Howe Arena** is jammed for high school basketball games every Friday night in the winter. Named for Jim and Bill Scherr, brothers who became hometown heroes when they competed as Olympic wrestlers in the 1980s, and for celebrated South Dakota artist Oscar Howe, the arena is still in use a half-century after it was constructed. The custodian gladly lets visitors gaze at 10 of the most unusual murals in the state. Painted by Howe under a Works Progress Administration grant in 1942, the murals represent some of the artist's early realistic work—not the abstract, colorful movement that defines Howe's later painting—and portray the history of the Plains Indians who inhabited the Mobridge area, from traditional ceremonies and depictions of everyday Sioux life, to the arrival of the missionaries. Of these 30-foot (9-m)-tall murals, one, called *Sundance*, bears particular mention: Lakota Indians sing and pound their drums in the background, while a Sioux warrior with the skin of his breasts pierced performs the sacred dance—a ritual in which a participant dances in the sun until overcome by a trance vision. It is a powerful painting filled with pain and pride, themes which resurfaced frequently in Howe's subsequent work.

■ SITTING BULL COUNTRY

Long before engineers and bridge builders came to the prairie land north of Pierre and near the town of Mobridge, it was home to the Arikara and later to Sioux Indian tribes, as well as to Sitting Bull, North America's most famous medicine man and Indian leader.

Sitting Bull was born in this rolling riverfront terrain in 1831, on the Grand River a few miles west of the town of Mobridge—and he died at the very same place. During his life, Sitting Bull was alternately praised as a hero and condemned as a coward by his own people. Sitting Bull was not a hereditary chief, but gained the power he possessed through his undying resentment of white encroachment on tribal lands and his ability to convey that message in a powerful and sometimes eloquent way. Credited with masterminding Indian strategy at the Battle of the Little Bighorn, Sitting Bull had to live in exile in Canada for several years following Custer's defeat. Later, he starred in Buffalo Bill's Wild West Show as it toured the United States and Europe, signing thousands of autographs for the then-princely price of 50 cents each. Even in death, he remains controversial, mysterious, and a continuing reminder of Native Americans' proud struggle for independence.

In 1881, Sitting Bull returned from exile with his starving band of sympathizers and surrendered to the U.S. Army. He was placed under house arrest on the Standing Rock Reservation in extreme southern North Dakota, where he grudgingly submitted to reservation life and the humiliation that he feared most—dependence on the U.S. government for all he wore and all he ate. Even after a long period of quiet drudgery and brief stints tending a small garden plot with his compatriots, Sitting Bull was still regarded as a "hostile" by Indian officials who feared his power and his potential to arouse the anger of reservation Indians.

When the Ghost Dance religion came to South Dakota (see "HISTORY"), offering Indians hope that they might rid themselves of the whites and welcome home the buffalo and their departed brothers, Sitting Bull did nothing to quell the dancing among his people. This angered government officials who, in turn, concluded that the Ghost Dance would lead to hostile action against whites and that the aging Sitting Bull was responsible and should be arrested.

Fearing that the use of Union soldiers in the arrest of Sitting Bull would result in unnecessary bloodshed, military officers assigned the task to 42 Indian policemen. As dawn approached the Dakota plains on December 15, 1890, the "metal breasts," so called because of the badges on their chests, swept into Sitting Bull's encampment. They found him asleep on the floor of his cabin with his two wives, and rousing him, told him he was under arrest. Sitting Bull, 59 years old, reconciled himself to imprisonment and slowly shuffled from his cabin at gun point. As he came into view, he found the entire camp surrounding his home. Braves harassed the Indian policemen. Women screamed and called upon the men to drive the police from the camp. And finally, Sitting Bull's son Crowfoot taunted his father for submitting to the will of the police.

That was enough, and in his last act of defiance, Sitting Bull loudly proclaimed that he was not going anywhere. In the ensuing struggle between reservation police and Sitting Bull's warriors, the chief was shot twice in the back and killed.

As the firefight continued, its smoke obscuring the fallen bodies of those mortally wounded, the horse that had accompanied Sitting Bull in the Wild West Show sat down, lifted one leg, and performed circus tricks. When the smoke cleared in the gray dawn light, seven members of Sitting Bull's faithful bodyguard lay dead, scattered among four bodies of Indian police. Army troops arrived a short time later, restored order, and loaded the bodies of the policemen and the chief like cordwood on a supply wagon, Sitting Bull on the bottom, and transported them to nearby Fort Yates in North Dakota. There, with no ceremony and little respect, the army buried Sitting Bull in a corner of a post cemetery, interred in a rough wooden box. When Fort Yates was abandoned as a military post years later, the bodies of soldiers buried in the cemetery were removed and Sitting Bull became the lone occupant of an all but abandoned graveyard in a place he never knew.

In 1953, a group of descendants of Sitting Bull sought permission from North Dakota authorities to remove the Sioux leader's remains from the neglected gravesite at Fort Yates to a new memorial near Mobridge. When their request was denied, the group alerted the Indian agent at Fort Yates, and, in his presence, took the bones. The descendants buried them on a high bluff five miles (8 km) from Mobridge on U.S. 12, close to Sitting Bull's home grounds. Following the removal, North Dakota officials were incensed. But a U.S. circuit judge ruled that only the family and the federal government could determine where the great Sioux leader would finally rest.

At the site today, a seven-ton granite bust of Sitting Bull by the late Crazy Horse Memorial sculptor Korczak Ziolkowski looks out over a horseshoe bend

Sitting Bull's grave site near Mobridge.

in the scenic Missouri River valley where the chief once roamed. Although isolated by the changed route of the highway and mowed only occasionally, this somewhat desolate memorial nonetheless conveys the resiliency, the intelligence, and the quiet pride of a great Sioux leader.

■ STANDING ROCK AND CHEYENNE RIVER RESERVATIONS

Approximately 70,000 Sioux live in South Dakota—as much as three times the population 200 years ago—and of the nine Sioux tribal governments in the state, six have reservation boundaries. Reservations within the state cover 4,960,881 acres, or about 10 percent of the total acreage in the state. Just west of Mobridge on U.S. 12 is the Standing Rock Indian Reservation, 846,291 acres of vastness and desolation, which extends in the north into North Dakota. Past the reservation's southern border lies the Cheyenne River Indian Reservation, the second largest of South Dakota's Indian reservations with 1,400,614 acres.

Together these two enormous reservations cover a tract of land larger than Delaware, with none of that state's diversity. Although residents use the medical and retail services of Mobridge to the east and Pierre to the southeast, there is little interaction between these two worlds. For the most part, whites and Indians remain indifferent to one another.

These two reservations are among the most sparsely populated areas in South Dakota and cover three counties of remote grasslands and mind-numbing tundra-like expanses. Motorists traveling the two main arteries, U.S. highways 212 and 12, through the two reservations should check the condition of their own vehicles before attempting a cross-country trek in this very remote region. Except for the asphalt and gravel roadways and an occasional community, this land is little changed from the Civil War era. Residents live far apart in small towns, most with less than 500 people, with names that echo the area's Native American past: Thunder Hawk, Eagle Butte, Whitehorse, Green Grass, and Iron Lighting. Each is marked only by reduced speed zones, cigarette stops, and gas pumps.

Look-alike government housing dots the prairie—the paint, though fading, in stark contrast to the brownness of the surrounding land.

VISITING GRANDMOTHER ENGLAND

In the late 1870s, Black Elk toured with Buffalo Bill's Wild West Show, performing across the United States and abroad, and even visiting with Queen Victoria.

*T*hey put us all on a very big fire-boat, so big that when I first saw, I could hardly believe it; and when it sent forth a voice, I was frightened. There were other big fire-boats sending voices, and little ones too.

Afterwhile I could see nothing but water, water, water, and we did not seem to be going anywhere, just up and down; but we were told that we were going fast. If we were, I thought that we must drop off where the water ended; or maybe we might have to stop where the sky came down to the water. There was nothing but mist where the big town used to be and nothing but water all around. We were all in despair now and many were feeling so sick that they began to sing their deathsongs . . .

❖ ❖ ❖

One day we were told that Majesty was coming. I did not know what that was at first, but I learned afterward. It was Grandmother England. . . . We stood right in front of Grandmother England. She was little but fat and we liked her, because she was good to us. After we had danced, she spoke to us. She said something like this:

"I am sixty-seven years old. All over the world I have seen all kinds of people; but to-day I have seen the best-looking people I know. If you belonged to me, I would not let them take you around in a show like this." She said other good things too, and then she said we must come to see her, because she had come to see us. She shook hands with all of us. Her hand was very little and soft. We gave a big cheer for her, and then the shining wagons came in and she got into one of them and they all went away.

—John Neihardt,
Black Elk Speaks, 1932

Black Elk. (South Dakota State Historical Society, Pierre)

SOUTH-CENTRAL
AND BADLANDS

VAST TRACTS OF SOUTH DAKOTA ARE WITHOUT CIVILIZATION. Across miles of open plain, scarred over ages by creek-cut coulees and incessant winds, few signs of human habitation exist. So it is with south-central South Dakota—an area bounded on the north by I-90, on the east by the Missouri River, on the west by the Black Hills, and on the south by South Dakota's border with Nebraska. Today, except for the relatively populated Black Hills region, the West River area has only about two persons per square mile.

Much of the south-central plains lack any one measure of distinction. Formed by the same lift that created the Rocky Mountains, the land slants east and drains into the Missouri River. Unlike the flat basins and gently rolling hills of lowland eastern South Dakota, the plains' topography is high buttes, deep canyons, and badlands. It's home to surprising changes in a landscape that ranges from cool wooded ravines and lazy rivers to national grasslands and some of the most godforsaken country man has ever seen.

South Dakota journalist Bob Mercer claims that western and eastern South Dakota essentially grew up as twins separated at birth by the Missouri River and the vast Indian reservations which have historically run down the middle of the state. In the 1870s and '80s, when Yankton, Bismarck, and a host of other communities fought to be named the Dakota Territory capital, nonconformists in western South Dakota sought to break away and form their own separate territory to be called Lincoln. As the region grew, its residents developed two distinct personalities. By and large, residents of western South Dakota are a bit less mainstream and a lot more down to earth than their eastern counterparts who, they sense, probably look down their noses at the West River residents' less refined ways. Even in 1993 an eastern South Dakota public relations worker—who might consider a new vocation—said, "I believe the East River and West River people are different in the ways of their women. The women on the West River chew tobacco and the women on the East River don't." Truth is, only a few western South Dakota women chew tobacco, but they're hell on whiskey and cigars.

■ HISTORY

The first inhabitants of this land were hunters of the giant bison herds that roamed the Great Plains. Not surprisingly, white settlement of this infertile region came late. While the fertile farmlands of eastern South Dakota attracted sod-busters after the 1861 establishment of Dakota Territory, the plains west of the Missouri were designated for Indians under treaties with the U.S. government. But when the bison herds were gone, living off this land became extremely difficult for the Sioux, and only when they turned to the Black Hills could the Indians find game to supplement the government's rations.

In the 30 years following the initial gold rush to the Black Hills, enormous areas of western South Dakota still remained remote and untouched by white settlement. In the 1880s, the main routes to the Black Hills from the east were two wagon trails leading to Deadwood: one from Bismarck, North Dakota; and one from Fort Pierre in central South Dakota. The first rail line into western South Dakota came not from Sioux Falls, but from Chadron, Nebraska, through Buffalo Gap in 1885–86. No railroads directly connected eastern and western South Dakota until 1906–07. Public bridges didn't span the Missouri until 1924,

When George Catlin painted this scene, tens of millions of buffalo roamed the Great Plains. (Buffalo Bill Historical Center, Cody, Wyoming. Gift of Paul Mellon)

with one at Mobridge first, and later others at Forest City, Pierre, Chamberlain, and Rosebud.

In 1904, the Rosebud Indian Reservation was opened to homesteaders, and widespread white settlement came to western South Dakota outside of the Black Hills, and homesteading occurred on other reservations throughout the ensuing decade. In 1907, Edith Eudora Kohl (née Ammons) and her sister, Ida Mary, joined more than 100,000 others who contracted "homestead fever" and sought a stake near "the land of the Burnt Thigh," otherwise known as the Lower Brule Indian Reservation, then located around present-day Gregory County on the west side of the Missouri. The exploits of the two young women, both in their twenties and "timid as mice," are told in *Land of the Burnt Thigh,* published in 1938 by Minnesota Historical Society Press. A classic account of the quiet, heroic settlers of this vast region, the book offers rare insights into the legion of women who sought their own simple investment in the future by "proving up" their own land claims. The sisters ran a newspaper, taught school, operated a post office and general store, helped others who had come to settle, and found time to battle prairie fires, rattlesnakes, and raging blizzards—all in an effort to keep 160 acres. While Edith Kohl's narrative pales in comparison with those of other noted prairie writers, such as Pulitzer Prize-winner Hamlin Garland, her descriptions of the carnival atmosphere surrounding the opening of the Rosebud Indian Reservation—the last government land lottery in the United States, and yet another affront to the Sioux tribe—portray both the naiveté and the desperation of many pioneers who sought to settle land in South Dakota.

In the first decade of the twentieth century, thousands of single women "marched" as homesteaders into western South Dakota. Some sought a prudent investment, some sought a husband, and still others sought a way to support themselves and several children after the loss of a spouse through death, divorce, or desertion. Claim records indicate that nearly 12 percent of all homesteaders were women—and committed women at that. Those same records reveal that 42.4 percent of the women proved up their final claims, while only 37 percent of their male counterparts did the same.

LAND LOTTERY AT ROSEBUD

*A*t the stroke of midnight a cry went up from the registrars. At 12:01 under the dim flicker of coal-oil lanterns and torches hung on posts or set on barrels and boxes, that most famous of lotteries began. The uproar and confusion of the hours before midnight were like a desert calm compared with the clamor which broke out. Registrars lined both sides of the street. 'Right this way, folks! . . . Register right here!' And there, on rough tables, on dry-goods boxes, anything upon which a piece of paper could be filled out and a notary seal stamped thereon, the crowd put in their applications as entries in the gamble, raised their right hands and swore: 'I do solemnly swear that I honestly desire to enter public lands for my own personal use as a home and for settlement and cultivation, and not for speculation or in the interest of some other person . . .'

In the excitement and chill of the October night, fingers shook so that they could scarcely hold a pen . . . Into the slits in the huge cans which held the applications dropped a surprising number of items. People became confused and used it as a mail box, dropping in souvenir cards. One applicant even dropped in his return fare. And some, shaking uncontrollably with excitement, were barely able to drop their applications in at all.

And somewhere, off in the dark spaces beyond the flickering lights, lay the million acres of land for which the horde was clamoring, its quiet sleep unbroken.

—Edith Eudora Kohl, *Land of the Burnt Thigh*, 1938

■ ROSEBUD INDIAN RESERVATION

Of the estimated 70,000 Lakota (Sioux) living within South Dakota, about three-fourths claim reservation residence. Two Indian reservations in this region, Rosebud and Pine Ridge, cover well over two million acres amid the sticky gumbo soil and the buffalo and western wheat grasses. Most urban Indians in the state either live on reservations part-time or make frequent visits to them to maintain cultural and family ties, while they take advantage of employment and educational opportunities offered in towns and cities. In western South Dakota, where few employment opportunities exist close to the reservations, the Lakota tend to be among the most disadvantaged people in the United States.

Eighteen miles (29 km) west of Winner on U.S. 18 is the Rosebud Indian Reservation, a 527,640-acre tract once home to an early Native American leader who strove for peace between Indians and whites. Following a series of conflicts in the 1850s between Indians and the U.S. Army, Spotted Tail (Sinte Gleska) of the Brules became a proponent of peace. As a chief of the Brule, a sub-tribe of the Teton Sioux, Spotted Tail was certain that his tribe could not emerge victorious against the superior numbers and weapons of the white soldiers. After he persuaded most of the members of his tribe to sign the Fort Laramie Treaty in 1868, which created the Great Sioux Reservation though further diminishing what was once an eight-million-acre Sioux stronghold, the Brules were moved from Nebraska to land near the Missouri River in South Dakota, where they were encouraged to take up farming. When tribesmen refused, Spotted Tail traveled to Washington and attempted to persuade the Secretary of the Interior to relocate the agency farther west and to preserve Sioux hunting lands in the Black Hills. Spotted Tail was allowed to move his agency, but the Sioux agenda to save the Black Hills was eventually defeated de facto by the discovery of gold in the Black Hills and the subsequent rush to the area by white settlers. This further angered members of the Brule Sioux and many left the reservation to join hostile bands, including that of Spotted Tail's nephew, Crazy Horse. These bands, under the leadership of Crazy Horse and Sitting Bull, ultimately toppled Custer at Little Bighorn. Crazy Horse returned to an agency, Sitting Bull fled to Canada, and Spotted Tail selected the site of a new agency near Mission. The agency was first named for the peace-seeking Sioux leader, but later was changed to Rosebud Agency.

The landscape of the Rosebud Indian Reservation hasn't been altered much since the days when Spotted Tail rode bareback over its grassy buttes and into its quiet creek beds. Only two main highways now bisect what was once marked only by buffalo herds and a few Indian ponies. Standing on a rise in the surrounding prairie, buffeted by the ceaseless winds, the low drone of a few passing vehicles is the only indication that twentieth-century man has ever visited this place. Were you to fly over it on a moonless night, only a few yard lights would stare back from the darkness.

Electricity and plumbing have come to the main buildings in the communities of the Rosebud Reservation. But in the outback, where gravel roads and a few dirt tire tracks lead the way to the horizon, there are few amenities. Dirt-floored shanties, mobile homes, and brightly painted government houses are found at the

A lone schoolhouse graces the high plains in the western part of the state.

end of those lonely litter-lined roads, and little else. In the few towns—really just wide spots in the road—such as Okreek, Mission, Olsonville, Saint Francis, Rosebud, and Parmelee—children go to school each morning and grown-ups to coffee, just like every other rural town in South Dakota. The town of Rosebud, southwest of Mission, is home to the reservation's only medical center, as well as the state's only college on an Indian reservation. Sinte Gleska College offers courses in Native American studies and liberal arts degrees. Just west of Rosebud in Crazy Horse Canyon is **Ghost Hawk Park,** about fifty thousand acres of stark beauty. Southwest of town, the nine-hole, grass-green **Spotted Tail Golf Course** gives residents one of the few opportunities to tee off in southwest South Dakota.

■ ST. FRANCIS
During his presidency (1869–77), Ulysses S. Grant attempted to establish the first peace policy toward Native Americans. Meanwhile, various Christian missionaries had established their churches on most reservations. To simplify his supervision of the reservations, Grant's policy assigned each reservation one and only one Christian denomination. The Rosebud Reservation was first designated Episcopalian,

Father Beuchel, a Jesuit priest who wrote a number of books in the Lakota language and introduced their culture to many non-Indians. (Marquette University Archives, Milwaukee)

Sioux dolls from the collection of the Cultural Heritage Center in Pierre. (South Dakota State Historical Society, Pierre)

but Spotted Tail argued that many of the Brule had been converted to Catholicism by Father De Smet. In addition to acquiring Catholic status for his tribe, the Brule chief was able to persuade U.S. authorities to allow a Catholic mission to be constructed, finished in 1885 by Franciscans and Jesuits who had been expelled from Germany by Prince Otto von Bismarck. These missionaries also plowed adjoining fields and planted trees. By 1900, with 500 students enrolled in elementary and vocational education, the St. Francis Mission in the present-day town of St. Francis had become the largest Indian mission school in America and eventually expanded to include a full high school curriculum.

Although many priests have stood at St. Francis' altars and blackboards, one of the most remarkable was Father Beuchel, a Jesuit who took an intense interest in the Sioux and introduced the Native culture to thousands of non-Indians. Beuchel collected artifacts and photographs, deciphered the Lakota language, and wrote a number of books in Lakota, including a Bible history and grammar guides. His collection is the cornerstone of the **Beuchel Memorial Lakota Museum** on the campus of the St. Francis Mission and School. Preserved there are a variety of Teton Sioux materials, including historic photographs of Spotted Tail, as well as a 300-plant herbarium.

LAKOTA BOARDING SCHOOL

*I*t is almost impossible to explain to a sympathetic white person what a typical old Indian boarding school was like; how it affected the Indian child suddenly dumped into it like a small creature from another world, helpless, defenseless, bewildered, trying desperately and instinctively to survive and sometimes not surviving at all . . .

Oddly enough, we owed our unspeakable boarding schools to the do-gooders, the white Indian-lovers. The schools were intended as an alternative to the outright extermination seriously advocated by generals Sherman and Sheridan, as well as by most settlers and prospectors over-running our land. "You don't have to kill those poor benighted heathen," the do-gooders said, "in order to solve the Indian Problem. Just give us a chance to turn them into useful farmhands, laborers, and chambermaids who will break their backs for you at low wages." In that way the boarding schools were born. The kids were taken away from their villages and pueblos, in their blankets and moccasins, kept completely isolated from their families—sometimes for as long as ten years—suddenly coming back, their short hair slick with pomade, their necks raw from stiff, high collars, their thick jackets always short in the sleeves and pinching under the arms, their tight patent leather shoes giving them corns, the girls in starched white blouses and clumsy, high-buttoned boots—caricatures of white people. When they found out—and they found out quickly—that they were neither wanted by whites nor by Indians, they got good and drunk, many of them staying drunk for the rest of their lives.

—Mary Crow Dog with Richard Erdoes, *Lakota Woman*, 1990

Lakota students pose with a nun on the reservation.
(Marquette University Archives, Milwaukee)

■ MURDO

Forty-five miles (72 km) north of Mission at the intersection of U.S. 83 and I-90 is Murdo, home to 679 residents and a collection of rare, classic vehicles, from a 1902 Oldsmobile to one of Elvis Presley's motorcycles. The 10-acre, 39-building **Pioneer Auto Museum and Antique Town** is worth a stop for anyone interested in the finest vehicles America has produced, as well as 100 other collections ranging from fine china to hand organs. Down the street, and there aren't that many streets in Murdo, the **McKen-Z Doll Museum** boasts hundreds of cloth, bisque, china, and wood-faced dolls, some of which arrived on the first wagon trains in South Dakota in the 1850s, others of which have been collected from around the world.

■ BEEF AND BUFFALO

Traveling in south-central South Dakota can be a serenely pleasurable experience. A full moon can light the prairie on a summer night. In winter, that same moon can cast a glow across a wind-swept tundra, silhouetting coyotes, deer, and antelope as they forage for food. And on some nights the unexpected happens, the occasion no one planned. Such was the case in the mid-1950s when Beef met buffalo.

Stanton Uhlir had grown up in the area of **Kadoka**, a small rural town of ranchers about 50 miles (80 km) west of Murdo. As long as anyone around those parts can recall, Stanton had always been big. By the time he reached high school, his friends were kidding him that he would have to use the truck scale at the grain elevator just to be weighed. Stanton's bulk earned him the nickname "Beef," and his six-foot-six (2-m) height earned him center spot on the Kadoka High basketball team. Even though the team never won the State B championship, Stanton's heroics on the court are legendary in the community. More than family and friends still remember the night Kadoka traveled to the Corn Palace in Mitchell to compete for the State B Consolation Championship. It was Stanton's last game in high school, the tennis shoes would be put in the closet for the winter, and the graduating senior undoubtedly hoped to end his career with a bang. When the final buzzer sounded that night in 1950, Beef had scored an incredible 50 points—a record that still stands in South Dakota B basketball.

Following graduation, Stanton headed off to South Dakota State University to earn a degree in agriculture. A bum knee sidelined him from sports, but following graduation he came home to Kadoka with a new degree and a real desire to teach veteran farmers how to manage their land. As the newest agent for the Agriculture,

Stabilization and Conservation Service, Stanton traveled the backroads, conducting classes in all the small communities of south-central South Dakota.

One winter night, after teaching a small group of White River farmers and ranchers the latest in tillage techniques, Beef headed for home in his big old Buick. It was nearly midnight when he spotted the lights of Murdo over the northern horizon. Friends say Big Beef was probably thinking about stopping "for a hook or two" before making the last leg into Kadoka, but perhaps he was just mulling over the next day's schedule, or dreaming about a soft pillow and a warm bed.

As his speeding Buick crested a rise in State Highway 83, Beef probably had a micro-second to analyze what lie before him—a herd of bison that had broken a fence and found a firm footing on the asphalt roadway. Buffalo have been known to outrun horses, but these didn't budge. What happened next has been described as the "crimson splash." The Buick bashed into the buffalo and neither prevailed. The car was totaled. Two buffalo were killed instantly and more than half a dozen were wounded. Miraculously, Beef wasn't hurt—a testament to his 300-pound (136-kg) frame. After assessing the situation, Stanton decided that Murdo was close enough to call for help and he elected to hoof it to town.

As he slid from the mangled car into the surrounding darkness, he detected a strange sound over the escaping steam of his broken radiator. Two bulls, each about seven times heavier than the Big Beef, were less than pleased by the introduction of a car into their world. The death of others in their group and the pungent smell of fresh bison blood splashed on frozen ground had excited them, and they were mad. Beef slowly backed to the car as the bulls pawed the pavement and snorted their intentions. Beef knew when he was licked.

About an hour later, another motorist was driving up State Highway 83 when he came upon a sight even stranger than Beef had literally run into. There, in his headlights, was a man sitting on top of a wrecked car with dead, bloodied, and angry buffalo all about. "His buddies gave him a hard time about those buffalo until the day he died," Beef's uncle, Vernon Uhlir, says with a chuckle. "But there aren't too many people who can run into a herd of buffalo and live to tell about it. The pure size of Big Beef, he was just solid. To visit with him, you'd think he was as mean as anyone in the world. But inside he had a heart of gold and he was just like a big kitten." Stanton died in September 1990, but around Kadoka, the story of Beef and the Buffalo lives on.

West of Kadoka, I-90 passes through one arm of 590,000 acres of rolling prairie known as **Buffalo Gap National Grassland.** Early morning and dusk are the best times to roam the grasslands in search of the deer, antelope, grouse, wild turkey, and prairie dogs that live there. On the northern edge of this section of the park is the town of Wall, home to massive Wall Drug. (See essay, "How Many Miles to Wall Drug?") Known the world around, at least by name, the store more than dominates the local economy in this tiny town.

■ BADLANDS NATIONAL PARK

Just south of Wall, the landscape changes quickly. Rolling grasslands abruptly give way to chiseled spires, ragged ridges, and deep canyons—the setting for the Badlands, the strangest area in the state. So stark is Badlands National Park that it has been described as "hell with the fires burned out." In this land so ruthlessly ravaged over ages by the wind and rain, ridges, gullies, spires, and knobs are a powerful reminder of the forces of nature. Their fossil-laden soils, which erode with each new season, offer mementos of giant beasts which once lurked in the region.

The plains suddenly give way to the ragged buttes of the Badlands south of Wall.

According to Jay Shuler, a National Park Service naturalist who studied and wrote about the park in the 1980s, the Badlands are the result of

. . . *A* natural history that began about the time the dinosaurs died out, sixty-five million years ago. The shallow Pierre Sea, which divided the continent into eastern and western land masses, drained away, making North America whole again. A jungle developed on the exposed seabed, transforming the dark mud and shale to a bright yellow soil. From about thirty-seven million years ago to twenty-three million years ago, the climate gradually became cool and dry. Intermittent-sediment loaded floods swept over the area, depositing layer upon layer of volcanic ash and mud. Between floods, plant-eating mammals fed on the lush vegetation, and some fell prey to a variety of flesh-eaters. Their bones were buried by the sediments and fossilized. These fossils comprise the best and most complete record of the Oligocene Epoch, the Golden Age of Mammals, which had reached the species diversity and body size to occupy the living space left vacant by the dinosaurs.

About half a million years ago erosion began to slice through the prairie and the fossil-rich layers of mudstone beneath it, creating a landscape so chaotic and spectacular—so difficult to travel across—it came to be called the "Badlands." The word badlands then became the generic geologic term for all barren, severely eroded landscapes, whether in Montana or Mongolia, on the Moon or Mars.

The French fur traders who explored the western United States in the early 1800s referred to the area as *les mauvaises terres a traverser,* or "bad lands to travel across." The Lakota labeled it *mako sica,* or "land bad." Despite the harshness and apparent inhospitable topography of the Badlands for these more recent arrivals, this area has been supporting humans for more than 12,000 years. Ancient mammoth hunters were the first to visit the Badlands. Much later, the Arikara came to the area around the White River—which today runs through Pine Ridge Reservation— because of the huge herds of buffalo that darkened the grasslands. Later, the Lakota drove out those rival bands, and they dominated the region for about 100 years. By the mid-nineteenth century, trappers, followed by other Europeans, soldiers, miners, homesteaders, and cattlemen, supplanted the Lakota.

BADLANDS "ARCHITECTURE"

In 1935 Frank Lloyd Wright traveled through South Dakota and was greatly moved by the unique landscape of the Badlands. In this letter to Robert D. Lusk, Wright reveals his reverence for natural forms and his appreciation for their apparent architectural qualities.

*D*ear Bob:

Speaking of our trip to the Big Bad Lands, Black Hills, and Spearfish Canyon: I've been about the world a lot and pretty much over our own country; but I was totally unprepared for that revolution called the Dakota Bad Lands. From Mitchell, Paul Bellamy was driving a fair seventy over the brown Dakota prairie to reach the Bad Lands before sunset. About four, afternoon, something came into view that made me sit up straight and look at Bellamy to see if he saw what I saw. "Oh," said he, "you've seen nothing yet." But I had. What I saw gave me an indescribable sense of mysterious otherwhere—a distant architecture, ethereal, touched, only touched with a sense of Egyptian, Mayan drift and silhouette. As we came closer a templed realm definitely stood ambient in air before my astonished "scene," loving but scene-jaded gaze. The streamline working on a vast pleateau of solid cream white clay, something like "calichi," had sculptured this familiar world into one unfamiliar but entrancing.

Endless trabeations surmounted by or rising into pyramid (obelisk) and temple, ethereal in color and exquisitely chiseled in endless detail, they began to reach to infinity spreading into the sky on every side; an endless supernatural world more spiritual than earth but created out of it. As we rode, or seemed to be floating upon a splendid winding road that seemed to understand it all and just where to go, we rose and fell between its delicate parallels of rose and cream and sublime shapes, chalk white, fretted against a blue sky with high floating clouds; the sky itself seemed only there to cleanse and light the vast harmonious building scheme.

—letter from Frank Lloyd Wright, 1935

(following pages) Weather and shadows combine to create a dramatic effect in the Badlands.

Despite efforts to tame this vast wasteland, the Badlands soon became regarded as a geologic wonder worthy of preservation. Authorized by Congress in 1929, Badlands National Monument was proclaimed by President Franklin D. Roosevelt in 1939 "to preserve the scenery, to protect the fossils and wildlife, and to conserve the mixed-grass prairie."

In 1976, the size of the monument more than doubled with the addition of 133,300 acres of the **Pine Ridge Reservation,** which is administered by the National Park Service in agreement with the Oglala Sioux Tribe. Then, in 1978, Congress recognized the enduring value and uniqueness of the Badlands by elevating it to National Park status.

Altogether, these banded pinnacles, sawtooth spires, and steep canyons cover 244,000 acres in the southwest region of the state. The Badlands formations can be eerie to some, picturesque to others. The **Ben Reifel Visitor Center** at **Cedar Pass,** nine miles (14 km) south of I-90 on State Highway 240, and the **White River Visitor Center** in the southerly Stronghold Unit off BIA (Bureau of Indian Affairs) Highway 27, help visitors become acquainted with the area. Few paved roadways exist within the park. Many areas are accessible only by four-wheel-drive vehicles or on foot or horseback.

In 1976, Congress set aside 64,250 acres of the park as the **Sage Creek Wilderness Area.** While this roadless area is protected from development, it is open to hiking, backpacking, and other activities. The only trails within the wilderness area have been created by the tread of bison. Hikers, who have been known to get lost in the maze of canyons and layered cliffs, are encouraged to purchase a topographical map before adventuring into the backcountry. There are several other caveats for those who leave the comforting confines of air-conditioned autos and hotel rooms during a visit to the Badlands. Climbing the Badlands formations can be dangerous as slopes are often steep and crumbly. Weather can change suddenly, and lightning, hail, high winds, and sun require caution during the summer months. Take water along, even on the planned short hikes. Bison can be extremely dangerous. A large bull often weighs as much as a small car and can travel nearly as fast. Venomous prairie rattlers are common within the park.

As dangerous as an excursion into the Badlands may sound, these few simple precautions can guarantee a wondrous experience. The Badlands are one of the last vestiges of one of the world's great grasslands, and even today they support thousands of species of wildlife and plants. Prairie grasses once covered nearly a quarter of the United States from southern Alberta almost to Mexico, and from the Rockies to Indiana. While much of that grassland has vanished beneath the plow, in the Badlands those strains of grass still billow in a timeless wind, and wildflowers still bloom in the crags and crevices of this harsh landscape.

From afar, this land can look dead and dry. Up close, it is teeming with life. In every draw that drains the surrounding prairie, plant life is either blooming or awaiting a warm sun to spread its color. In the spring, the bloom of the star, sego, and gumbo lilies mirrors the receding snowdrifts, just an instant before the earliest of the wildflowers, the pasqueflower, bursts into bloom. From June through August, prairie coneflowers lift their bright yellow petals above the short grasses, while plains pricklypear and Missouri pincushions provide colorful, close-to-the-ground displays. All told, nearly 50 different grasses and almost 200 types of wildflowers grow in the Badlands.

Although summer temperatures may top 100 degrees F (38° C), and in winter the wind chill regularly drops below zero, an abundance of animals call the Badlands home. Hundreds of prairie dogs busily build their "towns," while badgers, bobcats, foxes, and coyotes may linger nearby, eager to make a meal of one of them. Antelope and Rocky Mountain bighorns, the latter introduced into the park after the extinction of the native Audubon bighorn, are often found on the rocky cliffs or grazing on the grassy tables, while mule deer favor the wooded draws. Cottontails and jackrabbits race through the tall grass, careful to avoid the prairie rattlers, yellow-bellied racers, and bullsnakes scavenging for food. White-throated swifts and cliff swallows nest on the faces of cliffs, and rock wrens build their homes in the crevices. Golden eagles have been known to rear their young on high, inaccessible buttes within the park, while the burrowing owl prefers ground level and often builds its nest in prairie dog holes. On the grasslands, long-billed curlews search for insects to the song of the western meadowlark. In late spring and early summer, small cinnamon-colored calves join the park's 500 head of bison.

Sunup and sunset reveal a panorama of color in this seemingly barren land, as light plays with the layers of sedimentation in the rock, casting varying hues of purples, reds, grays, and golds in contrast to the deep greens of the prairie grasses. At night these lands, located far away from the glow of city lights, provide the ideal spot to view the stars. The sky is commonly so clear that satellites can be seen in orbit around the Earth. A full moon can illuminate the way for starlight hikers as the ragged ridges draw a wicked line against the horizon.

HOW MANY MILES TO WALL DRUG?

You could walk clear across South Dakota and still know nearly every step of the way how many miles you were from the tiny high-plains community of Wall. Catchy and sometimes, corny, phrases are attached to virtually every billboard along the way: "Have You Dug Wall Drug?" and "Who Has the Gall to Bypass Wall?" are two standards. Then there are signs that inform motorists they've missed the place.

The signs were the brainchild of Ted and Dorothy Hustead, who, back in 1936 were owners of little Hustead Drug Store on Main Street in Wall. One sizzling Sunday afternoon, Dorothy observed the cars zooming out of the Badlands and heading for Rapid City on unpaved U.S. 16. Those tourists, thought Dorothy, were probably hot and thirsty, and here she sat with a mountain of ice and no customers. Why not put up roadside signs strung along the fence rows reading "Free Ice Water/Wall Drug/Wall, S.D."?

In short order, her husband had boards painted, postholes dug, and signs planted along the neighboring highway. Before he returned to the store, customers already had arrived for their free ice water. The rest, as they say, is history. At last count, there were more than 3,000 Wall Drug signs in all 50 states. In fact, Wall Drug signs have been posted in countries around the world, including Italy, Holland, England, Wales, Germany, and India, and in spots in Africa and the Arctic Circle. In World War II, a Wall Drug sign was suspended from the harbor bridge in Sidney, Australia, and a helicopter-mounted sign which noted that it was 10,659 miles to Wall Drug survived the Tet Offensive in Vietnam in 1968.

Today, Wall Drug in Wall takes up a full city block and features far more than pharmaceuticals. A legion of South Dakotans and a number of regular, cross-state travelers have grown up enjoying the drugstore's two "cowboy bands"—actually animated mannequins—who perform every 15 minutes or so. The store also serves some of the best pancakes and donuts in the state, and sells Black Hills gold jewelry, Native American arts and crafts, books, and fine Western apparel and tack. In summer, it's hard to find a parking spot among the out-of-state cars, motorhomes, and motorcoaches that clog the narrow streets of this small town. In winter, the tables at Wall are frequented by uniformed personnel from nearby Ellsworth Air Force Base and warmly clothed ranchers who sit side by side enjoying coffee and donuts.

(right) The famous "jackalope," part rabbit and part antelope, is one of the many tourist attractions at Wall Drug.

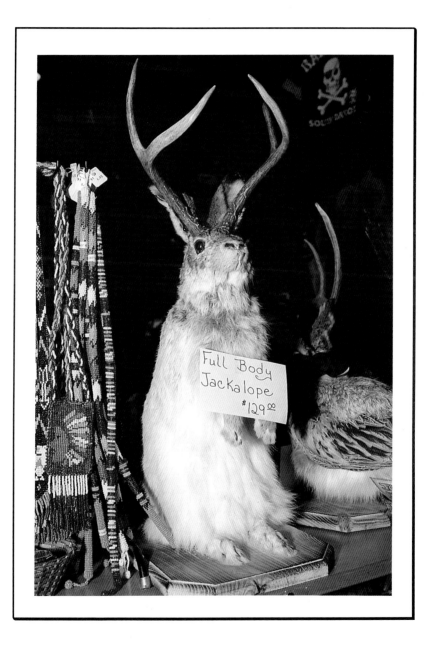

■ PINE RIDGE INDIAN RESERVATION

Along Badlands National Park's southern edge is the northern boundary of the Pine Ridge Indian Reservation. With 1,783,741 acres, the home of the Oglala Sioux is second in size only to Arizona's Navajo Reservation. And it is nearly as desolate, as evidenced by any South Dakota map. Amid a smattering of towns with names such as Red Shirt, Potato Creek, Porcupine, and Wanblee, visitors find an abundance of buttes with monikers like Buzzard, Eagle Nest, Snake, and Slim.

Shannon County, which covers more than two-thirds of the Pine Ridge Reservation, is consistently ranked as the poorest county in the nation. Unemployment hovers at 85 percent and alcoholism and infant mortality rates are high. Only 47 percent of the residences in Shannon County have telephone service, while 94 percent of South Dakota households have that utility.

The towns and their residences reveal the poverty of the region. Adults sit on porches and steps with little to do, as their children play in grassless yards. The trading posts, stores, gas stations, and laundromats are the center of activity, except during the powwows, when the whole town turns out to celebrate.

Eight miles (13 km) from the White River Visitor Center, the **Cuny Table Cafe** offers what are inarguably the best Indian tacos in South Dakota. Served on fry bread (instead of a hard tortilla) and filled with seasoned ground beef, lettuce, and cheese, they're best eaten with a fork. Three miles (5 km) west of **Kyle,** on BIA Highway 2, Oglala Lakota College provides the area's only four-year accredited college and a bookstore with a respectable collection of Native American literature. The major community celebration—the **Wazi Paya Oyate Festival and Kyle Fair**—is held in mid-August.

On the reservation's extreme southern edge, near the border of Nebraska, is the town of **Pine Ridge,** home to the **Oglala Nation Fair & Rodeo** held the first weekend in August. The three-day rodeo and four-day powwow feature drum and dance contests, and golf, horseshoe pitching, and softball tournaments. The **Sioux Nation Shopping Center** offers a lean selection of groceries, hardware, clothing, books, and arts and crafts.

The **Red Cloud Indian Mission School,** a few miles north of Pine Ridge on U.S. 18, presents the Indian Art Show with a collection of 300 works of art representing 30 different tribes. Forty paintings from the school's permanent collection are on display. The Indian star quilts are exquisite, and its gift shop offers genuine bead and quill work at reasonable prices.

Brandon One Feather at a powwow at Pine Ridge Reservation.

A rare photo of a dejected looking Chief Sitting Bull, with his wife and two babies (white woman unidentified), shortly before his murder at Standing Rock Reservation on December 15, 1890. (Center for Western Studies)

■ BATTLE AT WOUNDED KNEE

Tucked in the south-central area of Pine Ridge, in a place few but avid historians and Native Americans ever visit, is the town and National Historic Site of Wounded Knee. Just east of town on BIA Highway 27, near the silent hardwoods of Wounded Knee Creek, stands a simple stone marker erected to honor those slain here on a cold winter day in 1890. But to those who live on the reservation, and to those who drive past this solitary pinnacle on a regular basis, the soul of the nation may well be buried here.

In the years immediately following the loss of the Black Hills to the U.S. government, some Sioux leaders resisted removal of their people to reservations and agencies which the treaties demanded. Big Foot, known to some as Spotted Elk, was a hereditary chief of the Minniconjou Sioux of the Cheyenne River Reservation. Regarded as an outstanding chief and a strong believer in the way of life the Indians had known prior to the arrival of the whites, Big Foot eagerly accepted the Ghost Dance religion, taught by the Paiute religious leader Wovoka. Big Foot encouraged his people to faithfully perform the ceremony and in so doing rid themselves of the whites, welcome back their departed warriors, and return to a way of life robbed from them over time.

On December 15, 1890, Sioux spiritual leader Sitting Bull was killed on the Standing Rock Reservation in north-central South Dakota. As tension mounted

A Grand Council between Indian chiefs at Pine Ridge on January 17, 1891, just two and a half weeks after the Massacre at Wounded Knee. (Center for Western Studies)

among Indians throughout South Dakota, Chief Big Foot decided to leave his en-campment on the shores of the Cheyenne River and journey with his band to Pine Ridge, where he hoped to join Red Cloud, another Lakota chieftain. En route, Big Foot was joined briefly by more than 40 of Sitting Bull's warriors who had fled Standing Rock following the shooting of their leader. As he neared Wounded Knee in the dead of winter, the exhaustion, cold, and the 150-mile (240-km) trek had clearly taken a toll on his band of followers—350 men, women, and children.

On December 28, Maj. Samuel Whitside and about 200 members of the Seventh Cavalry (the same regiment wiped out at the Battle at Little Bighorn in 1876) caught up with Big Foot's band and escorted them into camp along Wounded Knee Creek. Whitside and his officers made plans to disarm the Indians the next morning, take many of the warriors prisoner, and transport them to Omaha, Nebraska, for detainment. Suffering from pneumonia and exhaustion, Big Foot willingly acceded to the demands.

The next morning, December 29, 1890, the army of 500 surrounded the Indian camp. At its center, a white flag was hoisted as a sign of peace, while Big Foot lay

(above) Participants prepare at dawn for the next leg of the annual Wounded Knee Memorial Ride, which retraces the route taken by Big Foot and his band before the massacre.
(right) The memorial to those killed at Wounded Knee on December 29, 1890.

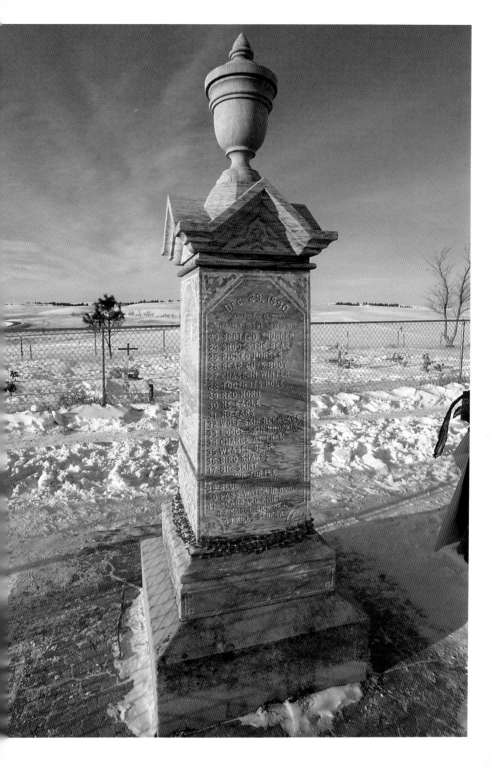

in a heated army tent. Though the Indians were ordered to give up their weapons, only a few guns were surrendered, so officers began searching tepees. This alarmed the Indians and in the commotion, a shot was fired. Soldiers responded with a barrage of bullets, killing nearly half of the warriors in the first round of gunfire. Then the Hotchkiss guns opened up, firing on the Indian camp. In only a few minutes, about 200 Indians were dead. Bodies of unarmed women and children were found as far as three miles (5 km) from the initial confrontation, shot down as they ran for their lives across the plains. Twenty-five of the military were killed. Big Foot was shot down in the first volley, his body photographed for posterity. (He was buried in a mass grave with the other victims of the Massacre at Wounded Knee.) That night, a sudden blizzard passed through, covering the bodies in a thick blanket of snow.

In the following days, newspapers and government officials referred to the confrontation as a "battle," but it was none other than wholesale slaughter. Within a year, the army had awarded 23 Medals of Honor to members of the Seventh Cavalry for "valor" shown in the carnage. But there was no cover-up of this affair. Even whites were incensed, and from this point on, the systematic extermination of the Indian people ended. With the earlier deaths of Sitting Bull and Crazy Horse, and the final tragedy at Wounded Knee, settlement of the last true frontier in the West was assured. The blood in the snow at Wounded Knee melted in the spring of 1891, and as it thawed and ran across the prairie in a thousand rivulets, it carried with it a way of life for the American Indian.

"The Wounded Knee Massacre marks a major turning point in world history," former Harvard University instructor turned Oglala Lakota College official Patrick Cudmore wrote in the *Rapid City Journal* on the hundredth anniversary of the tragedy. "It symbolizes more than just the massacre of Chief Big Foot's ragged band, more than just the ending of America's Indian Wars and more than just the closing of America's 'last frontier.' The deeper meaning of the Wounded Knee Massacre is that it symbolized the end of almost 400 years of unrelenting war against the indigenous people of the Americas . . ."

■ TRAGEDY REVISITED AT WOUNDED KNEE

In April 1973, violence returned to Wounded Knee when members of the **American Indian Movement** (AIM) took 10 hostages and barricaded themselves in the Sacred

This photograph of plantiffs suing for the return of the Black Hills to the Sioux was taken in 1923. The recovery of some of those lands continues to be debated in Congress today. (Marquette University Archives, Milwaukee)

Heart Church at Wounded Knee. The occupation at Wounded Knee (whose perimeter included grounds where nearly 200 Lakota had been massacred by U.S. troops 83 years earlier) followed a February 6 riot at the Custer County Courthouse. That protest was incited when a white man who had killed an Indian was charged with manslaughter rather than murder. Three weeks later, on the evening of February 27, a caravan of 40 cars headed to Wounded Knee where AIM members occupied several buildings and took the hostages in an effort to draw attention to the federal government's violation of the 1868 Fort Laramie Treaty and alleged corruption in tribal government and in the Bureau of Indian Affairs. Federal authorities soon circled the village and even called in armored personnel carriers. At the height of the confrontation, AIM members and supporters swelled to about 300 in number and exchanged hundreds of rounds of fire with federal marshals and BIA police. By the time the siege ended on May 8, after 71 days, only about 40 were left in the occupying forces, the rest having crept away exhausted and discouraged. The occupation resulted in the deaths of two members of the occupying force, Buddy Lamont and Frank Clearwater, as well as injuries to nine others, including federal Marshal Lloyd Grimm of Omaha, who was paralyzed from a chest wound.

Soon after the occupation of Wounded Knee ended, the Sacred Heart Church burned to the ground. From its ashes came change on the Pine Ridge Reservation. The siege raised international awareness of the plight of the Lakota people. Calls to return sacred lands in the Black Hills to the Lakota gained backers on the reservation and in Congress. The Oglala Sioux tribe formed its own police department, and the white governor of South Dakota declared a year of reconciliation between Indians and non-Indians.

Days after the first massacre at Wounded Knee, when the blizzard finally left southwestern South Dakota, U.S. soldiers dug a huge hole in the ground and buried many of the Indians killed at Wounded Knee in a common grave. Today, that inornate stone pillar marks the burial site. Descendants of the victims of the massacre have petitioned Congress to designate Wounded Knee as the nation's first tribal park. It seems only fitting that those who died in this place be remembered, perhaps finally putting the troubled spirit and the tragedy of Wounded Knee to rest.

The Oglala Nation Powwow at Wounded Knee. (above)

Pale purple coneflowers grace the high plains. (opposite)

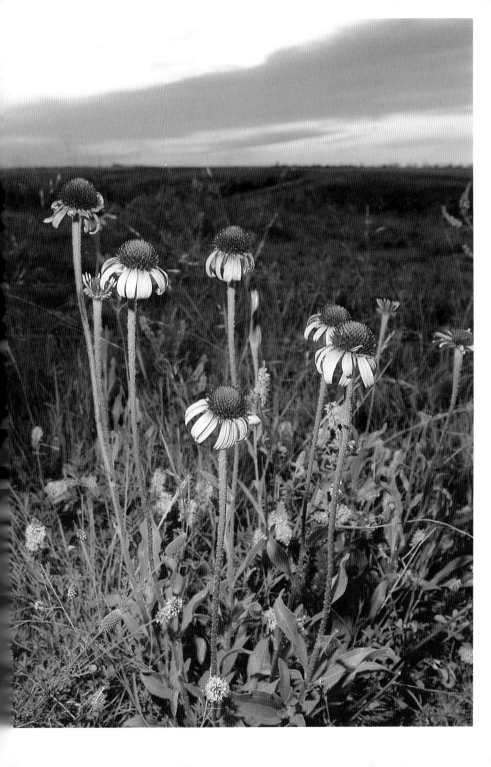

BLACK HILLS

AFTER AN EXPANSE OF SEEMINGLY ENDLESS PRAIRIES, South Dakota's Black Hills, the oldest mountains in America, unfold on the western horizon. At first appearing as a dark cloud on the edge of the rolling range, they gradually grow in size, casting a silhouette against the sky. Then the true height of the Black Hills becomes apparent. Eighteen of its peaks are higher than 7,000 feet (2,134 m), and they are capped by Harney Peak, at 7,242 feet (2,202 m).

Residents of neighboring Wyoming and Montana, proud of their own state's Rockies, often scoff at the size of the Black Hills. The former once placed a billboard just over the Wyoming-South Dakota border which read, "You've Seen the Hills, Now Come See the Mountains." Meanwhile, South Dakota's northerly brother posted the self-effacing phrase, "North Dakota Proudly Announces the Completion of Its Mountain Removal Project." South Dakotans say it's all a matter of perspective. After all, Harney Peak is the highest point between the Rocky Mountains and the Swiss Alps.

Altogether, the Hills cover an area roughly 50 miles (80 km) wide and 120 miles (192 km) long. Two-thirds are located in South Dakota, the remainder in eastern Wyoming. Within the Hills are four areas administered by the National Park Service: Mount Rushmore National Memorial, Wind Cave National Park, Jewel Cave National Monument, and Devils Tower National Monument, the latter located in extreme northeastern Wyoming.

Some 60 million years ago—roughly the same time dinosaurs disappeared from the face of the Earth—an igneous intrusion below the flatlands formed the dome-shaped hills, as well as the labyrinth of large caves beneath. Lakota Sioux called them "Paha Sapa," or "Hills of Black," and from afar, their pine-clad cliffs do appear as dark shadows. Within their borders, 1,000-foot (305-m) limestone palisades flank streams bordered by quivering aspens and ponderosa pines. Lush forests are home to deer, elk, mountain lions, wild turkeys, Rocky Mountain goats, porcupines, raccoons, and bighorn sheep; and stream banks to beavers, muskrats, and minks.

To the Cheyenne Indians, who practiced their vision quests in the isolation of these wooded hills and valleys, and later to the Lakota Sioux, the Black Hills were sacred, far removed from the rigors of everyday life, a place of solitude and introspection. One of the most important focal points to connect with Wakantanka —the Great Spirit—is Bear Butte, a 1,200-foot (366-m) cone-like geologic rarity located east of Sturgis. Both tribes also often avoided the Hills because of strange noises that emanated from within. Those noises can still be heard today, as wind whistles past the finger-like granite spires of the Needles, and thunder crashes off hundreds of canyon walls during frequent spring and summer storms.

■ TRAVEL BY ROAD AND TRAIL

Travel through the Black Hills is enhanced by fine roads, thanks in large measure to the state-owned South Dakota Cement Plant in Rapid City. Its product has been used in miles of scenic highways that chase gurgling creeks and weave their way through the pine-covered canyons of these mountains. Make no mistake, though. There are more curves on these roads than there are in a bronc rider's cowboy hat and enough hills to overheat your brakes. However, except in extreme weather conditions, most roads are well maintained and passable in a family sedan.

Though highway travel is easy in the Black Hills, something about the windshield gets in the way of truly experiencing their beauty and ruggedness. They are best enjoyed close up, with dirt and pine needles underfoot. The 111-mile (178-km) **Centennial Trail** spans the entire Black Hills from north to south. First dedicated during the state's centennial in 1989, the trail is intended to represent the diversity of South Dakota's landscape. Crossing prairie grasslands near **Bear Butte State Park** northeast of Sturgis, the trail gradually climbs into the Black Hills high country, skirting seven lakes and a myriad of streams, abandoned gold camps and ghost towns, through the **Black Elk Wilderness Area** and **Custer State Park**, before returning to the wildflowers and prairie pines at **Wind Cave National Park** near Hot Springs.

The attraction of this trail is not only its length and the variety of landscapes and geologic formations which users encounter, but the large number of access points and campgrounds along its route and the ways in which that trail may be traveled. The Centennial Trail features 22 trailheads which allow hikers, bikers, and horseback riders access to the pines, creeks, and coulees of Black Hills National Forest. Many portions of the trail follow the paths of long-gone flumes which carried water to townsites and gold-mining sluices in the late nineteenth century. As a result hikers will discover a trail that is surprisingly level, with the exception of spots where small bridges and trestles have rotted and disappeared over time.

While all of the trailheads have ample parking, four of them are designated as "horse camps," allowing extra room for horse trailers for those who want to hoof it through the forest. Horseback riders are encouraged in all but Wind Cave National Park, and mountain bikers may use the majority of the trail, with the exception of Wind Cave and the Black Elk Wilderness Area. In winter, more than 600 miles (966 km) of additional trails throughout the Hills are open to cross-country skiers and snowmobilers.

One of the most scenic and easily accessible portions of the trail begins at the **Flume Trailhead,** a half mile south of Sheridan Lake on Forest Road 439. The trail follows the gentle shoreline of the lake before heading into the forest. Along the way, a spur trail takes hikers over the earthen dam and across a sturdy footbridge that spans Sheridan Lake's spillway. This segment of the trail, as well as the **Rapid Creek Trailhead** off U.S. 385 below the dam at Pactola Reservoir, are ideal for a quiet picnic or bobber fishing from shore. For a brochure on the Centennial Trail and information on other trailheads, contact the Black Hills National Forest Supervisor's Office at (605) 673-2251.

Trail rides and hikes are a favorite recreation for visitors to the Black Hills. (Paul Jones)

BLACK HILLS

0   10   20
miles

Elevation
7,242
6,000
5,000
4,000
3,000
2,400
1,800
1,200
feet

■ WEATHER

Extreme temperatures, at least by Midwest standards, are infrequent in this region, sometimes labeled the "Banana Belt" because of its warm temperatures. Yet winds known as **"chinooks"** often race through the Hills, melting snow and bringing a warm respite from the winter months—and causing some of the greatest variations in temperature in one day that can be found in the United States.

The most famous chinook was that of January 1943, when the greatest change in temperature ever recorded in the United States occurred in the northern Black Hills community of Spearfish. The mercury rose from 4 degrees F below zero (-20° C) to 45 degrees F above zero (7° C) in less than two minutes. So quick was the temperature change that large plate glass windows cracked throughout town, and cattle that had been standing on frozen ground had to work to stay on their feet in the slippery mud of feedlots. As the chinook's warm winds blanketed the town of Lead, thermometers soared to 52 degrees F (11° C). Meanwhile, less than three miles (5 km) away, residents of the city of Deadwood still shivered in temperatures of 16 degrees F below zero (-27° C). In Rapid City, the thermometer at Montana-Dakota Utilities showed 9 degrees F (-13° C) at 10:30 A.M., and in the next half hour rose to 57 degrees F (14° C), then fell to 10 degrees F (-12° C). The following day, the *Rapid City Daily Journal* reported:

> The phenomenon was striking at the Alex Johnson Hotel corner at
> 11 A.M. On the east side of the hotel, winter was in all its glory, biting
> legs and faces, while around the corner on the south side, not 50 feet
> away, spring held sway.

■ RAPID CITY: GATEWAY TO THE BLACK HILLS

On the eastern edge of the Black Hills is Rapid City, a former cowtown that grew up to become the state's second largest population center and the eastern gateway to the Paha Sapa. Located at the intersection of I-90 and state highways 44 and 79, the city has become a regional center for shopping and medical services. Its 55,000 residents work in a variety of industries, from timber to tourism, and because of the state's low wage scale, seem content to take part of their pay in blue skies, trout streams, and ponderosa pine. The dream of most blue-collar workers in this community is to be able to afford a house in the trees, where "you can hunt deer from your deck."

Rapid City was founded in 1876, when John Brennan persuaded a ragtag group of unsuccessful miners to establish a commercial center at the base of the Black Hills to provide supplies for the gold fields. Despite Brennan's best intentions, most stagecoaches and wagon trains continued into the heart of the Hills where other settlements already were booming. Fortunately for Rapid City, in 1886 residents persuaded the Missouri, Fremont & Missouri Valley Railroad to lay tracks through town, and soon after, Rapid City began to prosper.

Topography determined much of Rapid City's subsequent development. Residential and commercial buildings wrapped themselves like a horseshoe around a large hill in the center of town, separating the east and west sections of town. Today, residential development to the north and east is middle class and sprawling. Homes on the west and south sides of town tend to be newer and tucked in the pines or built on the ridges that afford commanding views of the surrounding night lights. **Skyline Drive** creeps down the hill's spine, providing an impressive

Crowds gather to watch a parade in Rapid City, circa 1900. (Center for Western Studies)

RAPID CITY

0   1   2
miles

view of the entire community. Incongruously, replicas of seven life-size green dinosaurs guard the ridge at **Dinosaur Park,** a reminder of the Works Progress Administration crews that constructed the kid-climbers from concrete in the 1930s.

The center of downtown boasts a **commercial historic district** consisting of 38 buildings constructed between 1881 and 1930. Typical of the period, the buildings have flat roofs and were built of stucco, brick, limestone, and clapboard. Few have been restored to their original grandeur, which perhaps wasn't all that grand, but the **Buell Building** at Seventh and St. Joseph streets, the **Firehouse Brewing Company** at 610 Main Street, and its next-door neighbor, the **Prairie Edge** building, have undergone substantial renovation.

At Seventh and Quincy downtown, the **Dahl Fine Arts Center** rotates exhibits of paintings and sculpture by area artists. One of the center's largest rooms is dedicated to a cyclorama of American history, a 200-foot (61-m)-long, 10-foot (3-m)-high mural which, at the push of a button, brings on special lighting and narration and leads visitors around the room and through the evolution of the United States.

Farther east on State Highway 79 South in Rapid City, the **Museum of Geology** on the campus of the South Dakota School of Mines and Technology provides a rare glimpse of prehistory. "Talking" dioramas narrate the history of the Big Bad-lands and the strange creatures that once inhabited the area. The museum also houses what is arguably the finest collection of fossilized bones from giant dinosaurs, marine reptiles, and prehistoric mammals in the state, as well as exten-sive collections of rare and wonderful agates, fossilized cycads, rocks, gems, and minerals. And in South Dakota, which has a confirmed propensity for collecting and displaying such items, assembling the finest collection is no small task.

The **West Boulevard Historic District** covers portions of 18 blocks southwest of the downtown business area. Its homes are set back from a wide, tree-lined boule-vard, giving the area a stately and quiet atmosphere. Architectural styles include nineteenth-century Queen Anne homes and early twentieth-century Colonial.

The Journey, a $12.5 million state-of-the-art museum, opened in May 1997 and combines art, artifacts, and memorabilia from five outstanding public and private collections. Located in a 48,000-square-foot bulding off New York Street north of downtown, the Journey takes visitors on a 2.5-billion-year trip through the history of the Black Hills.

Live animals, nursery-rhyme displays, and play areas grace the grounds of **Story-book Island,** on Sheridan Lake Road between Canyon Lake Drive and Jackson

Contemporary Indian art pieces, such as this painting by Don Montileaux titled "Badlands Singer," are available in Rapid City's finer art galleries.

Boulevard. The free fairyland park is Rapid City's most popular attraction and its fountains, trains, castles, and Children's Theatre make it a perfect side trip for those traveling with children. Just a few minutes away in a tree-lined meadow stands the 1969 **Stavkirke Chapel** on Chapel Lane Drive off State Highway 44 West a replica of the 830-year-old Borgund Church in Norway. The park-like setting, intricate wood carvings, strange dragon heads, and the church's unusual pegged construction make this an interesting stop.

Rapid City is also home to a wide variety of events ranging from the **Black Hills Stock Show & Rodeo** in late January and early February and the **Central States Fair** in August, to Broadway productions and International Basketball Association action. The arena of the massive **Rushmore Plaza Civic Center** was christened by Elvis Presley in "the King's" last performance, and serves as the focal point for most community activities, concerts, and events.

Rapid City is not known for its nightlife, although a few sports bars and hideaways do keep city fathers from rolling up the streets at 7 P.M. The **Boot Hill Saloon,** 826 Main Street, offers the best toe-tapping country-and-western bands, and the cowboys and their gals who frequent the place dance the most authentic two-steps, jitterbugs, and line dances between Billy Bob's in Fort Worth, Texas, and the Blue Moon Saloon at Whitefish, Montana. The **Firehouse Brewing Company,** 610 Main Street, is the region's only brew-pub, and as these on-premise breweries go, the suds at the Firehouse rank with the best at similar establishments in Portland, Minneapolis, and Chicago. Its lagers, ales, and stouts are best served with the brewery's traditional German fare—the smell of the bratwursts would make a Wisconsinite's tastebuds water. In good weather, sample the suds in the Firehouse's outdoor beer garden, where local musicians are regularly showcased.

Just west of town on scenic State Highway 44 are two lovely places to eat and sleep: **Fireside Inn,** seven miles (11 km) past Canyon Lake, (605) 342-3900; and **Audrie's Cranbury Corner Bed & Breakfast,** at (605) 342-7788. (For more information on both these places see "Lodging and Restaurants," pp. 272–275 in "PRACTICAL INFORMATION.")

■ ELLSWORTH AIR FORCE BASE

Rapid City's economy receives a major boost from nearby Ellsworth Air Force Base, located seven miles (11 km) east of the city on I-90. Home to a third of the nation's B-1B bombers, and one of the largest military installations in the United

States, Ellsworth also has some worthwhile activities for visitors. A low-cost tour of the base takes participants near one of the strategic, low-level bombers, along the base flightline, and stops to view restoration work being conducted on vintage aircraft in one of the hangars. More entertaining value, however, is the **Air & Space Museum**, located just outside the Main Gate at Ellsworth. The museum features a steadily growing collection of more than 20 static aircraft, including Gen. Dwight Eisenhower's personal Mitchell B-25 bomber, a scaled-back version of the Stealth bomber, fighters, and cargo and utility aircraft.

■ STURGIS

Home to the world's largest motorcycle rally, the tiny town of Sturgis is tucked against the eastern foothills of the Black Hills about 30 miles (48 km) north of Rapid City on I-90. Sturgis is normally a quiet town of two-story storefronts and 5,200 people, unless it's August. Then the town swells to a couple hundred thousand bearded bikers who roar in for the annual **Sturgis Rally & Races.** (See "Bikers' Bash," pp. 196–197.)

Sturgis has hosted one of the most interesting frontier attractions in the Hills for more than a century: the **Fort Meade Museum.** Fort Meade opened as a peace-keeping fort in 1878, two years after the Seventh Cavalry's disastrous defeat by the Sioux at the Battle at Little Bighorn. Its initial mission was to keep whites out of the Black Hills in accordance with U.S. government treaties with Indian tribes. When that proved impossible, its troops protected white settlers and gold miners. After it became an active fort, remnants of the defeated Seventh Cavalry, minus Lt. Col. George Custer, eventually regrouped here. And Comanche, the horse of Capt. Myles Keogh and the only living creature found by the U.S. Army on the Custer battlefield following the massacre, arrived at the fort and was retired by Col. Samuel Sturgis, commander of the fort.

Colonel Sturgis had lost his son, Lt. Jack Sturgis, in that fateful 1876 fight against the Sioux, and the story goes that the colonel had it in for Maj. Marcus Reno, accused (and later acquitted) of negligence at Little Bighorn. Major Reno, a confirmed drunk and carouser, developed a crush on the colonel's daughter, Ella. Colonel Sturgis refused to grant Reno permission to date his daughter, but that didn't stop Reno from ogling the young maiden through her bedroom window. When Colonel Sturgis discovered the paneful romance being conducted under his

BIKERS' BASH

It was "Bike Week" in the Black Hills back in 1990—the fiftieth anniversary of the Sturgis Rally and Races—and I had just shared a few brews with a friend who was tending bar at the Pyramid Beer Gardens. The hot August sun scorched my retinas as I stepped onto Main Street, and, fumbling for my sunglasses, I saw that the curb was lined with Harley Davidsons of every era—an assortment of old-time Knuckleheads, Shovelheads, and Panheads mixed with the modern stream-lined beauties called Wideglides, Softtails, and Dressers, complete with farings, luggage bins, stereos, and a lot of chrome.

The streets were packed for the fiftieth observance of the largest motorcycle rally in the world. Two-wheelers had traveled from around the globe to enjoy rock concerts, motorcycle racing, hill climbs, and scenic highways. The radio had warned local residents for weeks to brace for the expected 400,000 bikers for rally week. As I navigated the crowded street, suitably dressed in jeans and a black T-shirt, it appeared to me that the radio announcers had been right. Beards and bandannas were de rigueur, and from all the halter tops and short-shorts you'd think you were at Daytona Beach over spring break. The smell of stale beer and portable toilets mixed with motorcycle exhaust wafted over the sun-baked parchment, so it all stopped somewhat short of euphoria.

Vendors hawked a mountain of T-shirts to bikers from every state in the Union, ten Canadian provinces, and more than three dozen foreign countries. As I walked down Main Street, watching biker women "headlight" tourists holding Sony camcorders, I wondered why they all came. Sometime between that thought and the speculation of how badly beaten a guy would get if he accidentally set one of these bikes on its side and triggered a domino-like catastrophe on Main Street, a strange thing happened. The crowd began to part for me. I was no longer bumping shoulders with hairy, badly groomed men who slept in sleeping bags and forgot to brush their teeth. They were literally stopping in front of me, stepping to the side, and smiling. Initially it was so odd and disconcerting that I thought perhaps my fly was down or I'd worn my Suzuki baseball cap. With a glance I dismissed each of those possibilities, but still they stared. Surely they didn't mistake me for the far grayer and infinitely more wealthy Malcolm Forbes, who used to like to bring his hot air balloons and Capitalist Tools to the rally each year.

After a block of continuous examination from passersby, I was frazzled. After all, nobody goes to a party with a half-million people—many of them Harley owners—hoping to get noticed. Why were all these burly boys looking at me? My underarms began to get moist and I was grateful that, at the very least, my Right Guard was performing admirably. But still they looked, they smiled, they got out of the way. Finally, in a pure act of desperation just short of running screaming through the throng—I stopped and turned around.

There, behind me, following me step for step was one of the most beautiful women I had ever seen. I admit I don't recall her face, though I'm sure it was surrounded by blonde hair freshly rinsed with spring water and lemon. Come to think of it, the only thing I recall was her black, knee-high calfskin boots and the body paint, because that's all she wore. As she smiled, I think I saw perfect teeth, and I stepped aside and returned the grin like every other doorknob on the block, simultaneously feeling sorry for the next sorry sap who inadvertently walked in front of that woman.

Hundreds of thousands of motorcycle enthusiasts descend upon the town of Sturgis every year for the world's largest bikers' rally.

roof, he had Reno charged with window-peeping, which in military parlance translated into conduct unbecoming an officer and a gentleman. Reno was found guilty and was forced from the army. Eventually, he died penniless and was buried in a pauper's grave in Washington state. But the story didn't end there. In 1967, Reno's grandnephew petitioned the federal government for a review of the charges, and Maj. Marcus Reno received a full pardon, was restored to rank, and received an honorable discharge. The remains of Major Reno were then reburied with his comrades on the bluffs overlooking the Little Bighorn.

Fort Meade's history also encompassed events far more violent than a flirt and a court-martial. In June 1884, Alex Fiddler, "a white man of a desolate character," was jailed for beating and robbing a German immigrant. Shortly after his arrest and transport to the Sturgis jail, an angry mob forced his release and transported him to the nearest large tree, where they hanged him. The tree was referred to afterwards as "Fiddler's Tree." A year later, a trooper named Ross Hallon was arrested and accused of killing a local doctor. Another group of vigilantes visited the jail and told the guards it was time for dinner break. The next morning, Hallon's body was found hanging from Fiddler's Tree.

Historic documents are on display at the museum, among them original papers signed by Custer, Reno, and Sturgis. The most intriguing and poignant may well be letters written by common soldiers to their wives and children. In one such beautifully penned letter, dated June 8, 1876, Henry C. Dose, a trumpeter for the Seventh Cavalry, wrote his wife: "General Terry said that if we get Sitting Bull and his tribe soon, then we are going home, but if we don't we will stay three months and hunt for him. I wish for mine part we would meet him tomorrow." Little more than two weeks later, Dose got his wish and lost his life. In addition, the museum displays countless old uniforms, guns, and photographs depicting the fort's history and the men—like the all-black 25th Cavalry unit, and the all-Sioux Indian Troop L of the Third Cavalry—who served here. In the mid-twentieth century, Fort Meade was used to house workers for the Civilian Conservation Corps and even German prisoners of war before it was turned over to the Veterans Administration in 1944.

Seven original buildings constructed in the 1880s still stand on the grounds, as well as a number of other buildings erected between 1904 and 1906. Three of the original stables survive and some of the historic houses still serve as homes for the staff of the **Fort Meade V.A. Medical Center,** located on the grounds. Also on the grounds are the **South Dakota Military Academy's officer training school,** and the **South Dakota National Guard,** which is working to restore two barracks.

FROM CUSTER TO HIS SUNBEAM

*M*y Darling Sunbeam—Your dear Bo can't send a very long letter, tho with volumes to say. After dinner, when we reach camp, I usually take an escort to search out a few miles of road for the following day, and when I return I am ready to hasten to my comfortable—but Oh so lonely—bed.

Reveille regularly at a quarter to three, so that it behooves one to go to bed early. Reynolds leaves in the morning for Ft. Laramie, so to-day is letter-day. I am going to explore in that direction some 25 or 30 miles. I take five companies with me. Two companies left this morning in another direction. Both absent three days.

Breakfast at four. In the saddle at five. First I have my official dispatch to attend to, then a letter to the "World."

The expedition has surpassed most sanguine expectations. We have discovered a rich and beautiful country. We have had no Indian fights. We have found gold and probably other valuable metals. All are well. I did not expect my wagon-train . . . and here it has followed me all the way.

—Lt. Col. George Custer, letter to his wife written from
Harney Peak, Dakota Territory, July 2, 1874

■ SPEARFISH

Nestled in a quiet valley on the northern tier of the Black Hills, about 15 miles (25 km) northwest of Sturgis on I-90, is the idyllic community of Spearfish. Known for its beautiful location at the mouth of Spearfish Canyon, the town contains the Black Hills State University campus, an unobtrusive Main Street, and sleepy residential neighborhoods. Add low crime and unemployment rates, and a friendly, small-town atmosphere, and it's obvious why this was the fastest growing community in South Dakota in the late 1980s and early '90s.

Spearfish first stepped into the history books in 1833, when a band of prospectors dodged Indian tribes and snuck into the Hills in search of their fortune. Judged by the evidence today, it appears that this group truly "discovered" gold in the Hills 40 years before the Custer Expedition confirmed its presence. However, as the ragged party headed for home, they were discovered and attacked by Indians near Spearfish. In 1887, Spearfish stonemason Louis Thoen was on Lookout Mountain near town when he uncovered a rock on which had been scratched:

> Came to these hills in 1833 seven of us DeLacompt, Erza Kind, G.W. Wood, T. Brown, R. Kent, Wm. King, Indian Crow. All died but me Erza Kind. Killed by Ind. beyond the high hill, got our gold in 1834. Got all gold we could carry, our ponys all got by Indians. I have lost my gun and nothing to eat and Indians hunting me.

Because dating the stone accurately has proved difficult, a few historians may doubt the authenticity of the **Thoen Stone**. Nonetheless, its presence has spurred queries into who really first searched for gold in the Black Hills. Today the Thoen Stone can be viewed, with its easily read etchings, at the **Adams Memorial Museum**, 54 Sherman Street, Deadwood.

The first to pioneer Spearfish Valley came in 1876, to take advantage of steady streams of clear water flowing from the nearby hills and rich, black soils. Its first store opened in 1877, and students began attending the town's first school a year later. Spearfish Normal School, now Black Hills State University, graduated its first class in 1887. The **D. C. Booth Historic Fish Hatchery** at 423 Hatchery Circle, one of the West's oldest, was established in 1898.

The **Matthews Opera House** at 614 1/2 Main Street, opened in 1906 and was immediately hailed as the focal point of an otherwise culturally bleak region. It hosted vaudeville in the 1930s, a shooting gallery in the 1940s, summer melodramas in the 1950s, and, after its restoration in 1966, the summer theater of the local college. Refurbished and reopened in the late 1980s, the opera house continues its tradition with a mix of music, vaudeville, and comedy. Performances take place most Mondays, Wednesdays, Fridays, and Saturdays mid-June through mid-August.

In 1939, one of Europe's oldest productions, the Luenen Passion Play, came to America from Germany and became a permanent Black Hills institution. More than 55 years later, the **Black Hills Passion Play** is still powerful. For information call (605) 642-2646. Staged three nights weekly from June 1 through August 31 in a 6,000-seat outdoor amphitheater, the production uses 22 scenes and an ensemble of 250 actors to re-enact the last seven days in the life of Christ, taking the audience on a journey from Jerusalem to Gethsemane and the Ascension.

The Booth House at D. C. Booth Historic Fish Hatchery in Spearfish.

As pretty as the town of Spearfish is, **Spearfish Canyon** is prettier. In any season, the limestone palisades that flank either side of U.S. 14A are breathtaking. A National Forest Scenic Byway, the road meanders along Spearfish Creek, past waterfalls, quaking aspens, sweet-smelling spruce, and ponderosa pines. For about three weeks each fall, the canyon fills with the colors of changing leaves, as spectacular as any Vermont countryside. The upper reaches of the canyon provided the backdrop for the closing scenes in the movie *Dances With Wolves.*

■ DEADWOOD

Gold was discovered near Deadwood in 1876 and within a year, 6,000 gold-hungry diggers had swarmed into the area to stake their claims. Soon arrived the camp followers—mule skinners, merchants, madams, card players, outlaws, and con artists. Among them was James Butler, alias **Wild Bill Hickok**—a sometime spy, scout, stagecoach driver, and sheriff—and his pal, **Martha "Calamity Jane" Cannary Burke.**

Standing left to right: Deadwood Dick, Edgar Howard, Charles R. Norden, Doc W. F. Carver, Buffalo Bill. Seated left to right: Capt. L. H. Norik, Pawnee Bill, and Diamond Dick Janner. (Center for Western Studies)

When Hickok heard of the 1876 gold rush, he left his new bride in Wyoming and galloped to Deadwood, where he hoped to relieve recently wealthy miners of some of their earnings at the gaming tables. Because Hickok was renowned as a gunman and marshall in the Kansas towns of Hays City and Abilene, Deadwood folks thought maybe Hickok could bring "a semblance of order to the lawless element of the camp," as the local newspaper stated at the time. But that wasn't to be. On August 2, as he sat in a poker game with his back to the door at Saloon No. 10, a hooligan named Jack McCall crept up behind Hickok and shot him in the back of the head. As McCall escaped, the dying Hickok fell forward, spilling pairs of black aces and eights on the table—a combination that forever after would be known as "the dead man's hand." Even though McCall was quickly captured and a vigilante jury was assembled, the defendant argued that Hickok had recently killed McCall's brother. To everyone's surprise, the jury acquitted McCall, who quickly left town. His freedom, however, was short-lived. After drunkenly bragging about his manipulation of the Deadwood jury, he was arrested by Nebraska authorities and turned over to a U.S. Marshall in South Dakota. Just four months later, a Yankton jury found McCall guilty of killing Hickok, and on March 1, 1877, he was hanged outside of town, his corpse buried in an unmarked grave.

Meanwhile, Hickok's body was laid to rest high above town at Deadwood's own Boot Hill—the **Mount Moriah Cemetery**. Even today, throngs of travelers visit the fenced gravesite. Nearby are the final resting places of other legends of Deadwood Gulch, including Calamity Jane, Preacher Smith, Potato Creek Johnny, and Madam Dora DuFran.

Two fires and a flash flood obliterated Deadwood three times in the next 10 years, and lawlessness continued. Finally, civilization came to town in the form of millionaire George Hearst (father of William Randolph Hearst) and two fellow California investors. Together, they bought the Homestake Mine in the nearby town of Lead, and big industry entered the picture. Shafts thousands of feet deep were dug to reach ore deposits. Bankers built banks, publishers began printing newspapers, and wary merchants began constructing buildings from non-flammable bricks and stones. Many of those buildings still stand today.

When South Dakota gained statehood status in 1889, gambling was outlawed in Deadwood, but that didn't stop the betting parlors and brothels from conducting a steady trade right into the next century. Gambling flourished until a major crackdown in 1947, and discreet bawdy houses continued operations until 1980. The city's reputation for exciting nightlife never did die, but by the late 1980s,

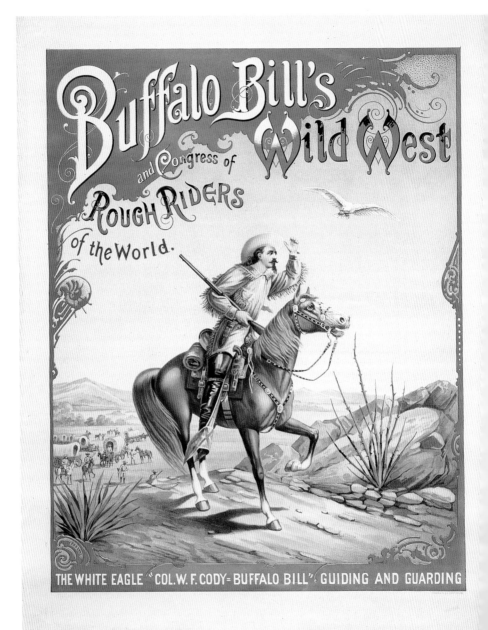

Poster advertising Buffalo Bill's Wild West Show circa 1890.
(Buffalo Bill Historical Center, Cody, Wyoming)

Deadwood's historic Main Street began to take on the appearance of a dying town. Storefronts were boarded up. Once impressive Victorian facades were crumbling, and instead of a quaint Wild West business district, visitors encountered drab and virtually deserted streets in all but the busiest summer months.

That all changed in the fall of 1989 when legalized gambling returned, and changed the face of Deadwood. Between 1989 and 1993, more than $80 million in public and private funds were invested in renovating everything from the original period street lighting and cobblestone streets to area churches, museums, and downtown buildings, some of which required as much as $5 million in restoration work. What had been a town in steady decline is now a model of historic preservation, and the entire town is listed as a National Historic Landmark.

Eighty gaming halls now line the streets of Deadwood. Tired, old, run-down stores on Main Street that were worth less than $30,000 in 1988, suddenly sold for $1 million a year later. The negative aspects of the gambling boom include the depletion of nearly all the downtown retail outlets and the cacophony of slot machines stuffed in every nook, cranny, and convenience store.

The **Bullock Hotel,** 633 Main, is one of the finest examples of historic restoration in South Dakota. Built in 1895 by Seth Bullock, the town's first sheriff and a close friend of President Theodore Roosevelt, it features the finest guest rooms in

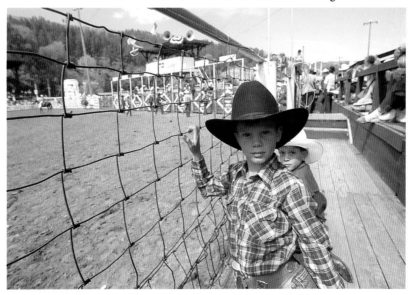

Rodeo fan in Deadwood during the Days of '76 Festival.

CALAMITY JANE

Martha Jane Cannary Burke, a.k.a. "Calamity Jane," has been the subject of so many stories and legends that it is difficult to distinguish fiction from fact. Notorious for drinking, smoking, sexual promiscuity, a foul mouth, and wearing pants, she was an ace shot, a part-time prostitute, and a one-time soldier (until a skinny-dipping episode ended her military career). Her claim to be a companion to Wild Bill Hickok, King of the Pistoleers, was enough to make her famous. But who *was* Calamity Jane?

Supposedly, she was born in 1852, in Iowa or Missouri, and moved west to Montana with her family. She eventually reached Deadwood, South Dakota, where she may or may not have known Bill Hickok, and acquired her significant reputation. According to her own story, she was at various times a Pony Express Rider, an Indian fighter, a stagecoach guard, and a scout under Custer. In 1878, she is said to have ministered to victims of smallpox. She got married once to a Mr. Clinton Burke in 1891, and had children both in and out of wedlock.

In her own day, Calamity Jane was somewhat of a legend. Dime-novel writers in the East, eager for a heroine and thrilled with the chance to hook someone up with Wild Bill Hickok, portrayed Calamity Jane as a femme fatale. Their Calamity possessed a graceful, womanly form, girlish beauty, and tresses of raven hair reaching down to a "peerless" waist. This Goddess of the Plains was always galloping out of

Calamity Jane looking somewhat tougher than Mae West's
Hollywood version. (Library of Congress)

the hills on her cayuse pony in time to notice deserving men on flagging horses pursued by thieves or Indians. With a couple of shots she'd knock out the villains, and the hero would turn around on his horse to see bad guys biting the dust, done in by a pretty little thing with a luscious figure and cherry red lips—a "wonderful little woman to have around in a calamity." The hero would then ask Calamity what her name was and if she might want to get together. She'd answer, "If you want to find me, ask around. Everyone knows who I am," and she'd trot off into the hills. This is the Calamity Jane portrayed by Mae West in the Hollywood version of the story.

The most frequently published photograph of Martha Jane Cannary reveals a plain and rather shabby woman in a slouch hat and stained, fringed, buckskin jacket. The photograph published in this book shows a confident, physically powerful woman, nicely mounted and well dressed in mannish Western clothes.

Whoever she was in fact, Calamity Jane was one of the most infamous heroes of the West, a woman whose motto was, "Never go to bed sober, alone, or with a red cent left in your pocket." When she died in 1903, she was buried next to Bill Hickok.

—Jessica Fisher

town, each appointed with nineteenth-century Victorian furnishings, as well as spacious gaming parlors with blackjack, poker, and one-armed bandits. The cut-stone building, with its fancy cupolas and cornices, is purportedly haunted by Bullock's ghost, which has shown up too frequently to be easily discounted. Guests are more inclined to have a face-to-face encounter with actor Kevin Costner, who stays at the Bullock during his frequent visits to Deadwood, where he and his older brother, Dan, own **The Midnight Star,** 677 Main. The Star actually is three establishments in one—a casino on ground level, a richly wooded sports bar called **Diamond Lil's** on the second floor, and **Jakes,** South Dakota's only four-diamond restaurant, on the third tier. The costumes Costner wore in nearly all of his films—from *Field of Dreams* to, of course, *Dances With Wolves*—are displayed on the walls of Diamond Lil's, but the real dream is found in the food at Jakes. The rib-eye with mushrooms sautéed in amaretto is a better bet than any poker game in town.

A host of other Main Street casinos, including the **Silverado, Gold Dust, Four Aces,** and **Miss Kitty's** have invested hundreds of thousands of dollars to dazzle visitors as soon as they cross the threshold. Some casino owners have even purchased their own limousines and buses to transport customers past the other establishments to their own front doors. But the real fun in Deadwood is often found in just roaming the streets, watching the tourists, and stepping in and out of doorways. **Durty Nelly's** Irish pub in the **Historic Franklin Hotel,** 700 Main, hosts some of the best bar bands and jazz in the Black Hills, and there's something half-cocked over at the **Old Style Saloon No. 10,** 657 Main, which bills itself as the only museum in the world with a bar. After two shots of red-eye and a walk through sawdust, past walls and rafters jammed with thousands of artifacts, historic photographs, and even Wild Bill's wedding license, you may be hard-pressed to argue the point. Across the street, even teetotalers stop in to admire the massive carved oak bar of the **Bodega,** 662 Main.

In addition to the Bullock Hotel, a number of other hotel/casinos offer good rooms at fair prices. Each of the properties is served by the **Deadwood Trolley,** which rolls past nearly every important place in town about every 15 minutes. **The Mineral Palace Hotel,** 607 Main, has fireside dining and one of the largest gaming complexes in Deadwood, while the **First Gold Hotel,** 270 Main, attracts huge crowds (including thousands of Canadians) each year because of its good food and

Deadwood is nestled in a lush Black Hills valley. (Paul Jones)

Miners have risked life and limb in their pursuit of gold in the Black Hills over the last century. (Adams Museum, Deadwood)

friendly dealers. The **Deadwood Gulch Resort,** south of Main Street on U.S. 85, offers comfortable accommodations, pool, spa, and plate-sized T-bone steaks in a creekside location. The Gulch also boasts the region's only amusement park, as well as a great miniature golf course, a quiet campground, horseback rides, a convenience store, and several spacious casinos and full-service bars.

■ LEAD

Most of the mile-high community of Lead (pronounced "Leed," as in an auriferous gravel deposit) sits perched on steep hillsides. Visually, it is dominated by the gray metallic Homestake Gold Mine, with its 8,000-foot (2438-m)-deep shafts and high hoist. Homestake has dominated the region's economy for nearly 120 years, and though several mining companies continue to search for gold in the Black Hills, none has had the lasting and profound impact of Homestake, the longest continuously operating gold mine in the world.

Four fortune-hungry prospectors originally worked the Homestake claim, but quickly sold out to a group of capital-rich Californians who brought in the machinery necessary for large-scale ore mining in 1877. The company hired large numbers of immigrant miners from Italy, Great Britain, the Balkans, and Scandinavia, and quickly made South Dakota one of the leading gold-producing states.

A company town, Lead is marked throughout with the presence of gold mining on a colossal scale. Its massive "open cut" signifies the spot where an entire mountain was moved, scoop by scoop, in search of the precious metal. The **Homestake Gold Mine Surface Tour** on Main Street is offered May through September and exposes visitors to the giant hoists, ore-crushing machinery, and final refining processes of this industry. At 323 West Main Street, the **Black Hills Mining Museum** examines the history of the mining industry, from carbide lamps and timber stopes to compressed-air locomotives and gold-panning techniques.

As much as 15 feet (4.5 m) of "white gold," also known as snow, falls at this altitude in the Black Hills each winter, bringing thousands of skiers to the Lead area for outdoor recreation. **Terry Peak Ski Area,** three miles (5 km) southwest of Lead off U.S. 85, has a 1,200-foot (366-m) vertical drop, more than 20 miles (32 km) of ski trails, and beginner, intermediate, and expert runs. Nearby **Deer Mountain Ski Area** boasts a 700-foot (213-m) vertical drop, 25 trails, and lighted night skiing.

A 100-ounce gold bar from the Homestake Gold Mine.

A view of Harney Peak's summit, at 7,242 feet the highest point between the Rockies and the French Alps.

■ SCENIC DRIVES FROM THE NORTHERN BLACK HILLS

Although virtually every paved highway, gravel road, and cow path constitutes a scenic byway, the roadway used to get from Point "A" to Point "B" can often mean the difference between a common road trip and an adventure. U.S. 85 from Lead winds through the heart of the Black Hills all the way to Nebraska, and it's a relatively quick and pretty drive past towering pines, rock outcroppings, **Pactola Reservoir,** and **Sheridan Lake,** and the towns of **Custer** and **Hot Springs** farther south.

A road less traveled (which generally means a combination of cattle guards, gravel, and dust) will test your savvy and your vehicle's shocks. One of the best afternoon excursions in any season (but winter) takes motorists about three and a half miles (5.6 km) south of Lead on U.S. 85, before turning left onto County Road 17 to the all-but-abandoned town of **Rochford.** Tracing the path of the North Fork of Rapid Creek for about 15 miles (24 km), the road winds its way to Rochford. (The suddenly faint or carsick should take left turns on County Roads 216 or 255 for a five-mile [8-km] trip back to the blacktop of U.S. 385.) A small grocery store, the **Green Acres Saloon,** and a number of deer hunters' shacks make up the town of Rochford. To continue, stay on County Road 17 for just a couple of miles before it connects with County Road 187 to **Castle Creek.** At the bottom of the hill, the road leads past slate-lined slopes, ponderosa pines, and wildflowers, to one of the loveliest creeks in the Black Hills, Castle Creek, as it flows on its slow, meandering course from **Deerfield Reservoir** to its confluence with **Rapid Creek.** Unimproved camping sites are available, and the creek is an ideal place for a picnic.

Rimrock Highway, also known as U.S. 44 West, provides a splendid scenic drive through one of the prettiest canyons in the Black Hills. Leading from west Rapid City to its junction with U.S. 385, Rimrock Highway follows Rapid Creek and some of the most heavily stocked fisheries in the Hills. A favorite with motor-cyclists who love to visit the **Rimrock Tavern** and **Jerry's Johnson Siding Store,** the roadway has many curves but is well-maintained. A half-mile (1 km) past the well-marked **Thunderhead Falls** turn-off, the highway leads through **Big Bend,** a wicked and wonderful canyon. (Some say this was the site of a thunderous colli-sion between two locomotives in 1907, but no one seems able to find the exact location of the disaster.) On the steep canyon wall, remnants of a flume which car-ried water to Rapid City are still visible, and at various times, bighorn sheep, goats, and deer have been spotted in the area, as have rattlesnakes, minks, muskrats, beavers, and a variety of waterfowl.

Chilly Rapid Creek, with its alternating slow and fast currents, is a popular place for inner-tubers, as well as for fishermen who wet their lines and waders in search of elusive brown trout. In South Dakota, public access to creeks and rivers can be gained at most bridges, or by asking landowners permission to cross their private property. Those same waterways are regarded as a public thoroughfare up to the high water mark, even if they flow through private property. Consequently, once in the water, fishermen and tubers can proceed unimpeded.

Creekside residences are plentiful in the canyon, and many original home builders took advantage of an abandoned railroad right-of-way on which to con-struct their houses. The **Crouch Line** was often called "the crookedest railroad in the world." Along its 30-mile (48-km) path between Rapid City and **Mystic,** the railroad crossed Rapid Creek 110 times and the train made the equivalent of 14 complete circles in one trip. Nearly every rail was bent to fit the curves of the canyon, and locals joked that the bends were so sharp that the brakeman in the caboose could pass a chew of tobacco to the engineer manning the locomotive. The railroad, a dream of Charles D. Crouch, was founded in the early 1890s and was closed in 1947. Few signs of it exist today.

■ RAPID CITY TO RUSHMORE

Along U.S.16 south of Rapid City—the road to Mount Rushmore—travelers encounter a myriad of private tourist attractions ranging from drive-through wildlife parks and go-cart tracks to RV resorts and waterslides. One of the oldest is the **Reptile Gardens,** six miles (9 km) south of Rapid City. Founder Earl Brockelsby got a start in 1937 exhibiting fearsome rattlesnakes and selling trinkets. Today the attraction is still fresh and fun. Sporting the world's largest collection of reptiles, including snakes, lizards, and crocodiles, it also features an array of birds, orchids and other tropical and desert plants, under a massive walk-through skydome. The trained animal act is a bit corny, but three other shows—Birds of Prey, Alligators, and Snakes—are intriguing and worth the admission price. The Reptile Gardens is also home to the **Black Hills Raptor Rehabilitation Center,** which receives injured birds such as hawks, owls, and eagles, nurses them back to health, and whenever possible, releases them back to the wild.

Other nearby attractions include **Bear Country,** home to the largest captive collection of black bear, as well as deer, elk, bison, bighorn sheep, timber wolves, and a giant grizzly bear. **Rushmore Waterslide Park** has nine slides, some 400 feet (122 m) long; and **Ranch Amusement Park** features go-cart races, bumper boats, and miniature golf. **The Gaslight** in **Rockerville** has a dining saloon, antique shop, and the best old-fashioned soda fountain and candy shop in the region.

■ HILL CITY

A century after it was founded, Hill City resembles numerous Black Hills communities that were settled by gold miners, faltered when the strike waned, then figured out a way to stay around. The tiny town of 650 residents continues to cater to traffic on U.S. 385: tourists in the summer months, and hunters, fishermen, snowmobilers, and cross-country skiers in the off-season. Historic Main Street is so rustic that it's hard to believe horses aren't tied to the posts in front of the buildings. Nonetheless, the street is home to some delicious food and interesting shops. The **Alpine Inn** in the Harney Peak Hotel on Main Street has a pleasant Bavarian atmosphere and some of the best beef in the region. **Gregson's Fine Dining and O'Bryan's Pub,** 349 Main Street, are two great places to eat in one historic 1902 brick building. More formal dinners are served at Gregson's upstairs, while microbrews and pub fare are offered downstairs at O'Bryan's.

Railroad buffs can get their fill aboard **The Black Hills Central Railroad.** Departing four times daily in the summer season, **The 1880 Train** makes a two-hour trip from Hill City to Keystone with a vintage steam locomotive and passenger cars. The train offers a perfectly relaxing excursion through the Black Hills backcountry, past creeks, pines, canyons, and trestles. Boarding can be done in either town, but the Hill City stop offers great food in the High Liner Restaurant car and the gift shop is the only place in the region with railroad memorabilia.

■ KEYSTONE

The only town closer to Mount Rushmore than Hill City is the less-than-scenic Keystone. After traveling quiet country byways, smelling fresh pines, and listening to streams babble past granite outcroppings, the town at the base of Mount Rushmore turns out to be filled with T-shirt shops, jewelry stores, fast food outlets, neon-lined blocks of blacktop, and false storefronts. For a dollar, a rumpled,

Carnivals have always played a part in the rural life of South Dakota. Here a horse race through downtown draws sponsors and crowds. (Center for Western Studies)

(right) Mountain man Dewey and his tepee at one of South Dakota's annual "rendezvous."

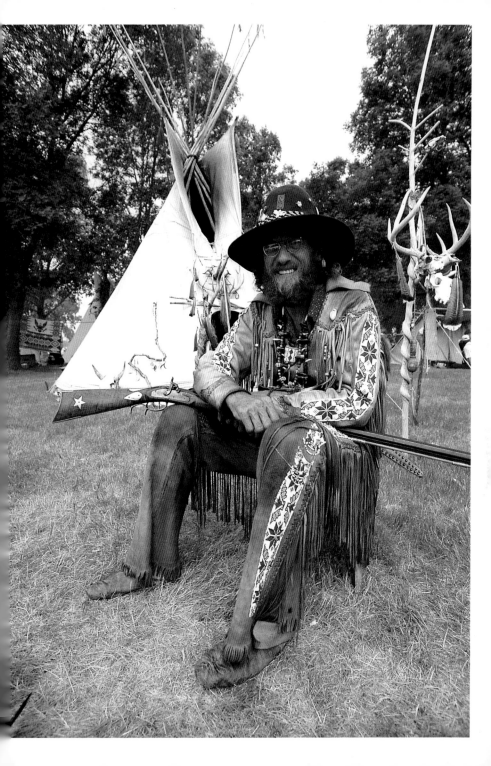

stubbly-chinned "miner" and his pack mule will pose for placement in your photo album.

Keystone's 400 motel rooms, 40 gift shops, and proximity to Mount Rushmore make it one of the busiest towns in the Black Hills for about five months of the year. A former gold mining community that went from boom to bust, then boom again with the carving of America's largest rock group, Keystone seems content to make a buck during the tourist season, then cover its lone traffic light and wait out the winter.

One establishment which provides historical insight is the **Rushmore-Borglum Story,** a museum dedicated to exploring the life story and work of sculptor Gutzon Borglum prior to his arrival in the Black Hills. The Borglum Story also features models used by the sculptor in carving the mountain memorial, as well as a Mount Rushmore newsreel narrated by newscaster Lowell Thomas. The **Historic Ruby House** has an impressive collection of classic rifles displayed in an 1890 Victorian cathouse setting, replete with green and red velvet tassels and draperies. Five miles (8 km) east of Keystone on State Highway 40 is **Beautiful Rushmore Cave**, discovered by gold seekers. Available today are tours of colorful "dripstone" formations including stalactites, stalagmites, ribbons, columns, and helectites.

Immediately southwest of Keystone on U.S. 16A is the **Iron Mountain Road,** a brainchild of former South Dakota governor and U.S. senator Peter Norbeck. Norbeck personally laid out the entire course of this scenic highway—much to the disappointment of the engineers and contractors who then had to build it. "This is not a commercial highway," Norbeck snorted when objections were raised. "It's a scenic road. To do the scenery half-justice, people should drive 20 mph or under; to do it full justice,

Gutzon Borglum inspecting some face rock during carving of Mount Rushmore in the 1930's. (National Park Service)

they should get out and walk!" What Norbeck wrought is still visible today in a roadway that is both a wonder of engineering and a motorhome driver's nightmare.

Iron Mountain Road is well known for its pigtail bridges—three consecutive loops over rustic timber trestles that avoid standard switchbacks commonly used in mountain road construction. As you drive through three of the narrow tunnels on the roadway, you'll have perfectly framed views of the four faces of Mount Rushmore. Scenic turnouts along the route provide far-off views of Mount Rushmore, vast landscapes of jagged peaks jutting up from the surrounding forests, and hillscapes so large that visitors can watch the dark shadows of clouds race across the treetops from windswept mountain tops to quiet valleys.

■ MOUNT RUSHMORE NATIONAL MEMORIAL

In 1924, South Dakota historian Doane Robinson envisioned an enormous sculpture carved on the Needles in the Black Hills of some of the Old West's legendary heroes—Lewis and Clark, Buffalo Bill Cody, and the great Sioux warriors. After enlisting the support of South Dakota's senator Peter Norbeck, Robinson wrote a letter of invitation to sculptor Gutzon Borglum, then involved with a massive Confederate memorial being carved at Stone Mountain, Georgia.

When Borglum arrived in the Black Hills in the summer of 1925, he decided the Needles, a grouping of finger-like granite spires that rise from the surrounding pine forests, were too brittle for carving, and the spires disproportionate to the sculpting of the human body. Borglum chose Mount Rushmore instead for its sound granite. In addition, the mountain's carveable surface faced southeast, allowing direct sunlight for as much of the day as possible. Furthermore, Borglum surprised Robinson and Norbeck by informing them that the subjects of the South Dakota sculpture would be national, rather than Western, figures.

Together Robinson, Norbeck, and Borglum chose four presidents for the memorial who would represent the birth, growth, preservation, and development of the United States: George Washington, "father of the nation;" Thomas Jefferson, facilitator of the Louisiana Purchase; Abraham Lincoln, preserver of the Union; and Theodore Roosevelt, builder of the Panama Canal and a frequent visitor to the Black Hills.

In 1927, President Calvin Coolidge arrived to help dedicate the beginning of work on the memorial. For the next 14 years, Borglum and his drill-dusty crew of

(following pages) Mount Rushmore is at its most dramatic at sunrise.

unemployed miners drilled, blasted, and chiseled the gnarled face of the mountain into the visages of the four presidents. Deep fractures in the rock forced Borglum to change the concept of the carving nine times; funds often ran out; and severe weather caused frequent delays. When Borglum died in March 1941, the unfinished work was taken over by Borglum's son, Lincoln, who carried the work to its close on October 31.

As you approach the monument on Gutzon Borglum Memorial Highway (State Highway 244), just outside Keystone you'll see the presidents peeking at you through the trees. It's best to go in the early morning hours, when sunlight from the east casts a warm glow on the four faces. On the main viewing terrace, visitors gaze up at Borglum's work and often speak in hushed tones, as if the imposing sculptures could hear.

More than 2.5 million visitors flock to the memorial each year, making Mount Rushmore one of the most popular national parks. Increasing crowds and outdated facilities led the non-profit Mount Rushmore Society to raise more than $23 million nationwide in conjunction with the memorial's fiftieth anniversary in 1991.

Completed in 1997, a Presidential Trail leading to the base affords visitors several vantage points from which to view the four Presidents. The Visitor Orientation Center at the memorial's entrance acquaints travelers with the park's layout, and the park's concessionaire opened its new $10 million restaurant and gift shop in 1996. A grand amphitheater was dedicated in 1997; construction of an impressive Interpretive Center, with interactive exhibits, theaters, and a bookstore, followed quickly on its heels.

■ CUSTER STATE PARK

Iron Mountain Road enters Custer State Park on its extreme northeastern edge, then connects with the lone east-west roadway through the park. Here, more than 1,500 bison roam free on the 73,000-acre preserve established by Sen. Peter Norbeck in 1919. "Buffalo jams" are more common here than bumper-to-bumper traffic, and burros often interrupt motorists to beg for something to munch. They'll eat about anything they're given, and if they're not given anything, these wild donkeys will leave slippery saliva on car windows as an expression of their annoyance.

Lincoln's face begins to emerge from the rock in the midst of the memorial's construction. (Courtesy of Tom Griffiith)

CRAZY HORSE MEMORIAL

The Sioux called Crazy Horse their "strange one," believing he had mystical powers, and the white soldiers he engaged in combat may have held those same beliefs. As a leader, Crazy Horse is partially credited with Lt. Col. George Custer's spectacular defeat at the Battle at Little Bighorn, and has inspired a great deal of curiosity, controversy, and respect. Today, the legend of Crazy Horse is the inspiration behind a massive mountain memorial being carved in the Black Hills: Crazy Horse Memorial, five miles (8 km) north of Custer on U.S. 385.

The idea for the memorial began in 1939, when Korczak Ziolkowski (pronounced "Core-jock Jewel-CUFF-ski" an assistant to sculptor Gutzon Borglum at Mount Rushmore, received a letter from Chief Henry Standing Bear stating that the Sioux "would like the white man to know the red man has great heroes, too." Seven years later, Korczak agreed to sculpt a memorial for the great Sioux warrior Crazy Horse.

Korczak Ziolkowski and his wife, Ruth, decided the sculpture would be the largest ever undertaken—a colossal 563-foot (170-m) statue of Crazy Horse pointing over his stallion's head to the sacred Black Hills.

(above and opposite) The massive Crazy Horse Memorial
gradually takes shape in the Black Hills.

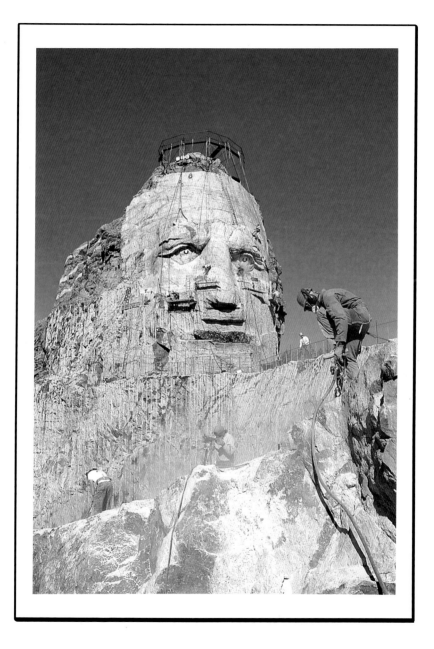

The first few decades of work on the mountain were long and arduous. Korczak Ziolkowski most often worked alone, wielding a jackhammer and setting his own dynamite charges. In the early days, he had to climb 741 steps up to his workplace on top the mountain, and every time his pneumatic drill stalled he had to descend the stairs again to fiddle with his generator. In 1982, when Korczak realized he was dying, he said to his wife, "I cannot carve Crazy Horse from the grave. There are some decisions you have to make." In the early 1990s, Ruth began carving the face of Crazy Horse, rather than the head of the stallion, which Korczak had envisioned for the first detail work. The results have been remarkable, and Ruth, with the help of seven of her ten children, projects that the face will be completed by 2000.

Visitors driving by the area often hear dynamite blasts on the mountain, a sign that work is progressing. When night blasts are set, they tend to be among the most spectacular events in the Black Hills. Visitors to the area may wish to stop by the Indian Museum of North America at Crazy Horse, home to one of the most extensive collections of Plains Indian artifacts in the country. The pieces in the three large exhibit halls represent tribes throughout the United States, Canada, and Mexico. The museum's gift shop features authentic Indian-made items.

Custer State Park boasts the largest and most diverse population of wildlife, the best accommodations and facilities, and the most spectacular natural resources of any park in the state. Custer's 83 square miles (212 sq km) of land alternate between rolling foothills, pine forests, and the finger-like granite spires of the Needles. Tucked in the forests in separate corners of the park are four resorts owned by the state and operated by the Custer State Park Resort Company. Each is distinctly different, with facilities ranging from comfortable lodge rooms to rustic lakeside cabins. (See p. 264 in "Practical Information.")

The **State Game Lodge** served as the summer White House for President Calvin Coolidge in 1927 and was visited by President Dwight Eisenhower in 1953. The historic stone and wood lodge has only seven guest rooms, but 40 nearby motel rooms and 20 cottages supplement the supply. For information call (800) 658-3530. Its dining room features excellent pheasant and buffalo dishes, and from the lodge, visitors can embark on a four-wheel-drive excursion into the bison herds. Hiking trails and trout fishing also are located nearby. **Legion Lake Resort** is centrally located in the park, close to buffalo herds, a golf course, summer theater productions at the **Black Hills Playhouse,** and hiking and horse trails.

The **Blue Bell Lodge and Resort,** State Highway 87 South, provides a guest ranch setting for secluded cabins, camping, hayrides, chuck wagon cook-outs, trail rides, hiking, and fishing.

The most incredible setting, however, is reserved for **The Sylvan Lake Lodge and Resort.** Set high atop the Black Hills, overlooking a small but stunning lake, the lodge is rustic and comfortable. There may be no better place in the state to settle down with a cocktail and ponder the events of a day than its veranda, which has a splendid view of the Harney Range. Some guest cabins, set apart on the rugged, wooded hills near the lodge, feature fireplaces and waterbeds. Paddleboats, canoes, and mountain bikes are available for rent near the lake. From the lodge, the **Needles Highway** takes motorists and mountain bikers on a 14-mile (22-km) adventure through pine forests and past the eponymous granite spires to the highest reaches of the park. Vehicles zigzagging among the towering pillars and squeezing through skinny tunnels seldom exceed 30 mph (48 kph). Among the special spots on the route are the **Needle's Eye,** a slit in a spire about four feet (1.2 m) wide and 40 feet (12 m) long, and the **Cathedral Spires,** unique formations of granite towers that rise from the forest floor heavenward as a Registered National Landmark.

Other popular attractions within Custer State Park include the 18-mile (29-km) **Wildlife Loop Road,** the observation deck of the **Mount Coolidge Fire Lookout,** and the historic **Gordon Stockade,** site of the first—albeit brief—white settlement in western South Dakota. In 1874, a small group of miners defied U.S. government–Sioux agreements and snuck into the Hills, remaining in this spot for all of 90 days before being arrested by the army for violating the Laramie Treaty of 1868. There's also the cozy log cabin of South Dakota's first poet laureate, Badger Clark, best known for his "Cowboy's Prayer." The **Badger Hole,** as it has come to be known, is constructed of native stone and wooden shingles. Its porch extends around a large pine tree that Clark just couldn't cut down. The thoughtful writer scorned electricity and carried water by hand from a nearby spring. The cabin—with original library and furniture—remains just as it was when Clark sat by the light of a kerosene lantern and penned his short stories, novels, poems, and lyrics.

Hikers will find an extensive network of trails. Among the most popular are the **Harney Peak summit trail,** a 22-mile (35-km) segment of the 111-mile (178-km) Centennial Trail, and the **Cathedral Spires Trail.** The Resort Company offers trail rides into the backcountry, and the park provides a horse camp and riding trails. In addition to helping visitors locate bison herds and hot fishing spots, Custer State Park staff conduct guided nature walks, gold panning demonstrations, junior naturalist programs, and patio talks throughout the summer months. Call (605) 255-4515.

Just east of Custer State Park at the intersection of State Highway 89, U.S. 16, and U.S. 385 stands the city of **Custer,** a thriving community of 1,741 residents whose friendly nature makes it the ideal headquarters for exploring the Black Hills. All told, the town's not much to look at. The main business district has expanded until it now stretches in a "T" too far along U.S. 16 and northward up U.S. 385. But the city's proximity to natural attractions found in nearby parks and monuments, along snowmobile and hiking trails, and numerous scenic byways is coupled with a glad-you-came atmosphere provided by residents who are as gracious at the local chamber of commerce as they are at the service station down the street.

In 1874, Lt. Col. George Custer gave glowing accounts of the beauty of this future townsite in his journals. Confirmation of gold in the Black Hills was made just east of Custer, in French Creek, when a member of Custer's expedition named

(above) By 1900, American bison were hunted to near extinction, but through the efforts of conservationists and cattlemen, freely roaming bison herds, like this one in Custer State Park, now graze in protected areas of the Great Plains.

(right) Cathedral Spires dwarf snowmobilers in the snowy winter months. Over 100 inches of snow usually fall in the higher elevations of the Black Hills each winter, allowing for a myriad of winter sports.

Horatio Ross found "colors" in his pan. But the 1,200-man expedition also discovered the enduring beauty of the region, and it wasn't long before Custer became the first city founded in the Hills. Residents recreate the memorable moments in their history with the **Pageant of Paha Sapa** each July, recounting the discovery of gold and the creation of the town.

Fans of TV cartoon characters Fred, Barney, Wilma, Betty, and Dino won't want to miss the **Flintstones Bedrock City** west of town on U.S. 16. The Stone Age theme park has train rides, play areas, and Brontoburger stands. Wood carving enthusiasts should visit the **National Museum of Woodcarving**, U.S. 16 West, which boasts hundreds of works by Dr. H. Niblack, the original animator of Disneyland. **Dakota Badlands Outfitters** can put you in the saddle or a mule-drawn wagon for trips into South Dakota's backcountry. Participants taste dust and sweat. Excursions range from one-day jaunts to full-blown four-day pack trips complete with pack mules, packers, and guides. For those who want to get above the smell of saddle blankets, campfire smoke, and baked beans, **Black Hills Balloons** provides flights past Mount Rushmore, Crazy Horse, herds of grazing bison, elk, and deer, and scenic lakes and granite peaks. Though it's expensive, there may be no other experience quite like a sunrise or sunset hot air balloon ride over the Hills, away from the switchbacks, gas gauges, and hot tires of earth-bound travelers.

■ WIND CAVE NATIONAL PARK

Sharing the southern boundary of Custer State Park, Wind Cave National Park combines 28,000 acres of wildlife preserve above one long cave. Bison, elk, deer, and antelope roam the woodlands and high prairies, while only people crawl through the dark—71 miles (114 km) of mapped passageways rank Wind Cave as the seventh longest cave in the world. Within its interconnecting corridors are fragile gypsum beard (that will sway gently from the warmth of a spelunker's carbide lamp); tangled mineral-laden bushes resembling small, intricate crystal Christmas trees; and delicate helicite balloons found on the cavern walls that will burst at the touch of a finger. On the surface of Windy City Lake, 650 feet (198 m) below the earth's surface, float tiny calcite rafts.

Wind Cave is part of a great cave system that lies beneath the Black Hills—a system some scientists believe has been only five percent mapped. At Wind Cave and at **Jewel Cave National Monument**—the world's fourth longest cave, west of Custer on U.S. 16—a maze of rare and unusual boxwork, frostwork, and popcorn formations, as well as of more common stalactites, stalagmites, and calcite crystals, awaits those with enough nerve (and a heavy sweater) to travel underground. Park rangers conduct regular tours of both caves ranging from standard sightseeing excursions to genuine spelunking and candlelight expeditions.

In 1987, the author of this book accompanied a group of veteran spelunkers into Wind Cave. We wound our way through a maze of interconnecting passageways which might best be suited for contortionists. While squeezing through holes narrower than my shoulders and dragging myself through an 18-inch (45-cm)-high passage, my battery pack fell off my belt and I was left in blackness. After two and a half hours of slithering, the underground world opened up, revealing a giant ballroom (known as the Club Room) two football fields long (200 yards/183 m) and eight stories high. On the floor of the cave sat giant boulders the size of houses. We stopped there to rest and drink our water, hearing only our own labored breathing.

■ HOT SPRINGS

Years before settlers entered the Black Hills in search of gold, the Sioux and Cheyenne Indian tribes battled for control over the natural warm-water springs of present-day Hot Springs. According to legend, a skirmish raged in the hills high above the springs, on a peak now called Battle Mountain.

Farmers and ranchers followed miners into the area and settled Hot Springs, but in 1890 a group of ambitious entrepreneurs decided to turn the town into a health spa. Leading the pack was Fred Evans, who built **Evans Plunge** over a number of small sparkling springs and one massive thermal spring of warm mineral water. After the railroad arrived in 1891, and for some 20 years thereafter, trainloads of prosperous visitors disembarked at the Hot Springs depot intent on wallowing in the "healing water" of those therapeutic springs. Families combined mineral bath cures with vacations, enjoying picnic outings in the Hills and stagecoach rides to nearby Wind Cave. Liberal statutes and lax residency requirements turned the community into a divorce center, increasing business for hoteliers, restaurants, and attorneys. By World War I, however, most of that had changed.

Doctors were less likely to recommend mineral baths as a cure for ailments and changes in state law rendered quickie divorces a thing of the past.

Despite these changes, a visit to present-day Hot Springs is still enjoyable. A century after its construction, Evans Plunge still accommodates 87-degree F (31° C) water in its 50-by-200-foot (15-by-61-m) pool, the world's largest natural warm-water swimming pool. It's probably a lot more fun now than it was in the days of swimming caps and modest bathing suits. Three water slides, exercise facilities and Jacuzzis, a special kiddie pool and slide, and water volleyball and basketball allow options beyond leisurely bathing in sun and water.

The same warm waters that gave Hot Springs its name helped fund construction of a variety of beautiful buildings in the community. Intricate carvings and ornamental designs decorate the facades of many sandstone buildings, which blend perfectly with the surrounding sandstone cliffs and evergreen forests of Fall River Canyon. The city's **Historic District,** which includes homes, resort hotels, sanatoriums, and commercial buildings constructed between 1890 and 1915, comprises a large section of the old town, especially along River Street and Chicago Avenue.

(above) Dayton Hyde runs the Black Hills Wild Horse Sanctuary between Edgemont and Hot Springs.(right) The remains of over 50 mammoths have been uncovered at the Mammoth Site in Hot Springs.

As impressive as this city's history and architecture are, nothing is as unusual as the treasure trove uncovered in 1974 during the construction of a new housing project for Hot Springs. In June of that year, heavy-equipment operator George Hanson was leveling a hilltop when the blade of his grader struck an object that shone white in the sunlight. Hanson stepped down for closer inspection and found a tusk, about seven feet (2.1 m) long, that had been sliced in half. Further examination revealed a number of smaller bones. To his credit and that of landowner Phil Anderson, site preparation was stopped while scientists were contacted to determine exactly what had been uncovered. Arizona professor Larry Agenbroad arrived about a week later and determined that mammoth bones had been uncovered. He also realized that there must be more beneath the surface.

In 1975, Agenbroad and his foreman, Jim Mead (both professors of geology and quaternary studies at the Northern Arizona University in Flagstaff), led a team of students who began excavating the site. Over the next few years, as the number of mammoths uncovered at the site increased, the scientists began piecing together evidence of a giant sinkhole that had literally swallowed the giant beasts. The theory is that the pond was created by a collapsed underground cavern, and that water rising under pressure from an artesian well partially filled the sinkhole. About 26,000 years ago, when giant Columbian and woolly mammoths roamed the territory, the warm waters of the sinkhole acted as a magnet for the large animals. Once in the water, however, the mammoths were trapped by the steep, slippery sides of the sinkhole and died. Eventually, the source of the water became plugged and layers of reworked sand served as a hardened, protective shroud around the animal remains. The mammoth mausoleum went unnoticed for the next 260 centuries.

The fossilized remains of nearly 50 mammoths have now been uncovered at the **Mammoth Site**—the largest paleontological find of its kind in the world. In addition to the mammoth remains, a variety of other species have been unearthed, including the giant short-faced bear, gray wolf, mink, black-tailed prairie dog, western harvest mouse, meadow vole, frog, and minnow, giving scientists vital pieces to the puzzle of what the ancient environment and climate were like when mammoths roamed the grasslands 26,000 years ago.

A superb 20,000-square-foot (1,858-sq-m) building and educational center was constructed over the site by a non-profit foundation that oversees the project. Guided tours, junior paleontological digs, and one of the finest scientific bookstores in the region are all available here. Due to its uniqueness, The Mammoth

Site experience ranks with Mount Rushmore, Crazy Horse, and Deadwood as one of the four most exciting destinations in South Dakota.

Two other attractions in the southern Black Hills are worth mentioning. At a remote location west of Hot Springs—on a gravel road which runs west off State Highway 71—hundreds of mustangs, unclaimed through the Bureau of Land Management's Adopt-A-Horse program, run wild across open range. The **Black Hills Wild Horse Sanctuary,** also known as the **Institute of Range Management and the American Mustang,** is the first privately owned wild horse preserve in the United States. South of Hot Springs and immediately west of U.S. 385 lies **Angostura Reservoir.** On any given summer weekend, a convoy of vehicles pulling all sorts of watercraft leads through the Hills on its way to the calm waters of this shallow lake. For those in need of a swim, it's well worth a visit.

Cowboys grapple with a pair of recalcitrant ponies in this classic photo by frontier photographer Fred Farrar. (Center for Western Studies)

THE NORTHWEST

IT MAY BE MORE LIVABLE now than it was a century ago, but northwestern South Dakota is still the least inhabited region in the state. Interrupted only occasionally by randomly placed buttes, the northwest's flatlands are filled with gumbo, a clay soil that becomes incredibly sticky when wet. During the Indian Wars in the 1870s, half of Gen. George Crook's cavalry horses died of exhaustion trying to cross the gumbo flats in a rainstorm on the way to Slim Buttes. Today, that mud can be found in the wheel-wells of every pickup truck that travels this unforgiving terrain.

The wooded draws of these rolling grasslands are filled with the fossils of dinosaurs who first rumbled here 60 million years ago. Tepee rings, buffalo jumps, stone tools, spear points, stylized rock carvings, and other clues prove that people inhabited the **Cave Hills** and **Slim Buttes** of northwestern South Dakota as much as 9,000 years ago. Indians, and later whites, stalked buffalo, wolves, and grizzly bear through the narrow ravines and across the boundless prairie of the northwest. The history of the region is as sparse as the landscape. The most famous story northwestern South Dakotans tell about this region is the tale of Hugh Glass, which, they assert, proves the hardiness of the first pioneers.

■ LEGEND OF HUGH GLASS

In 1823, the Rocky Mountain Fur Company acquired a license to trade on the upper Missouri under the leadership of Maj. Andrew Henry and Gen. William Ashley. That year, brawny and bearded Pennsylvanian Hugh Glass was asked to join Ashley's trading party on an expedition into the territory. Hugh was hunting alone one day that summer when he came upon the fork of the Grand River southwest of present-day Lemmon. As he neared the stream of water, a female grizzly and her cubs appeared in a thicket. From his startled horse, Hugh fired his rifle. The bear charged and the frontiersman was forced to fight at close quarters armed with a knife barely longer than the bear's claws. When his comrades found him the following day, Hugh was broken, badly mauled, bleeding from gashes all over his body, and near death. The bear lay dead nearby. After digging Hugh's grave and waiting two days, General Ashley's party moved eastward, leaving two members behind to tend to what seemed to be the imminent burial of the unlucky man.

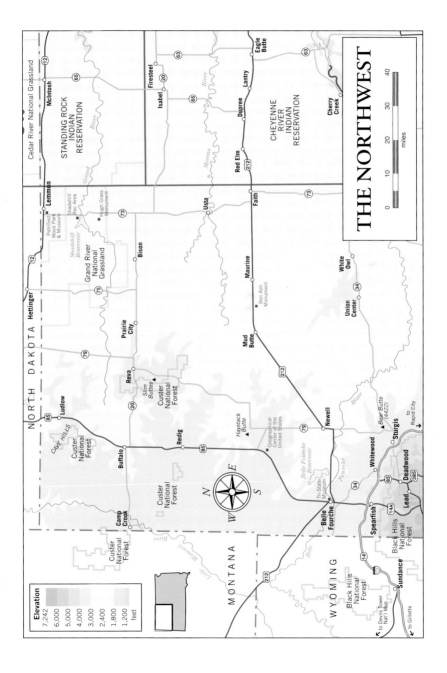

THE NORTHWEST

In spite of his broken bones, deep lacerations, and smashed face, Glass continued to cling to life for six more days as the two men watched his chest rise and fall with each labored breath. In between glances, they gazed at the nearby hillsides for sign of Arikara warriors. With no improvement in the big man's condition, the pair decided that Hugh was as good as dead. They gathered up Glass's gun, ammunition, and knife, saddled their horses and left him there on the banks of the Grand.

No one knows how long he remained unconscious. It may have been hours or days. But finally he awoke, in great pain. He drank from the river and was horrified at the bloodied and mangled face that stared back at him. After he surveyed the camp and noticed the yawning, shallow grave and the long-dead campfire, he became enraged that he'd been deserted in the wilderness, with no horse, no food, no gin, and no tools.

In his poem, *The Song of Hugh Glass*, John Neihardt contends that it was the burning desire to face those who had abandoned him that led the injured mountain man to survive and become one of the legends of the Old West. (The heroic story of Hugh Glass also formed the basis for the Frederick Manfred novel, *Lord Grizzly*.)

Dragging his broken leg behind him, Hugh began to crawl across the territory, drinking from mud puddles and creeks, and eating roots, berries, bugs, and about anything else within his grasp. Slithering through tumbleweeds, grass, and sun-parched prairie at night to avoid hostile Indians and weakened by his wounds and a lack of food and water, Hugh spotted the glow of a campfire and steered his course up a hillside to investigate. Instead of finding fellow frontiersmen, Hugh found only a campsite, abandoned except for a pack of wild dogs. Scavenging by the ashes, he found an old buck knife, which he used to kill one of the dogs.

After eating his fill and resting, Hugh spent the next several weeks crawling and hobbling more than 100 miles (160 km) to the Missouri River, then fashioned a crude raft and drifted another 100 miles to Fort Kiowa near present-day Chamberlain. When he eventually caught up to the men who had left him behind, as well as the rest of the Ashley party, Hugh forgave each of them. Ten years later, as he crossed the ice of the Yellowstone River near the mouth of the Bighorn, a band of Arikara braves killed him.

■ BATTLE OF SLIM BUTTES

After Custer's disastrous defeat at Little Bighorn in June 1876, Sioux leaders Gall and Sitting Bull fled to Canada with 400 lodges (families or small tiyospaye), and

SONG OF HUGH GLASS

. . . the lean dogs ran
And barked about him, for the love of man
Wistful, yet fearing. Surely he could find
Some trifle in the hurry left behind —
Or haply hidden in the trampled sand —

Long he sought
Without avail; and, crawling back, he thought
Of how the dogs were growing less afraid,
And how one might be skinned without a blade.
A flake of flint might do it: he would try.
And then he saw — or did the servile eye
Trick out a mental image like the real?
He saw a glimmering of whetted steel
Beside a heap now washed with morning light . . .

'Twixt urging hunger and restraining fear
The gaunt dogs hovered round the man; while he
Cajoled them in the language of the Ree
And simulated feeding them with sand,
Until the boldest dared to sniff his hand,
Bare-fanged and with conciliative whine . . .

—John Neihardt, 1915

Sioux bands gradually returned to their agencies, burning grass as they went to reduce the rations for any cavalry mounts that might be in pursuit. Generals Crook, Terry, and Miles began to hunt Indians and by September 7, Crook's ragged and weary column dispatched Capt. Anson Mills with 150 men to travel to Deadwood for supplies.

The next day Mills and his men discovered a village of 37 lodges on the eastern slope of the Slim Buttes, near present-day Reva. On September 9, the soldiers attacked. Within one of the tepees, buttoned up against the rain, was Oglala chief American Horse and his family. During the cavalry charge, American Horse and his wife and children fled to a nearby ravine with six other warriors. In the six-hour siege of the village and ravine, four of the warriors with American Horse and three of the soldiers died. American Horse, seriously wounded, surrendered with the survivors. Shortly before noon, the balance of Crook's army joined Captain Mills. It was none too soon. That afternoon, Crazy Horse and his 2,000-member band made a show of force and attacked the column of soldiers. With Crook's reinforcements, Crazy Horse could not gain the upper hand and the Battle of Slim Buttes ended in a draw. The next day, Crook's troops moved on toward Deadwood on a diet of horse meat, marking the end of a long and arduous summer campaign. Today, historical markers pinpoint the site of the battle east of Reva on State Highway 20.

Even though the Indians dealt a powerful blow to white encroachment with Custer's defeat and the stand-off at Slim Buttes in 1876, the U.S. government's long-term commitment of men and material to the Indian Wars and its precise and merciless strategy of cutting the enemy's food supply inevitably took their toll.

■ END OF THE HUNT

It is estimated that in the seventeenth century, 60 million bison, often called buffalo, darkened the grasslands of the Great Plains. The adult bull stands about six and a half feet (2 m) tall, and weighs more than 2,000 pounds (900 kg). Apart from eating its flesh, the Plains Indians relied on the shaggy bison's hide for clothing and shelter, its bones for weapons, toys, and utensils, and its droppings for fuel. In addition to the Ashley fur party, a hundred other groups of men traveled to the area to hunt

A buffalo-skin tambourine drum used in Sioux dances. (South Dakota State Historical Society, Pierre)

(right) Movie set of an Indian encampment near Sturgis.

on the open prairie, trap along the rivers, and trade with the remaining Indians. They discovered a vast expanse of rolling plains where thousands of bison lived. With the arrival of non-Indian hide-hunters and settlement of the plains came the depletion of the species, and by the early 1880s the last great northern herd of buffalo perished near the Little Missouri River in extreme northwestern South Dakota. As the number of bison dwindled, the last free-roaming bands of Plains Indians were forced to acquiesce to the will of the whites, and, hungry, to live on federal reservations.

With the threat of tribal retaliation gone, cattle ranges opened up, cowboys came, and thousands of Texas longhorns were herded to feed on the belly-high grass of South Dakota. Each year, cattlemen from the upper range along the Belle Fourche River would meet to plan two roundups of the giant herds—one in the spring to cut calves for branding, and one in the fall to ready animals for shipment to market. The unified South Dakota Stock Growers Association organized the last major roundup in 1904, just before homesteaders entered the open range.

Fast on the bootheels of cowboys came sheep herders and, later, farmers. A few of the farming communities became small towns, but few survived. Those that did watched their economy rise and fall with the market price for beef, mutton, wheat, and wool.

Although the twentieth century has brought improvements in transportation and electrical service for residents of northwest South Dakota, life in this land of barren buttes and mud flats is much as it was a century ago. Great distances separate ranch from ranch, town from town. Cars and pickup trucks make life somewhat more tolerable, but the region is still prone to severe winter weather and each family must be self-sustaining, able to wait out the plows for days after a blizzard.

A quilled Sioux saddle blanket. (South Dakota State Historical Society, Pierre)

■ CUSTER NATIONAL FOREST

The timbered hills of northwestern South Dakota were rare enough even by the turn of the twentieth century to motivate the federal government to preserve them. Twenty years before he became President, Theodore Roosevelt hunted bear in this region, and in 1904, he established forest reserves by presidential proclamation in the Cave Hills and Slim Buttes areas. President Roosevelt appointed his good friend and fellow Rough Rider, Capt. Seth Bullock, to serve as the forest's first supervisor. When farmers tilling marginal cropland went bankrupt during the '30s, the federal government acquired additional land and added it to the forest preserve.

All told, the lands of the Custer National Forest and the National Grasslands lie within 20 counties in South Dakota, North Dakota, and Montana. Four areas of the northwest, administered by the Sioux Ranger District, constitute South Dakota's 73,000-acre contribution to Custer National Forest. With ponderosa pine-covered hills and mesas rising above the surrounding plains, these areas are filled with deer, antelopes, coyotes, foxes, raccoons, minks, weasels, skunks, badgers, opossums, muskrats, and a variety of falcons, hawks, and eagles. Although these hills are not as user-friendly as the Black Hills—there are no designated hiking trails, even

Roundup of the longhorns in the northwestern part of the state photographed by John Grabill in 1887. The following winter, great blizzards wiped out most of the longhorn herds. (South Dakota State Historical Society, Pierre)

though ample hiking and riding opportunities exist—most of the ridges are open and afford spectacular views of the surrounding lowlands.

■ BELLE FOURCHE

Thirty miles (48 km) southwest of the geographic center of America stands Belle Fourche, an aging former railroad town that serves as the center of the sheep and cattle industries for northwest South Dakota, as well as parts of Wyoming and Montana. Though it's also the northern gateway to the Black Hills, its roots are in ranching, and Belle Fourche doesn't show the same flair for tourism as its southerly neighbors. A string of shops, taverns, and offices lines a narrow downtown business district that bustles while the sun's up, but slows to a crawl at night. The **Tri-State Museum** at 831 State explores the history of the town with exhibits and period paraphernalia. In 1981, a crew of ranchers and paleontologists extracted a Tyrannosaurus rex skeleton from Haystack Butte about 10 miles (16 km) east of Belle Fourche. Only the sixth T-Rex skull or skeleton find in the world, the dig ultimately yielded about 50 percent of the 65-million-year-old dinosaur's bones.

Owl Creek feeds the waters of **Belle Fourche Reservoir,** a few miles east of town on U.S. 212. A popular boating and fishing lake backed up by Orman Dam, the reservoir also is the site of one of the state's most impressive fireworks displays each July Fourth. The pyrotechnics follow the three-day **Black Hills Roundup,** one of the nation's oldest and best rodeos.

North of town, motorists either head for Wyoming or North Dakota. U.S. 212 veers northwest following the Belle Fourche River through a corner of Wyoming and past the Little Bighorn battle site in Montana before connecting with I-90 on its northerly run to Billings. Meanwhile, travelers on U.S. 85 leave the Black Hills and drop to the plains on a straight-line road that runs due north, then northeasterly for 21 miles (34 km) before reaching the exact geographic center of the nation near Castle Rock Butte.

For generations, the accepted **Center of the Nation** was near Smith Center, Kansas. When Alaska joined the Union on January 3, 1959, mathematical calculations shifted it into Butte County, South Dakota. Seven months later, when Hawaii became the fiftieth state, the center point was again relocated a few miles further southwest at the approximate intersection of 44° 58' North, with 103° 46' West. Today, the point is designated by a modest marker along the highway.

■ BUFFALO AND BISON

The old controversy over the name of those shaggy beasts that once roamed the prairie is reflected in the northwest by two towns. "Bison" is the correct appellation, while "buffalo"—actually the term for African and Eurasian species similar to the American bison—is more popular. The town of **Buffalo,** at the junction of U.S. 85 and State Highway 20, has a short business district, a new school, and 488 residents who cater to area ranchers and work in the natural gas industry, which has wells operating throughout Harding County. Similar in size and sophistication, **Bison** is located 55 miles (88 km) east of Buffalo on State Highway 20. Besides its bar, cafe, and store, Bison's main attraction is the **Anna Carr Homestead,** a sod house built in May 1907, which also served as the town's post office.

West of Buffalo on State Highway 20, near the South Dakota-Montana border, is **Camp Crook.** An isolated town of 146 friendly residents, the place had a larger population when its namesake, General Crook, stopped with his troops in the 1870s. It hardly looks any more permanent today. But with no crime, and stark beauty in the surrounding landscape, its inhabitants seem content to hang out at the **Corner Cafe,** where the prime rib is excellent. With no theater, bowling alley, or other form of entertainment, video movie rentals do a brisk business. On special occasions, some residents drive more than an hour south to Belle Fourche or north to Bowman, North Dakota, to take in a movie or do some shopping.

■ TIPPERARY

Arguably the most famous bucking horse ever to grace a rodeo ring was born and raised in this county, Perkins. Tipperary, a bronc buster's worst nightmare, was foaled in 1905 on a horse ranch near Camp Crook, and as a colt, his owner thought he had the makings of a good saddle horse. That was, at least, until a ranchhand tried to break him. Tipperary was a pacer, or as a cowboy from the Southwest would term it, a sidewinder. His legs moved in lateral pairs and his body would be alternately balanced on his right and then his left legs. That was unusual in a horse. Measuring 15 hands 3 inches tall and weighing in at half a ton, the blood bay gelding was not large—but he was tricky. Nearly 90 riders attempted to calm Tipperary between 1909 and 1926. Only two were successful in that 17-year career. In 1932, the fabled bronc was one of several horses stolen and trailed into Montana by thieves. With the law in hot pursuit, the horse thieves

(following pages) Rocky buttes dot the plains near the town of Buffalo.

abandoned the herd in a deserted barn. By the time he was discovered there, Tipperary was in poor condition. After being returned to his home range, the horse died in October 1932, at age 27, while standing in a snowstorm.

■ LEMMON

As close to the North Dakota border as any town in the state, Lemmon provides a large area of the northwest with medical, shopping, and recreational opportunities. The town's namesake, G. E. "Ed" Lemmon, is credited by the National Livestock Association with handling the largest number of cattle in a lifetime—one million—and for cutting, roping, and bringing to the branding iron the largest number of cattle in one day—more than 900 head. A successful rancher, Lemmon also helped found one of the last towns established in South Dakota. In November 1907, the Chicago, Milwaukee & St. Paul Railroad reached the newly founded town of Lemmon. The rancher sold 163 acres to the railroad on the condition that he be allowed first choice on a homesite. A year later, after selling all his cattle, Lemmon moved to town and built a house, which today is still used as a private residence. Most of the other buildings constructed during the town's birth were formed of embossed concrete blocks which provided a convenient and low-cost building material in an area that is virtually treeless.

In addition to a hospital, four motels, and five restaurants, Lemmon is also the site of the world's largest park dedicated solely to petrified wood and fossils. The free **Lemmon Petrified Wood Park** at 500 Main Avenue features more than 400 unusual structures constructed from specimens found within a 25-mile (40-km) radius of Lemmon. Nearly all the items displayed form spires, castles, pyramids, or other whimsical shapes. From 1930 to 1932, the park was the pet project of O. S. Quammen, who hoped to learn more about petrified wood, create a public display of the fossils, and provide work to men unemployed during the Depression.

The **Shadehill Recreation Area,** 12 miles (19 km) south of Lemmon off State Highway 73, is the only area for watersports in northwestern South Dakota. Fishing, hiking, boating, camping, and golfing are popular activities at the site during the summer. Significant populations of deer, small game, and birds keep hunters busy in the fall. In winter, outdoor enthusiasts prefer speedier sports, and when the snow flies, so do the snowmobilers.

WAKAN, ELUSIVE WOLF OF THE NORTHWEST

In the early twentieth century, northwestern South Dakota was plagued by a fierce and unusually clever wolf known as "Three Toes." The wolf's often gratuitous slaughters of sheep and cattle became legendary, and furious sheep herders and ranchers tracked "Three Toes" (or Wakan, Lakota for wolf) for years—but without success.

$\mathcal{E}$ntering the distant end of the pasture, [Three Toes] moved toward the docile critters. Without remorse, he killed every one of the fifteen lambs in the pen. After eating portions of only one, Wakan systematically dragged each lamb to a gate post next to the corral and placed them in a pile.

Wakan then returned to his observation post high on the hill and napped throughout the night.

The next morning the riders could not avoid seeing his handiwork as they saddled their horses to continue to stalk him.

As the sun rose, the wolf was alert to the movement around the cabin and corral. He heard one of the men shout obscenities when he discovered the slain lambs.

Obviously angry, the three riders quickly saddled their horses, swung the rancher's gate open wide, and started to search for the tracks leading away from the dead animals.

"It's Three Toes," one shouted.

"The bastard came in here last night and killed these sheep right under our noses," another declared.

Wakan could sense their exasperation and outrage as he watched them locate his trail and begin to follow.

Minutes later, Wakan stood up from his bed of grass and loped over the hill in plain view of the riders. They rode past the matted-down bed where he slept, pointing to the spot and commenting on how close the wolf had been to them as they slept the night before.

The chase began for a second day. Wakan maintained a steady pace, just out of rifle range, but close enough to give his pursuers hope that they could catch him.

About mid-day, Wakan scared up a jackrabbit. After a short chase, the wolf caught the unfortunate animal and devoured it. The riders found the rabbit's remains as they passed, still doggedly following his distinct trail.

When night came, the riders were still tracking Wakan but could not catch up to him. That day their pursuit changed direction. After leading them north for a day and a half, "Three Toes" was now heading east. . . .

—Gary Enright, *The Last Wolf: The Legend of Three Toes*, 1992

(following pages) A woman and two girls commemorate settler life at the Laura Ingalls Wilder Pageant in De Smet.

Transportation

PRACTICAL INFORMATION

■ TIME ZONES

South Dakota is located in the Central Time Zone and the Mountain Time Zone. Sioux Falls, located in the Central Time Zone, falls in the same zone as Minneapolis, Chicago, and Omaha with the dividing line generally running along the Missouri River. The Black Hills, which are located in the Mountain Time Zone, fall in the same zone as Denver, Salt Lake City, and Phoenix.

■ AREA CODE

The area code for all of South Dakota is 605.

■ TRANSPORTATION

For most visitors, South Dakota's appeal lies in its detachment from urban America. The population of its largest towns equals only that of suburbs of most metropolitan areas. Reaching South Dakota often requires more money and time than getting to more centrally located destinations, but the high cost of transportation is generally offset by a significantly lower cost of living. By most U.S. standards, touring South Dakota is a travel bargain.

■ BY CAR

The vast majority of visitors to the state arrive by car on interstate highways. The primary roadway, I-90, slices east-west through South Dakota from Minnesota to Wyoming. A second interstate, I-29, creeps up the state's eastern edge from Sioux City, Iowa, to North Dakota. State highways and secondary roads provide access to many of South Dakota's smaller communities and hidden treasures, while gravel roads and primitive logging tracks reach still deeper into the backcountry. No matter where you travel in the state, it's a good idea to check on weather and road conditions before leaving the pavement. Some parts of the state are known for a soil condition that allows even the slightest rain to turn clay into an impossibly sticky adhesive known as gumbo. The concoction can make vehicle travel and walking extremely difficult.

Highway rest stops and information centers appear infrequently along the interstates. The rest stops are always open, but the information centers close for the winter months. The South Dakota Highway Department does a superb job of maintaining roads in drivable condition year-round, but residents often quip that the state has only two seasons: winter and construction. Ground blizzards and heavy snows close down the interstates several times each year, and storms can strike anytime between October and mid-May. Smart motorists are prepared for the worst. Natives know that a candle in a tin can will heat the interior of a car. Although few carry items for every eventuality, the ultimate winter survival kit would include snow tires or chains, extra socks and warm clothing, insulated boots, a blanket or sleeping bag, a first-aid kit, non-perishable foods, a flashlight with extra batteries, a shovel, sand, gravel, or traction mats, matches or a lighter, and a window scraper.

South Dakotans are notoriously fast drivers, primarily because of the great distances between points, and state highway patrol officers generally will tolerate speeds of 60–65 mph (96–104 kph), even on secondary highways. The interstates, with the exception of small sections of roadway near Sioux Falls and Rapid City, are posted at 65 mph (104 kph), while motorists on all other highways are officially limited to 55 mph (88 kph). While patrolmen are somewhat tolerant of

Transportation

speeds exceeding those limits, they have little patience for nighttime speeders, and none for drunk drivers.

When traveling the Black Hills, commanders of motorhomes, buses, and trucks with trailers should examine maps of scenic highways for tunnel heights and restrictions. A fore-check can prevent wedging a perfectly good recreational vehicle between two slabs of granite.

■ BLACK HILLS TUNNELS

ROUTE	LOCATION	WIDTH	HEIGHT
US 16A	6 mi (9.7 km) SE of Keystone	13'6" (4.1 m)	12'6" (3.8 m)
U.S. 16A	4 mi (6.4 km) SE of Keystone	13'6" (4.1 m)	12'6" (3.8 m)
U.S. 16A	3 mi (4.8 km) SE of Keystone	13'6" (4.1 m)	12'6" (3.8 m)
U.S. 16A	1 mi (1.6 km) N of Keystone	20'0" (6.1 m)	10'3" (3.1 m)
S.D. 87	6 mi (9.7 km) SE of Sylvan Lake	9'0" (2.7 m)	12'0" (3.6 m)
S.D. 87	2 mi (3.2 km) SE of Sylvan Lake	8'7" (2.6 m)	11'5" (3.5 m)

■ BY AIR

South Dakota enjoys fairly good air service primarily due to its proximity to regional airline hubs in Minneapolis and Denver. Although wide fluctuations in price, arrivals and departures, and air carriers occurred in South Dakota in the 1990s, several of the nation's major airlines—Northwest, Delta, United, Mesaba, and Continental—serve South Dakota, although flights are often limited to the extreme eastern and western parts of the state, with passengers boarding and departing at Sioux Falls and Rapid City. Commuter flights link the cities of Pierre, Huron, Aberdeen, Mitchell, Yankton, Watertown, and Brookings. Other travelers charter flights from a large number of private aviators and flying services in the state.

■ MOTORCOACH CARRIERS

Greyhound Bus Lines. 301 N. Dakota Ave., Sioux Falls, 57102; (605) 336-0885.
Serving eastern South Dakota.

Jack Rabbit Lines and Powder River Lines. 333 Sixth Ave., Rapid City, 57701;
(605) 348-3300. Serving western South Dakota.

Balloons float serenely over the prairies of eastern South Dakota.

Climate

■ CLIMATE

South Dakota possesses one of the most extreme climates in the world. Positioned in the center of the North American continent and lacking any natural barriers to the Arctic Circle or the Gulf of Mexico, South Dakota sees virtually every type of weather (barring hurricanes). Over the past century, recorded temperatures have ranged from -58 degrees F (-50°C) to 120 degrees F (49°C). Yet in many respects the climate is pleasant. Low humidity, brilliant sunshine, and crystal clear skies are the rule rather than the exception.

CITY	FAHRENHEIT TEMPERATURE			ANNUAL PRECIPITATION	
	Jan. Avg. High/Low	July Avg. High/Low	Record High/Low	Average Rain	Average Snow
Sioux Falls	23 2	86 62	110 -42	26.43"	39"
Rapid City	32 9	87 59	110 -34	18.09"	46"
Pierre	28 8	88 64	115 -40	16.21"	28"
Aberdeen	20 -2	83 61	115 -46	23.96"	30"
Deadwood	30 8	79 52	101 -34	29.99"	70"

SOUTH DAKOTA'S SUNNY SEASONS

From a brochure for Sisseton, South Dakota, 1893.

Nothing is more misunderstood or misrepresented than the climate of South Dakota. This state is not a land of frosts and blizzards. On the contrary, it lacks little of being a land of almost perpetual sunshine. During eleven years' residence in South Dakota, but one blizzard has been seen which corresponds with the popular eastern conception of a blizzard. During almost any winter the East has storms which in all respects are worse than the much defamed blizzard of the Dakotas.

The atmosphere of this state is dry and invigorating, and one does not feel the cold as he does in a locality where the air is moist . . . Spring is a particularly delightful season in this county, all of the seeding being done before the 20th of April. The summer months are pleasant and sunny, and while the mercury is not ashamed to spend a good deal of time "cavorting" around among the nineties, the heat is not of a close, suffocating nature. Breezes are always blowing, and cases of sunstroke or heat prostration are very unusual. The nights are cool, and one always awakes with a feeling of refresh-

Climate

ment. The fall months bring the pleasantest weather of the whole year. The sun, dropping southward, sends his rays less directly, and the heat of summer subsides. Almost every day is bright and fair, and the air is laden with healthfulness. Cold weather sometimes occurs before the end of November, but for the most part winter weather is not looked for until the middle or latter part of December.

In New England much of the winter is rainy, cloudy and generally disagreeable, while frequently the heavy fall of snow makes traveling difficult. In South Dakota, at least every five days out of six are bright and cheery. There is seldom a heavy fall of snow, it rarely rains in winter, traveling is nearly always good, and the winter is generally unattended by the discomforts and disagreeable features which characterize that season in the East.

For health and long life, South Dakota beats the world. From the United States census report of 1880, the following death rate in proportion to the population is given for different localities:

Minnesota	1 in 86	All of the U.S.	1 in 66
Pennsylvania	1 in 67	Great Britain	1 in 46
Texas	1 in 64	Dakota	1 in 166

A tornado swirls across the landscape near Spearfish in August, 1954. Fortunately, little damage was done to the town. (South Dakota State Historical Society, Pierre)

(following pages) A tremendous electrical storm crackles over the Badlands.

Essay: Rapid City Flood

RAPID CITY FLOOD

For Glenn Anderson, a DJ at rock station KKLS, the night of Friday, June 9, 1972, started with a telephone call and a simple request to answer calls from listeners troubled by the rain. "The station had been getting some calls from people in the Hills who were concerned because of all the heavy rain and they had given reports of minor flooding," Andy recalls. "At about 9:15, a call came in from the Johnson's Siding area that said a 10-foot wall of water had just come down the canyon and you guys in Rapid City better brace yourselves."

Through that canyon west of Rapid City flowed the normally gentle Rapid Creek, a small stream about two highway lanes wide that was known for its excellent trout fishing. The creek ran into Canyon Lake, a small man-made reservoir on the city's westside, then flowed over the spillway and continued its meandering course through town on its way to the Cheyenne River. Andy and the station manager agreed that a live broadcast from Canyon Lake would bring listeners up to date on the storm.

Two blocks from the spillway, Andy stopped the car and delivered a broadcast message which told listeners that the creek was rising and urged them to stay away from the Canyon Lake area. After that, he signed off the air, started the car, and turned around to return to the station. He was just assembling his thoughts when a wall of water slapped the driver's side of the car and nearly flipped the vehicle on its side. As it righted itself, Andy felt the car floating. Not wanting to be trapped inside, he rolled down the window and climbed out into the chilly rainwater.

"The water was so forceful that it was tough to stand up. It was a raging torrent. One of the things I will never forget was knowing that I had been hit by a tidal wave. It was pitch black, and all you could hear was the water rushing and people screaming for help. You couldn't see them. You couldn't help. If you did you were throwing your life away. The screams would last two or three minutes and then they would fade away."

"Andy's attention quickly turned to his wife and daughter at home just five blocks away. He frantically searched for a telephone so he could alert them to the danger of the floodwaters.

"I had put our 17-month-old daughter, Nicki, to bed and I settled in to watch TV," Betty remembers, "when the phone rang. It was Andy and he said 'you need to get out of the house. There's a flood.' I said, 'What do you mean there's a flood?' He said, 'There's a big wall of water and it just knocked the car over and I crawled out and made it over to the nursing home . . .' Then the line went dead. I threw a blanket over Nicki and got out of the house."

With her infant daughter in hand, Betty tried to reach an elevated railroad grade behind the house, but high waters turned her back. At 5-foot-4 and 105 pounds, the 21-year-old mother surprised even herself by making it back to the house. In the darkness around her, screams filled the night. Standing on the porch with a shivering baby, she watched the water rise.

"I crawled onto the first board of the porch railing. I was holding Nicki in my left arm and the rafters with my other arm. I had been standing there for about 15 minutes when the next door neighbor's house exploded from leaking gas. I saw fire and debris just exploding way up in the air. For the next five hours, the only other sounds were the rushing water and the screaming and hollering."

At sun-up, Betty surveyed a scene of destruction. There was nothing left of her neighborhood. five nearby homes were gone and a pall covered the town.

"Rescue workers came by in a boat and I told them that the last time I had heard from my husband he had been over by Baken Park. He just looked at me with pity, and that look just alarmed me. I asked if anyone died in this. He said, 'I'm afraid so. I'm afraid a lot of people died in this. We've already found bodies. '"

Betty and Nicki were transported to the city auditorium which had been turned into a center for flood victims. Many were huddled around radios like punch-drunk prizefighters trying to figure out what just hit them—and to listen for the names of the missing. Andy found his wife and daughter at the refugee center later that morning. Others were not as fortunate.

The freakish thunderstorm had dropped more than 10 inches of rain over a 60-square-mile area. The heaviest rainfall was reported near Mount Rushmore, where 15 inches fell in six hours. More than 1 billion metric tons of water had fallen from the skies and saturated the pine trees, hillsides, and canyons with enough moisture to create a catastrophe. At final count, 238 people died. Five of those bodies were never recovered. More than 3,000 people were injured. Damages exceeded $165 million. Destroyed were 770 permanent homes, 565 mobile homes, and 5,000 vehicles. Nearly 3,000 other homes and 236 businesses were damaged.

"It's something none of us will every forget," Andy says. "When it rains hard, the memories return. You can't totally disassociate yourself from that. I don't think anyone who was alive here then will ever be able to do that."

Essay: Rapid City Flood

The snowiest month in South Dakota, March, leaves the Black Hills blanketed in white.

Camille Riner with a handful of hailstones, which in South Dakota sometimes reach the size of softballs.

Lodging and Restaurants

■ LODGING AND RESTAURANTS

By and large, costs associated with lodging in South Dakota change with the season, but room rates rarely exceed those of any tourism destination in the United States. Except in the peak periods—June through August and during motorcycle rallies, rodeos, and county fairs—rooms at low to moderate rates are readily available. Summer travelers are encouraged to call ahead. The best rooms, the most exquisite mountain cabins, and lakeside cottages fill up first. The following hotels, motels, and bed-and-breakfasts have been chosen because they have some special virtue, which may be price, location, or a better-than-average staff. For further information on accommodations in the state, contact the **South Dakota Innkeepers Association,** 2703 W. Seventh St., Sioux Falls, 57104, (605) 331-4194; or try the **Independent Motels of America,** P.O. Box 202, Winner, 57580, (800) 341-8000.

Eating is one of the least expensive pastimes in South Dakota, and dress is usually casual. Except for private country clubs, you'd be hard-pressed to find a restaurant in the state where ties are required. The following South Dakota restaurants, cafes, and roadhouses represent a good cross-section of the state's diverse eateries.

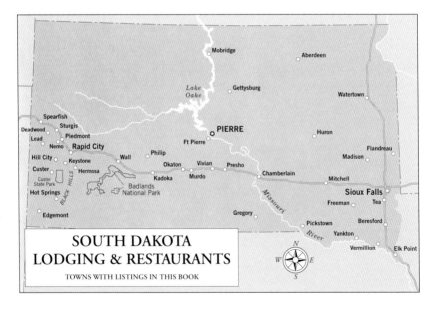

SOUTH DAKOTA
LODGING & RESTAURANTS
TOWNS WITH LISTINGS IN THIS BOOK

> *Room* rates:
> *(per room, double occupancy, one night)*
> $ = under $30; $$ = $30–80; $$$ = over $80
>
> *Restaurant* prices:
> *(per person, not including drinks or tip):*
> $ = under $8; $$ = $8–15; $$$ = over $15

ABERDEEN

White House Inn. 500 Sixth Ave. SW; (605) 225-5000 or (800) 225-6000 $
Conference rooms, continental breakfast included in rates, 96 units.

The Flame. 2 S. Main St.; (605) 225-2082 $$
Specializes in grilled steaks, ribs, and seafood. Open late by South Dakota standards. Child-sized plates available.

BADLANDS

Cedar Pass Lodge. Near park headquarters. 1 Cedar St., Interior; (605) 433-5460 $ - $$
There may be no better place to watch the sun rise. Open April through October.

Cedar Pass Lodge & Restaurant. Near park headquarters. 1 Cedar St., Interior; (605) 433-5460 $ - $$
Entrees include steaks and trout. Simple food, South Dakota style, is also available: buffalo burgers, Indian tacos, and fry bread. The fresh-baked desserts are wonderful. A cold beer or a glass of wine here are perfect after a walk.

BERESFORD

Conklin's Family Restaurant. East of I-29 on S.D. 46; (605) 763-2190 $
Complete menu with reasonable prices. Good breakfasts.

CHAMBERLAIN

Riverview Ridge Bed & Breakfast. 3.4 miles (5.4 km) north of Chamberlain on S.D. 50; (605) 734-6084 $$
Views of Missouri River. Breakfast includes homemade rolls, breads, and jellies.

Al's Oasis. I-90 at Exit 260; (605) 734-6054 $ - $$
Nickel-a-cup coffee and adequate food.

Casey's Cafe. Welcome West Plaza off I-90 at Exit 263; (605) 734-6530 $
Outstanding soups, sandwiches, and pastries. Try the pie.

CUSTER

Custer Mansion Bed & Breakfast. 35 Centennial Dr.; (605) 673-3333 $$ - $$$
Historic 1891 Victorian Gothic home; full home-cooked breakfast. Hiking, biking, fishing, and golfing nearby. No pets or smoking.

✗ **Bavarian Restaurant.** U.S. 385 and U.S. 16; (605) 673-4412 $
American and German dishes.

✗ **Chief Restaurant.** 140 Mount Rushmore Rd.; (605) 673-4402 $
Family-style dining. Hot dogs and pizza for the kids; prime rib for the adults.

✗ **Heritage Village.** 3 miles (5 km) north of Custer on U.S. 385 and U.S. 16; (605) 673-4761 $$
Large buffet and award-winning buffalo stew; roast chicken and pizza are also good. Music show.

✗ **Tortilla Flat.** 449 Mount Rushmore Rd.; (605) 673-5208 $
Pit-smoked barbecued ribs, pizza, sandwiches, and complete Mexican menu.

■ C U S T E R   S T A T E   P A R K

⌑ **Blue Bell Lodge & Resort.** In park on S.D. 87 S. 5 miles (8 km) south of Jct. S.D. 16A; (605) 255-4531 or (800) 658-3530 $$ - $$$
Rustic, secluded cabins, some with fireplaces. Enjoy a home-style meal or use the available grills and picnic tables. Campgrounds and hiking trails. Trail rides, hayrides, chuckwagon suppers, pack trips.

⌑ **Legion Lake Resort.** In the park on S.D. 16A, HCR 83, Box 67V, Custer, 57730; (605) 255-4521 or (800) 658-3530 $$ - $$$
Located near bison herds are these 25 cabins. Beach at lake, fishing opportunities, summer theater, horse trails, and more.

⌑ **State Game Lodge.** In the park on S.D. 16A, HCR 83, Box 74V, Custer, 57730; (605) 255-4541 or (800) 658-3530 $$$
"Summer White House" of two Presidents. In the main building are 68 rooms; also 21 cottages of various sizes. Hiking, fishing, fine dining. Jeep rides to the buffalo herds.

⌑ **Sylvan Lake Lodge.** On S.D. 87 a half-mile (1 km) west of Jct. S.D. 89; (605) 574-2561 or (800) 658-3530 $$$
Pristine 3-story mountain resort overlooking Sylvan Lake. Some rooms have fireplaces and balconies. Lounge, terrace, guest cabins with fireplaces or kitchenettes; access to outdoor activities.

✗ **Blue Bell Lodge & Resort.** S.D. 87 S.; (605) 255-4531 or (800) 658-3530 $$$
Downhome meals are served family-style in a rustic log dining room. Specialties include buffalo steaks and fresh trout.

✗ **State Game Lodge.** S.D. 16A; (605) 255-4541 or (800) 658-3530 $$$
Buffalo and pheasant specialties; luncheon buffet.

✗ **Sylvan Lake Lodge.** On S.D. 87 a half-mile (1 km) west of Jct. S.D. 89; (605) 574-2561 $$$
A spectacular view of Sylvan Lake and Harney Peak from the dining room and terrace, rainbow trout and buffalo specialties.

■ D E A D W O O D

⌑ **The Branch House.** 37 Sherman St.; (605) 578-1745 or (800) 336-1876 $$$
A good choice for a relaxing getaway or a business conference, this hotel offers some

attractive rooms, as well as suites with brick walls and skylights. Meeting rooms, business services, and exercise facilities are also available.

☎ **Bullock Hotel.** 633 Main St.; (605) 578-1745 or (800) 336-1876 **$$$**
Built in 1895 by Deadwood's first sheriff, Seth Bullock. Recently restored and furnished in elegant Victorian style. In the heart of Deadwood's gambling district.

☎ **Deadwood Gulch Resort.** U.S. 85 S.; (605) 578-1294 or (800) 695-1876 **$$**
Deadwood's newest resort features a 100-room hotel, indoor spa, outdoor pools, casinos, full-service bars, restaurant, store, large campground, and the Gulches of Fun amusement park, with bumper boats, go-carts, kiddie rides, miniature golf, snack bar, and a giant arcade.

☎ **Historic Franklin Hotel.** 700 Main St.; (605) 578-2241 or (800) 688-1876 **$$**
Historic hotel built in 1903. Free parking, Irish pub, wedding chapel, outdoor veranda, and sports lounge.

☎ **Mineral Palace.** 601 Main St.; (605) 578-2036 or (800) 84PALACE **$$ - $$$**
Deadwood's modern formal hotel. Business services, concierge, restaurant.

✗ **Bully's Bullock Hotel.** In the Bullock Hotel, 633 Main St.; (605) 578-1745 or (800) 336-1876 **$ - $$$**
Steaks and burgers in a quiet fireside atmosphere.

✗ **Chinatown Cafe.** Above Miss Kitty's. 649 Main St.; (605) 578-7778 **$ - $$**
A great break from burgers and steaks.

✗ **Creekside Restaurant.** At the Deadwood Gulch Resort, U. S. 385 S.; (605) 578-1294 **$ - $$**
Sizzling steaks, hearty lunches, and good breakfasts.

✗ **Deadwood Social Club.** Upstairs from the notorious Saloon No. 10. 657 Main St.; (605) 578-3346 **$$ - $$$**
A refreshing change of pace. Pastas, free-range chicken, and fresh salads.

✗ **The Depot/Motherlode.** 155 Sherman St.; (605) 578-3065 **$$**
Prime rib and shrimp scampi fo dinner, or check out the lunch buffet.

✗ **Diamond Lil's.** 677 Main St.; (605) 578-3550 **$ - $$**
Great burgers and chicken sandwiches in a sports bar atmosphere, surrounded by Kevin Costner movie memorabilia.

✗ **Historic Franklin Hotel Dining Room.** 700 Main St.; (605) 578-2241 **$$ - $$$**
Char-broiled steaks, buffalo, pasta, and vegetarian specialties are served in a Victorian dining room.

✗ **Jakes.** 677 Main St.; (605) 578-3656 **$$$**
The premiere restaurant in South Dakota, and the only one with four diamonds from AAA. Chef Dan's favorites include Cajun seafood, buffalo roulade, and pastas, but the rib eye with mushrooms sauteed in amaretto is the best bet in Deadwood. Elegant dining in an atrium-style dining room. Reservations necessary.

Lodging and Restaurants

✕ **Tradition.** 601 Main St.; (605) 578-2036 $$
Dine by the fireplace on cool nights. Exquisite prime rib.

■ D E   S M E T
✕ **Oxbow Restaurant.** U.S. 14; (605) 854-9988 $ - $$
Good breakfasts, lunches, and dinners at reasonable prices.

■ E L K   P O I N T
✕ **Edgar's.** Business loop downtown; (605) 356-3336 $
Authentic old-fashioned soda fountain, original wooden booths. Sodas and ice cream treats worth leaving the road for.

■ F L A N D R E A U
☎ **St. Vincent Hotel.** S.D. 32 and Wind St.; (605) 997-2221 $-$$
Historic hotel renovated with care.

■ F O R T   P I E R R E
☎ **Oahe Marina & Resort.** 20422 Marina Loop, Oahe Dam; (605) 223-2627 $$
Trailers for rent; restaurant. Boat and motor rentals, and bait and tackle available.

✕ **The Chateau.** Main St.; (605) 223-2402 $$ - $$$
Terrific barbecued steaks and outstanding onion rings waiting across the river from the capitol.

■ F R E E M A N
☎ **Farmers Inn Bed & Breakfast.** South of town on U.S. 81; (605) 925-7580 $$
Turn-of-the-century farmhouse decorated with antiques. Country gourmet breakfast.

■ G E T T Y S B U R G
☎ **Harer Lodge Bed & Breakfast.** U.S. 212; (605) 765-2167 $$
Five-bedroom country lodge on the prairie, nestled among evergreens. Within walking distance of Lake Oahe, fishing, hunting.

☎ **South Whitlock Resort.** 14 miles (23 km) west of Gettysburg on U.S. 212; (605) 765-9762 $$
Motel rooms and cabins; trailer rentals. Supper club and lounge. Boat ramp; guide services.

■ G R E G O R Y
☎ **Gray House Inn Bed & Breakfast.** R.R. 2 near U.S. 18; (605) 835-8479 $$
In the heart of pheasant country is this home with its eight rooms and loft. Gourmet breakfast with homemade breads, jellies, and caramel rolls.

■ H E R M O S A
☎ **Black Hills Health & Education Center.** Battle Creek Rd., off S.D. 40; (605) 255-4101 or (800) 658-LIFE $$$
Three-day packages available at this lodge, situated on 470 acres. Very up-to-date spa and the latest in health science; delicious vegetarian meals.

☎ **Bunkhouse Bed & Breakfast.** Lower Spring Creek Rd., off S.D. 79; (605) 342-5462 $$ - $$$
Working cattle ranch in the foothills. Facilities for horses, trail rides available. Ranch-style breakfasts.

■ H I L L   C I T Y

☂ **Black Hills Llama Lodge.** P.O. Box 109, 57745; (605) 574-2455 $$ - $$$
Stone guest house on 20 acres surrounded by forest. Furnished with antiques and family heirlooms. Take a llama for a walk.

☂ **Deerview Bed & Breakfast.** Five miles (8 km) west of Hill City on Deerfield Road; (605) 574-4204 $$$
Private wooded setting. Hunting, fishing, hiking, and snowmobiling on-site or nearby.

☂ **Edelweiss Mountain Lodge.** 13 miles (21 km) north of Hill City, just off U.S. 385, 2 miles (3 km) south of Pactola Reservoir; (605) 574-2430 $$$
Private home rentals: two- to four-bedroom homes. Waterbeds, steambaths or saunas, hot tub rentals. Open year-round.

☂ **High Country Ranch Bed & Breakfast.** 4 miles (7 km) west of Hill City; (605) 574-9003 $$ - $$$
Western-theme antiques, and Western-style breakfast, too. Free half-hour trail ride.

☂ **The Homestead.** 10 miles (16 km) from Mount Rushmore; (605) 574-4226 $$$
Spacious 5,000-square-foot (464-sq-m) luxury log home with guest house. Sleeps 2–24. Three fireplaces, satellite TV, large outdoor recreation area.

☂ **Mountain Shadow Chalets.** 25 miles (40 km) west of Rapid City; (800) 458-6830 or (605) 574-2742 $$$
Private vacation homes with two to five bedrooms; fireplaces, barbecues. Quiet in a lovely mountain setting.

☂ **Palmer Gulch Lodge.** 5 miles (8 km) west of Mount Rushmore on S.D 244; (605) 574-2525 or (800) 562-8503 $$$
Secluded mountain cabins with fireplaces and kitchens. Horseback riding, heated pool, restaurant, and lounge. Borders Harney Peak Wilderness Area.

✕ **Alpine Inn.** 225 Main St.; (605) 574-2749 $ - $$
German, traditional continental, and American dishes, but filet mignon is the only entrée on the dinner menu(!) The room does have a European flair. Fine steaks, and desserts that are to die for.

✕ **Gregson's Fine Dining and O'Bryan's Pub.** 349 Main St.; (605) 574-2400 $$ - $$$
A 1902 historic building with prime rib, seafood, and spaghetti upstairs; burgers, pizza, and suds downstairs.

✕ **Pauline's Ice Cream Parlour & Sweet Shop.** 351 Main St.; (605) 574-2423 $
Old-fashioned marble soda fountain and a 16-foot-long candy counter. Hard ice cream, sundaes, phosphates, and gifts.

■ H O T   S P R I N G S

☂ **Best Western Inn by the River.** 602 W. River; (605) 745-4292 or (800) 528-1234 $ - $$$
Downtown with easy access to the sights.

✕ **Dakota Rose Restaurant.** Jct. U.S 18 and S.D. 79; (605) 745-6447 $ - $$
Family dining.

Lodging and Restaurants

Lodging and Restaurants

(top) *Participants swap stories at a powwow at Pine Ridge. Luke Hjort and pal*
(bottom) on an errand to Sturgis.

(right) *Monique Ziolkowski, daughter of Korczak, with James Borglum, grandson of*
Gutzon, collaborate on a sculpture of Wild Bill Hickok. (Paul Jones)

Lodging and Restaurants

■ HURON

✕ **Crossroads Convention Center.** 100 Fourth St. SW; (605) 352-3204 $ - $$
The two restaurants here include **Festivals**, a steakhouse, and the more formal **Library**. Both offer a wide variety of entrees and desserts.

■ KADOKA

✕ **H&H El Centro Restaurant & Coffee Shop.** 105 S.D. 16 E.; (605) 837-2265 $
Homemade soups, sandwiches, charbroiled steaks, and chicken.

■ KEYSTONE

⌂ **Anchorage Bed & Breakfast.** 24110 Leaky Valley Rd.; (605) 574-4740 or (800) 318-7018 $$ - $$$
Private cottages in 20 acres of quiet forest.

⌂ **Kelly Inn.** S.D. 16A, Old Cemetery Rd.; (605) 666-4483 or (800) 635-3559 $ - $$
Sauna and whirlpool; family rooms with bunk beds.

✕ **Mount Rushmore Buffalo Dining Room.** Mount Rushmore National Memorial; (605) 574-2515 $$
Dine with the Presidents. Cafeteria-style dining, but the food's excellent, especially the fried chicken.

✕ **The Ruby House Restaurant and Red Garter Saloon.** Main St.; (605) 666-4404 $$
Steaks, seafood, and Italian dishes served in a Victorian dining room.

■ LEAD / TERRY PEAK

⌂ **Barefoot Condos.** Terry Peak, near Lead; (605) 584-1577 or (800) 424-0225 $$$
Great for summer vacations, winter ski trips, hunting excursions, even honeymoons. Kitchens, fireplaces, private saunas.

⌂ **Collins House Bed & Breakfast.** 616 W. Main St.; (605) 584-1736 $$ - $$$
Turn-of-the-century home, remodeled with whirlpool tubs, sun rooms. Rental options vary with the season, so call ahead.

⌂ **Mountain Streams Estates.** 38685 Cadillac Dr.; (605) 229-1619 $$ - $$$
Two vacation homes near Terry Peak, secluded in pines. A mountain stream runs nearby.

⌂ **Trailshead Lodge.** 21 miles (34 km) southwest of Lead on U.S. 85 South; (605) 584-3464 $$
Seven secluded cabins near trails for hiking, ATVs, cross-country skiing, horseback riding, and mountain biking. Snowmobile rentals available.

■ MADISON

✕ **F&M Cafe.** S.D. 34 W.; (605) 256-2051 $
Family dining with homemade cooking.

■ MITCHELL

⌂ **Anthony Motel.** 1518 W. Havens; (605) 996-7518 or (800) 477-2235 $ - $$
Pool, mini-golf, and family rooms.

☎ **Holiday Inn.** Off I-90 at Exit 330; (605) 996-6501 or (800) 888-4702 $$
Over 150 rooms, some with a balcony or patio. The "Holidome" boasts a putting green, pool, sauna, whirlpools, and arcade.

✕ **Block & Barrel Restaurant.** At the Holiday Inn (see above); (605) 996-6501 or (800) 888-4702 $$
Char-grilled steaks and burgers; chicken, and seafood in a typical chain atmosphere.

✕ **Chef Louie's Steakhouse.** 601 E. Havens; (605) 996-7565 $$ - $$$
Casual dining: steaks and barbecued ribs are specialties.

■ **MOBRIDGE**

☎ **Wrangler Motor Inn.** 820 W. Grand Crossing, a half-mile west on U.S. 12; (605) 845-3641 or (800) 341-8000 $$
Overlooking Lake Oahe. Indoor pool, sauna, whirlpool, and rec room.

✕ **Captain's Table.** Wrangler Motor Inn on U.S. 12; (605) 845-3641 $$
A superb view of the river. Good food.

✕ **Rick's Cafe.** Main St.; no phone $
The best chili in the state, bar none. Winner of the New York City Chili Cook-Off. *Casablanca* decor, gourmet hamburgers, and silly signs. But be prepared: opening hours are unpredictable.

✕ **Wheel Restaurant.** West U.S. 12; (605) 845-7474. $ - $$
Panoramic view of Lake Oahe with good food and homemade breads.

■ **MURDO**

☎ **Landmark Country Inn.** Exit 192 off I-90, then a quarter-mile south on U.S. 83; (605) 669-2846 $$
On 30 acres, with heated pool and suites with sunken tubs, hot tubs, whirlpools, or waterbeds. Open late May until October.

An old mountain resort in Spring Gulch in the Black Hills.
(Center for Western Studies)

Lodging and Restaurants

✗ **Star Restaurant.** Downtown; (605) 669-2411 $
Homemade burgers, meatloaf, and pies.

■ O K A T O N
▣ **Prairie Rose B&B.** 7 miles (10 km) north from Exit 183 off I-90; (605) 669-2529 or (605) 669-2271 $$
Take the kids out to the ranch at this bed and breakfast; $50 maximum per family per night. Pets welcome.

■ P H I L I P
▣ **Old West & Badlands Bed & Breakfast Association.** HCR 02, Box 100A, 57567; (605) 859-2120 or (605) 859-2117 $$ - $$$
Reservation service that puts visitors in touch with a farm or ranch family for lodging and breakfast at reasonable rates.

■ P I C K S T O W N
▣ **Fort Randall Inn.** South of U.S. 18 and U.S. 281; (605) 487-7801 $$ - $$$
Located near the Missouri River; bait and tackle available. Cafe.

■ P I E D M O N T
▣ **Elk Creek Resort & Lodge.** Exit 46 off I-90 near Piedmont; (605) 787-4884 or (800) 846-2267 $$
Scenic valley hideaway with guest cottages, furnished motel rooms, and a vacation home. Hiking trails, pool, and hot tubs.

✗ **Elk Creek Steakhouse.** North of Rapid City off I-90 on Elk Creek Rd.; (605) 787-6349 $$
Superb steaks and entertainment.

■ P I E R R E
▣ **Best Western Ramkota.** 920 W. Sioux St.; (605) 224-6877 or (800) 528-1234 $$ - $$$
On the banks of the Missouri River; 10 deluxe suites with Jacuzzis and wet bars; indoor pool, whirlpool, sauna, and a good restaurant.

▣ **Outpost Lodge.** 16 miles (26 km) north of Pierre, HCR Box 134, on S.D. 1804; (605) 264-5450 $$
On Lake Oahe with log cabins for sportsmen and families; guide services for hunting and fishing. Dine at the adjacent steakhouse.

▣ **Spring Creek Resort.** 10 miles (16 km) north of Oahe Dam on S.D. 1804; (605) 224-8336 $$ - $$$
Lakeside cottages; restaurant and lounge. Ideal for fishing trips: boat ramp, rentals, boat fuel, overnight or seasonal boat slips, bait and tackle, guide services.

✗ **Cattlemen's Club.** South of town on S.D. 34, HCR 531; (605) 224-9774 $$ - $$$
Terrific steaks are served in this Old West–style joint, where the floor is covered in sawdust.

■ P R E S H O
▣ **Sweeney's Bed & Breakfast.** 132 Main Ave.; (605) 895-2528 or 895-2586 $$
Renovated 1900s house. Full breakfast.

■ R A P I D   C I T Y
▣ **Abigail's Garden Bed & Breakfast.** 13137 Thunderhead Falls Ln.; (605) 343-6530 $$ - $$$

Peaceful streamside rooms, gourmet breakfast.

⊞ **Alex Johnson Hotel.** 523 Sixth St.; (605) 342-1210 or (800) 888-2539 $$ - $$$
Sioux Indian heritage and Western ambiance in a superbly restored hotel listed on the National Historic Register. Irish pub, gift shop, restaurant. Jacuzzis in suites.

⊞ **Anemarie's Country Bed & Breakfast.** S.D. 44 W.; R.R. 8, Box 840, 57702; (605) 343-9234 $$ - $$$
Country suite with hot tub. Austrian-style breakfasts.

⊞ **Audrie's Cranbury Corner Bed & Breakfast.** 23029 Thunderhead Falls Rd.; (605) 342-7788 $$$
Old World charm mixed with Black Hills hospitality. Antiques, fireplaces, hot tubs, wonderful breakfast. Open year-round.

⊞ **Barron's Bed & Breakfast.** 17 miles (27 km) southeast of town; (605) 342-1441 (call in the evening) $$ - $$$
Ranch setting with accommodations for eight. Horseback riding. Open year-round.

⊞ **Carriage House Bed & Breakfast.** 721 West Blvd.; (605) 343-6415 $$ - $$$
Historic Colonial-style home, with warm English-style interior. Close to downtown.

DAKOTA CUISINE

In 1883 Edmond Baron de Mandat-Grancey, a French nobleman and military officer, journeyed through Dakota Territory with companions Gifford Parker, an ex-Confederate soldier, and Frenchman Monsieur de Bouverie. After a month in the Black Hills, de Mandat-Grancey returned to France and published Cow-Boys and Colonels, *a journal of his travels which defined Dakota Territory for late nineteenth-century Europe.*

*A*las! In the course of ten minutes they bring us something smoking in a tin porringer, the strong putrescent odour of which has already reached our olfactory nerves. On inspection we find the contents to consist of rough pieces of venison, chopped with a hatchet and fried with rancid lard. Monsieur Bouverie immediately demands the receipt for this dish; he intends publishing a book that will form a supplement to the great work of M. Gouffe, *ancien chef de cuisine* of the Jockey Club, and will complete it. It will be entitled: "A Collection of Receipts to be avoided." He affirms that every meal he has taken in America furnishes him with matter for a whole chapter of this work, which will be for the cuisine of the future what in theology is the collection of the cases of conscience.

After dinner, and also during this execrable meal, a musical entertainment was

Lodging and Restaurants

Lodging and Restaurants

provided for us by the mosquitoes of the country, the old man living among them like a salamander in the fire. It seems he has served in the Confederate army. Parker wears also the grey uniform, and while these two old soldiers are entertaining one another with their exploits, I am sitting at a corner of the fire writing my notes in a cloud of smoke that makes my eyes run with water, while relieving me, however, in some measure from the persecution of the mosquitoes.

At eight o'clock, the master of the house makes his appearance on horseback. He takes a newspaper from his pocket and comes to read it at the table where I am writing, without saying a word to anybody.

What a charming country! and what charming people too!

❖ ❖ ❖

*T*oday the workmen are absent enjoying the after-fete of the 4th of July; we are therefore all alone. When Monsieur Bouverie was informed of the domestic arrangements, he declared that he would himself do the cooking. Hughes, therefore, has undertaken simply to make the nasty cataplasm which they call bread in this country.

Feeling ashamed of my idleness, I have offered my services, but they have thought proper to confide to me only the rough work. Consequently I am armed with a heavy hatchet, and I have to keep up the fire, which I do at the cost of some blisters on my hands in chopping a fir tree into convenient logs. When I came in with my load of wood I found old Hughes quite excited. He had just learnt that a mysterious composition, to which Monsieur Bouverie was giving the last touch, was that French dish, the renown of which had often reached the Black Hills, and which the epicure-ans of the Old World called an omelette. And it was really one with bacon, and, moreover, exquisite.

Old Hughes has tasted an omelette; he has lived seventy years, and this is the first time in his life! And the Americans pique themselves on their civilisation, forsooth! A single fact will give an example of their total ignorance of the culinary art. The Bordeaux fresh-water lobsters are unknown at Chicago, a city of 600,000 inhabitants, and these excellent crustaceans, positively swarming in the neighbouring brooks, and treated there with cold contempt, would actually boil with excitement if some Frenchman, while wandering along these brooks, would only give them a warm re-ception—in a saucepan!

—Edmond Baron de Mandat-Grancey, *Cow-Boys and Colonels,* 1887

☈ **Madison Ranch Bed & Breakfast.** 4.5 miles (8 km) west of Rapid City on Nemo Rd.; (605) 342-6997 $$ - $$$
Authentic 1920s rodeo guest ranch on 1,000 forested acres. Western museum collection. Full breakfast in the lodge.

☈ **Placerville U.C.C. Camp.** 10 miles (21 km) west on S.D. 44, follow signs; (605) 342-1390 $$
Main lodge with 14 rustic cabins along Rapid Creek. Fireplaces in some rooms and in main lodge dining hall.

☈ **Rushmore Plaza Holiday Inn.** 505 N. Fifth St.; (605) 348-4000 or (800) 465-4329 $$$
Eight-story atrium hotel, fountain court, piano lounge, indoor pool, sauna, whirlpools, and exercise room.

☈ **Town 'n Country Best Western.** 2505 Mount Rushmore Rd.; (605) 343-5383 or (800) 528-1234 $$
Conveniently located on the city's south side for a quick escape into the Black Hills. Black Hills tours; pools, playground.

☈ **Willow Springs Cabin B&B.** 11 miles (17 km) southwest of town, 11515 Sheridan Lake Rd.; (605) 342-3665 $$$
Secluded log cabins with antique furnishings; some have hot tubs. Breakfast delivered to each cabin.

✕ **Carini's.** 324 St. Joseph St.; (605) 348-3704 $$ - $$$
Authentic Italian cuisine. Sparse setting; high-quality food and enormous servings.

✕ **Firehouse Brewing Company.** 610 Main St.; (605) 348-1915 $ - $$$

Located in historic firehouse, the folks here brew a wide variety of beers and ales on the premises. Hearty pub fare, including fun dishes like gumbo and buffalo steaks.

✕ **Fireside Inn.** West S.D. 44; (605) 342-3900 $$ - $$$
The best prime rib, great steaks, and other fare in an appealing, comfortable setting.

✕ **Golden Phoenix.** 2421 W. Main St.; (605) 348-4195 $ - $$
Exceptional Chinese food at moderate prices, with friendly staff.

✕ **The Hall Inn.** 214 E. St. Joseph; (605) 343-9833 $
A dingy pool hall this may be, but the burgers are outstanding. Lunch only.

✕ **Landmark Restaurant.** Hotel Alex Johnson, 523 Sixth St.; (605) 342-1210 $$$
Fine food featuring buffalo, pheasant, and other regional entrees.

■ R O C K E R V I L L E

✕ **The Gaslight.** 12 miles (19 km) south of Rapid City on U.S. 16; (605) 343-9276. $$
Family dining in an Old West–style saloon, and an antique soda fountain where homemade ice cream is served.

■ S I O U X   F A L L S

☈ **Best Western Ramkota Inn.** 2400 N. Louise Ave., Exit 81 off I-29; (605) 336-0650 or (800) 528-1234. $$ - $$$
New indoor recreation center equipped with indoor and outdoor pools, sauna, whirlpool, racquetball courts.

Lodging and Restaurants

Lodging and Restaurants

⚐ **Holiday Inn Holidome City Center.**
100 W. Eighth St.; (605) 339-2000 or
(800) HOLIDAY $$$
Concierge services; "Holidome" recreation
center including indoor and outdoor pools,
whirlpool, putting green, and pool tables.

⚐ **Radisson Encore Inn.** Exit 77 off I-29;
(605) 361-6684 or (800) 333-3333 $$$
Adjacent to the Empire Mall. Indoor pool,
whirlpool, and athletic club. Shuttle service
to train station and airport.

✕ **Champp's Sports Cafe.** 2101 W. 41st
St. in the Western Mall; (605) 331-
4FUN $$
Heaping plates of barbecued ribs, ham-
burgers, fries, onion rings. Lively atmo-
sphere.

✕ **Louie's.** 400 S. Main St.; (605) 336-
3100 $$
Traditional Italian cuisine.

✕ **Minerva's 26th Street Market & Cafe.**
301 S. Phillips St.; (605) 334-0386 $$$
Wonderful deli lunches. Steaks, seafood,
and fish for dinner.

✕ **Spezia.** 1716 S. Western Ave.; (605)
334-7491 $$
Italian-inspired food: nearly forgotten old
recipes and newly adapted favorites served
in a warm and inviting room.

✕ **Theo's Great Food.** 601 W. 33rd St.;
(605) 338-6801 $$
Homemade pastas, seafood, and chicken.
Delicious pizzas, baked in a wood-fired
oven.

■ **S P E A R F I S H**

⚐ **Christensen's Country Home Bed &
Breakfast.** 432 Hillsview; (605) 642-
2859 $$ - $$$
The Passion Play is performed just a few
blocks away. Full breakfast.

⚐ **Eighth Street Inn Bed & Breakfast.** 735
Eighth St.; (605) 642-9812 $$
Listed on the National Historic Register,
this home (circa 1900) boasts a large porch,
a lovely parlor, and beautiful grounds.

⚐ **Spearfish Creek Inn.** 430 W. Kansas St.;
(605) 642-9941 $$
Creekside location that's still in the heart of
town. Pool, fishing.

✕ **Latchstring Restaurant.** U.S.14A in
Spearfish Canyon; (605) 584-3333
$$ - $$$
Sourdough pancakes, fresh trout, and
homemade pies.

✕ **Stadium Sports Grill.** 744 Main St.;
(605) 642-9521 $ - $$
Awesome quantities of nachos, burgers, and
grilled specialties served in a fun sports bar.

■ **S T U R G I S**

⚐ **Best Western Phil-Town Inn.** Exit 32
off I-90; (605) 347-3604 $$ - $$$
A favorite with friendly bikers during the
Sturgis Rally & Races. Restaurant, pool,
sauna, and whirlpool.

⚐ **Poker Alice House/Junction Inn.** Exit
32 off I-90, 1802 S. Junction Ave.; (605)
347-5675 or (800) 658-3695 $$
Stay in one of the 28 rooms or, better yet,
stay in the Poker Alice House, named for

the former owner who smoked cigars, drank whiskey, played cards, and ran a brothel.

■ **T E A**

✕ **Tea Steakhouse.** 215 S. Main St., 10 miles (16 km) south of Sioux Falls; (605) 368-9667 $$

Best kept secret in southeast South Dakota. The steaks are as big as the plate and nearly as tender as the cheese-and-onion-smothered hash browns.

■ **V E R M I L L I O N**

⊡ **Comfort Inn.** S.D. 50 off I-29; (605) 624-8333 or (800) 228-5150 $$

Rooms with wet bars and recliners. Meeting rooms and business services as well as indoor pool and whirlpools. Free continental breakfast.

■ **W A L L**

✕ **Wall Drug Store.** 510 Main St.; (605) 279-2175 $$

Country breakfasts, homemade cinnamon rolls and donuts, buffalo burgers, and nickel-a-cup coffee.

■ **W A T E R T O W N**

⊡ **Best Western Ramkota.** 1901 Ninth Ave. SW; (605) 886-8011 or (800) 528-1234 $$ - $$$

Connected to a bowling alley and lounge. Pool, whirlpool, and sauna.

✕ **Office Bar & Restaurant.** On U.S. 212, a half-block west of Jct. U.S. 81; (605) 886-2996 $$ - $$$

Prime rib, steaks, and seafood in a comfortable setting.

■ **W E B S T E R**

⊡ **Lakeside Farm Bed & Breakfast.** R.R. 2, Box 52; (605) 486-4430 $$ - $$$

Sample farm life—as well as homemade cinnamon rolls and hand-churned ice cream. Children welcome.

■ **Y A N K T O N**

⊡ **Lewis & Clark Resort.** S.D. 52 entrance to Lewis and Clark State Park; (605) 665-2680 $$

Adjacent to restaurant, playground, and marina, where there are boat docking and rental facilities. Close to a sandy beach; biking and hiking trails.

⊡ **The Mulberry Inn Bed & Breakfast.** 512 Mulberry St.; (605) 665-7116 $$

This beautiful inn, built in 1873, is on the National Register of Historic Places. Full of historic charm: there are two parlors with marble fireplaces, as well as a large porch.

✕ **JoDean's Steakhouse.** N. U.S. 81; (605) 665-9884 $$ - $$$

Good steaks, friendly atmosphere.

Lodging and Restaurants

Guest Ranches and Lodges

■ GUEST RANCHES AND LODGES

Guest ranches and lodges in South Dakota offer an alternative to chain hotels and motels, and many provide guide services to mainstream and off-the-wall attractions.

■ C U S T E R

Blue Bell Lodge & Resort. S.D. 87 S., inside park; (605) 255-4531 or (800) 658-3530. $$ - $$$
Rustic, secluded cabins, some with fireplaces. Home-cooked meals. Outings such as hay rides, trail rides, chuckwagon cookouts, camping, fishing, and hiking.

■ K E Y S T O N E

Spokane Creek Resort. U.S. 16A, 12 miles (19 km) east of Mount Rushmore; (605) 666-4609, fax (605) 666-4406 $ - $$
Cabins, RV, and tent camping by trout stream. Casual food: sandwiches, pizza, etc. Miniature golf Open May to September.

Triple R Ranch. U.S. 16A, 8 miles (13 km) southeast of Keystone. P.O. Box 124, Keystone, 57751-0124; (605) 666-4605. $$ - $$$
Includes all meals (family style), lodging. Horseback rides to a ghost town, Norbeck Wildlife Preserve, or Black Elk Wilderness. Breakfast and lunch rides. Trips to Mount Rushmore, Keystone, and Custer State Park. Swimming, cowboy supper show, wagon rides. Open June to early September.

L E A D

Cheyenne Crossing Store, Cafe, Bed and Breakfast. 8 miles (13 km) south of Lead in Spearfish Canyon; (605) 584-3510, fax (605) 642-1736 $$ - $$$
Meals include buffalo meat dishes, Indian tacos, *wojapi* (a Lakota Sioux dessert), sourdough pancakes, trout fishing, hiking trails, rodeos, Indian powwows, trips to Devil's Tower and Bear Butte, guides available. Open year-round.

■ N E M O

Nemo Guest Ranch. Nemo Rd., 16 miles (26 km) northwest of Rapid City. P.O. Box 77, Nemo, 57759-0077; (605) 578-2708, fax (605) 343-1916 $$
Cabins, campground, Western cafe and bar, general store, guided trail rides through National Forest. Open May to November.

■ V I V I A N

Rafter L Bar Ranch Bed & Breakfast. Exit 212 on S.D. 53; (605) 895-2202 $$ - $$$
Quiet ranch home on the banks of the White River. Horseback riding; home-style cooking.

■ W A L L

Shearer's Western Dakota Ranch Vacations. HCR 1, Box 9, Wall, 57790; (605) 279-2198. $$ - $$$
The best in Western vacations, from bed-and-breakfast and ranch home stays to sleep-outs in tepees or a sheep herder's wagon. Horse rides, chuck wagon suppers, bow rifle trophy deer hunting, posse and bandit games. Outfitters who will do it all.

■ CHUCKWAGON SUPPERS

■ CUSTER

Blue Bell Lodge and Resort. S.D. 87 South, Custer State Park. HC 83, Box 63, Custer, 57730; (605) 255-4531, fax (605) 255-4706.

The most popular group meal plan includes a hayride and chuckwagon cookout, complete with cowboy entertainment. Open mid-May through mid-October.

Dakota Badlands Outfitters. P.O. Box 85, Custer, 57730; (605) 673-5363

Authentic western backcountry experience on horseback in the Black Hills or remote Badlands areas. Day rides or tours of several days with chuck wagon meals provided.

■ RAPID CITY

Circle B Ranch. One mile (1.6 km) north of Intersection S.D. 44 West and U.S. 385. HC33, Box 3611, Rapid City, 57702; (605) 348-7358.

Cowboy-type supper with Western music show following. Trail rides, shoot-outs, and covered wagon rides. Gift shops. Open June, July, August.

Flying T Chuckwagon Supper and Show. Six miles (9.6 km) south of Rapid City on Mount Rushmore Rd.; P.O. Box 9351, Rapid City, 57709-9351; (605) 342-1905.

Chuckwagon supper with Western musical, comedy show. Open Memorial Day weekend through mid-September. Supper served nightly.

Hart Ranch Arena and Trailrides. Upper Spring Creek Road, south of Rapid City. P.O. Box 6500, Rapid City, 57709-6500; (605) 341-5702, fax (605) 341-1671.

Horseback riding including trail rides, breakfast rides, and chuckwagon supper rides. RV camping and motel with swimming pool. Indoor rodeos, golfing, and more, three miles from Hart Ranch Arena. Open year-round, more events from May through September.

■ WALL

Shearer's Western Dakota Ranch Vacations. HCR 1, Box 9, Wall, 57790; (605) 279-2198, fax (605) 279-2250.

Stay in a ranch home, cabin, sheepherder's wagon, or tepee. Wagon rides and chuckwagon meals with equipment and horses. Guests can go on a wagon train, participate in ranch activities, or spend a day touring the Badlands. Nine miles (15 km) north of Wall, on the Cheyenne River. Open year-round.

Chuckwagon Suppers

Ring-necked pheasant (top) and brook trout (bottom) are sought-after trophies for hunters and fishermen throughout the state. Bison bulls (right), at six and a half feet (2 m) tall and 1 ton (900 kg), must have intimidated hunters when the awesome creatures herded by the hundreds until a century ago.

Museums and Galleries

■ MUSEUMS AND GALLERIES

■ ABERDEEN
Dacotah Prairie Museum. 21 S. Main St.; (605) 626-7117. Free. Local east South Dakota history.

■ BADLANDS
Ben Reifel Visitor Center Museum. Cedar Pass, S.D. 240; (605) 455-5361. Park fee.

White River Visitor Center Museum. Off BIA Hwy. 27; (605) 455-2878. Park fee.

■ BELLE FOURCHE
Tri-State Museum. 831 State St.; (605) 892-3705. Free. Historical exhibits and paraphernalia.

■ BROOKINGS
South Dakota Art Museum. South Dakota State University, Medary Ave. at Harvey Dunn St.; (605) 688-5423. Free. Extensive collections of Sioux artist Oscar Howe and prairie painter Harvey Dunn, as well as Sioux craftwork and embroidery from the island of Madeira.

State Agricultural Heritage Museum. South Dakota State University, 11th St. at Medary Ave.; (605) 688-6226. Free.

■ CHAMBERLAIN
Akta Lakota Museum and the Lakota Visitors Center. St. Joseph's Indian School. Exit 263 on I-90 on N. Main; (605) 734-3452. Free. A historic look at Sioux life on the Great Plains before the arrival of European settlers.

South Dakota Hall of Fame. 100 W. Lawler St.; (605) 734-4216. Free. Exhibits of South Dakota writers and artists.

■ CUSTER
Crazy Horse Memorial Studio and the Indian Museum of North America. U.S. 16; (605) 673-4681. Fee. Houses one of the most extensive collections of Plains Indian artifacts in the country.

Jewel Cave National Monument Visitor Center Museum. U.S. 16 west of Custer; (605) 673-2288. Free. Large scale map of the cave; touch-screen interactive computer with information on cave minerals, spelunking, etc.

■ CUSTER STATE PARK
Peter Norbeck Visitor Center Museum. U.S. 16 east of Custer; (605) 255-4464. Park fee.

■ D E A D W O O D

Adams Memorial Museum. 54 Sherman; (605) 578-1714. Free.

■ F L A N D R E A U

Moody County Museum Complex. (605) 997-3191. Artifacts and artifacts from the region's past.

■ G E T T Y S B U R G

Dakota Sunset Museum. 207 W. Commercial Ave.; (605) 765-9480. Artifacts from Mandan and Arikara campsites.

■ H O T   S P R I N G S

The Mammoth Site. U.S. 18 Bypass; (605) 745-6017. Fee. Fossils of nearly 50 mammorths; educational programs.

■ K E Y S T O N E

Mount Rushmore National Memorial Visitor Center. (605) 574-4104. Free. Video about the memorial's construction; other historic exhibits.

■ L E A D

Black Hills Mining Museum. 323 W. Main; (605) 584-1605. Fee. Displays on the history of the mining industry.

■ L E M M O N

Lemmon Petrified Wood Park. 500 Main Ave.; (605) Over 400 unusual structures built from specimens found within 25 miles (40 km) of Lemmon.

■ M A D I S O N

Smith-Zimmerman Museum. Dakota State College; (605) 256-5211. Free. Farm implements and household items from 19th-century settlements.

■ M I T C H E L L

Friends of the Middle Border Museum of Pioneer Life. 1311 S. Duff St.; (605) 996-2122. Fee. Native American exhibits, antique autos, large collection of works by South Dakotan artists.

Mitchell Prehistoric Indian Village. Shores of Lake Mitchell; (605) 996-5473. Fee. The site of a town dating back to 900 B.C. Recreated buildings, visitors center, and museum.

Oscar Howe Art Center. 119 W. Third St.; (605) 996-4111. Free. An in-depth look at the life and work of the Sioux artist.

Soukup & Thomas International Balloon & Airship Museum. 700 N. Main St.; (605) 996-2311. Fee. History of ballooning from 1700 to the present.

■ M O B R I D G E

Klein Museum. 1820 W. Grand Crossing; (605) 845-7243. Free. Local pioneer and Sioux artifacts; restored schoolhouse. Changing art exhibits.

Scherr-Howe Arena. City Auditorium, 218 Main St.; (605) 845-3700. Free. Murals by artist Oscar Howe.

■ P I E R R E

Cultural Heritage Center. 900 Governors Dr.; (605) 773-3458. Free. The Verendrye Plate; exhibits regarding pioneer and American Indian history.

South Dakota Discovery Center and Aquarium. 805 W. Sioux Ave.; (605) 224-8295. Fee. Hands-on science and technology exhibits.

(left) The fare from today's "chuckwagon" establishments is probably a lot tastier than the grub served to cowhands when this photo was taken around 1900.

Museums and Galleries

Museums and Galleries

■ **PINE RIDGE**

Red Cloud Indian Mission School Heritage Center. 4 miles (6.4 km) north of Pine Ridge on U.S. 18; (605) 867-5491. Free. Works by artists representing 30 tribes; exquisite star quilts.

■ **RAPID CITY**

Dahl Fine Arts Center. 713 Seventh St.; (605) 394-4101. Free. Rotating exhibits of sculptures and paintings by area artists; 200-foot (60-m) cyclorama of American history on permanent display.

The Journey. 222 New York St.; (605) 394-6923. Fee. Museum exhibits of Black Hills history and culture.

Museum of Geology. South Dakota School of Mines & Technology, 501 E. St. Joseph St., 57701-3995; (605) 394-2467. Free. "Talking" dioramas of Badlands geologic and dinosaur history. Fossil, gems, agates, and other minerals.

South Dakota Air and Space Museum. Ellsworth Air Force Base near Rapid City. Exit 66 off I-90, 2.5 miles (4 km) north of Rapid City; (605) 385-5188. Free. Static aircraft and scaled-back versions of bombers and fighters.

Stavkirke Chapel. Chapel Lane Village off S.D. 44 W; (605) 342-8281. Free. Replica of 830-year-old Borgund church in Norway. Open seasonally.

■ **ST. FRANCIS**

Beuchel Memorial Lakota Museum. 350 S. Oak St.; (605) 747-2745. Free. Variety of Teton Sioux artifacts including photographs of Spotted Tail. Herbarium.

Jewelry made from Black Hills gold.

■ SIOUX FALLS

USS *South Dakota* Memorial Museum. Kiwanis Ave. and 12th St.; (605) 367-7060. Free. World War II mementos; memorial honoring the highly decorated ship and the 42 men who served on board. Open in summer.

Center for Western Studies. Mikkelsen Library at Augustana College. 2111 S. Summit Ave.; (605) 367-4007. Free. Norwegian rosemaled furniture, prairie art, Sioux Indian artifacts, and displays of prairie and plains history.

Civic Fine Arts Center. 235 W. 10th St.; (605) 336-1167. Free. Two galleries featuring contemporary regional artists.

EROS Data Center (Earth Resources Observation Systems). 10 miles (16 km) north of

Some fine examples of Indian bead and quill work. The vest at the top is a museum piece at the South Dakota State Historical Society in Pierre.

Museums and Galleries

Exit 402 on I-90; (605) 594-6189. Free. Data center of Department of Interior. Visitor center contains audiovisual exhibits, including photographs of Earth taken from satellites and aircraft.

Great Plains Zoo and Delbridge Museum of Natural History. 805 S. Kiwanis Ave. in Sherman Park; (605) 367-7059. Fee. Over 300 reptiles, birds, and mammals from all over the world. Museum houses hands-on exhibits and dioramas of different climatic zones.

Jim Savage Western Art Gallery and Historical Center. 3301 E. 26th St.; (605) 332-7551. Free. Mix of traditional, old, and modern Western art; pottery, jewelry, and collectibles.

Rehfeld's Dakota Galleries. 229 S. Phillips St.; (605) 336-9737. Free. Upper Midwestern, largely South Dakotan original art; prints and sculptures.

Siouxland Heritage Museums. 200 W. Sixth St.; (605) 367-4210. Free. Site includes **Old Courthouse Museum,** 1890 quartzite courthouse with displays of Siouxland history, and **Pettigrew Museum,** a historic house furnished to show life of state's first senator with galleries of local natural history.

■ SISSETON

Fort Sisseton State Park. 20 miles (32 km) west of Sissteton on S.D. 10 then south on S.D. 25; (605) 448-5701. 17 original and reconstructed buildings at this Civil War–era fort, previously known as Fort Wadsworth.

Tekakwitha Fine Arts Center. 401 S. Eighth St. W.; (605) 698-7058. Free. Impressive exhibits of over 30 local Indian artists.

■ SPEARFISH

D.C. Booth Historic Fish Hatchery and National Fish Culture Hall of Fame. 423 Hatchery Circle; (605) 642-7730. Free. One of the first in the West.

High Plains Heritage Center. 825 Heritage Dr.; (605) 642-9378. Fee. Western art, sculpture, cultural festivals.

■ STURGIS AREA

Bear Butte State Park Visitor Center. 6 miles (10 km) northeast of Sturgis off S.D. 79; (605) 347-5240. Park fee. Displays of American Indian history and culture.

Fort Meade Museum. Two miles (3 km) east of Sturgis on S.D. 34; (605) 347-9822. Fee. Old cavalry quarters, historic documents, including photographs of the all-black 25th Cavalry, and the all-Sioux Troop L, Third Cavalry.

■ VERMILLION

W. H. Over State Museum. University of South Dakota campus. 1110 Ratigen St.; (605) 677-5228. Free. Life-size diorama of Teton village; state history exhibits.

Shrine to Music Museum. University of South Dakota campus. Clark and Yale Sts.; (605) 677-5306. Free. Over 5,000 musical instruments from all over the world.

■ W A T E R T O W N

Kampeska Heritage Museum. 27 First Ave. SE; (605) 886-7335. Free. Pioneer and American Indian history.

Mellette House Museum. 421 Fifth Ave. NW;(605) 886-4730. Free. Family heirlooms, portraits. Open in summer.

Redlin Art Center. 1200 33rd St. SE and Mickelson Dr.; (605) 882-3877. Gallery visits are free; planetarium charges a fee.

■ Y A N K T O N   A R E A

Dakota Territorial Museum. Westside Park, 610 Summit St.; (605) 665-3898. Free. Sioux artifacts, steamboat displays.

■ FESTIVALS, EVENTS, AND RODEOS

■ M A R C H

Deadwood: St. Patrick's Day Celebration. A chance to play in the past in historic Deadwood, with green beer, corned beef, and cabbage; (605) 578-1876.

Freeman: Schmeckfest. A celebration of German heritage. Serving tables piled with bratwurst, cheese buttons, and kuchen.Colorful costumes and Old World demonstrations such as spinning and clock making; (605) 297-4150.

Oakwood Lakes State Park: Frozen Fat Tire Classic Mountain Bike Race. Bicycling for those unwary of weather; (605) 692-2708.

Sioux Falls: St. Patrick's Day Parade. A good Irish frolic through the central business district; (605) 336-1620.

■ A P R I L

Brookings: Jackrabbit Stampede Rodeo. Brahma bulls and saddle broncs; (605) 688-4727.

Huron: Collegiate Rodeo. The best in college rodeo action; (605) 352-5275.

■ M A Y

Clark: "Little Fellow's" Memorial Service. A celebration of the friendship between "Big Bill" Chambers and the "Little Fellow" he waved to from the train (see "Little Fellow of Clark," p. 114); (605) 532-5772.

Crazy Horse Memorial: Crazy Horse Memorial Open House. A free weekend for visitors who watch the carving in progress; (605) 673-4681.

Sturgis: Black Hills Balloon Rally. Colorful sunrise lift-offs against a ponderosa pine backdrop; (605) 347-5666.

■ J U N E

Clear Lake: Crystal Springs Rodeo. Saddle broncs, barrel racing, and beer; (605) 874-2499.

Deadwood: Charlie Utter Dayz. Typical "Deadweird" activities such as Min Street bed races, barstool volleyball, and free open-air concerts. (605) 578-1876.

Dell Rapids: Cootie Days. A wild small-town celebration; (605) 428-3499.

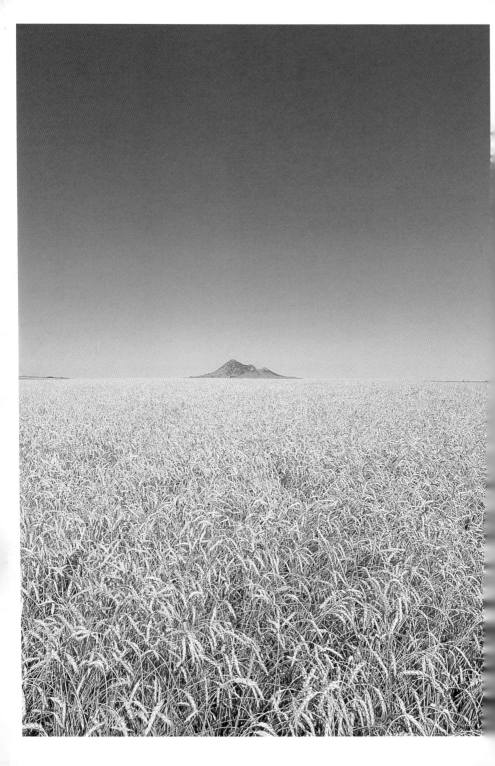

De Smet: Laura Ingalls Wilder Pageant. The premiere pioneer celebration in South Dakota, complete with butter churns, bonnets, square dances, and an outdoor pageant depicting stories from the *Little House on the Prairie* series; (605) 692-2108.

Fort Sisseton State Park: Fort Sisseton Historical Festival. Blue coats and bayonets gather for military exercises, muzzle-loading contests, and formal balls; (605) 448-5701.

Garretson: Jesse James Roundup. Fun times and a play recounting the day outlaws Frank and Jesse James outran a posse; (605) 428-3674.

Lower Brule: Native American Day Celebration. Recalling the way of life of the Plains Indian; (800) 658-4554.

Mitchell: Corn Palace Balloon Rally. Hot air ballooning with some of the finest crafts in the country; (605) 996-5567.

Rapid City: West Boulevard Arts Festival. One of the state's finest among many; (605) 342-6497.

St. Onge: Rough Riders Rodeo. A great tradition in cattle country, conducted the way they were a century ago; (605) 578-1655.

Sturgis: Black Hills Bluegrass Festival. A western hoe-down worth attending; (605) 394-4101.

Tabor: Czech Days. Tiny Tabor remembers the old country and its rich Czech heritage with polka music and plenty of *zelí* (sauerkraut), *koláče* (tarts), *knedlíky* (potato dumplings), and other Bohemian cuisine; 463-2331.

Webster: Sodbuster Fest. A celebration of pioneer heritage; (605) 345-4751.

■ JULY

Belle Fourche: Black Hills Roundup. One of the longest running rodeos in the nation; (605) 892-2676.

Custer: Gold Discovery Days. The oldest town in the Hills recalls its past; (605) 673-2244.

Deadwood/Lead: Gold Camp Jubilee. Another reason to celebrate in the northern Black Hills; (605) 578-1876.

Gettysburg: Civil War Re-enactment & Rendezvous. Recalling the trials of those who settled the region; (605) 765-2731.

Huron: Heartland Rodeo; (605) 352-8775.

Lead: Black Hills Jazz & Blues Festival. Trumpet mutes and raspy saxophones in a world-class affair; (605) 394-4101.

Mitchell: Corn Palace Stampede Rodeo; (605) 996-7775.

Mobridge: Sitting Bull Stampede. Rodeo action, entertainment, and enough refreshments to settle the dust in your throat; (605) 845-2387.

Rapid City: Black Hills Heritage Festival and Northern Plains Indian Powwow. Fine art, crafts, country bands, and a colorful powwow; (605) 394-4101.

Rapid City: Great Plains Indian Rodeo; (605) 341-5702.

Spearfish: Black Hills Corvette Classic. Lots of "vettes" touring the scenic byways of the Black Hills; (605) 361-2908.

(left) Wheat fields, azure skies, and brown buttes are the essence of the South Dakota landscape.

Festivals, Events, and Rodeos

Festivals, Events, and Rodeos

Spearfish: National Impala Convention. The largest gathering of Impalas and their owners; (605) 642-5868.

Watertown: Kampeska Days. A community celebration with pizazz; (605) 886-2555.

Webster: Glacial Lakes Stampede Rodeo; (605) 345-4613.

Winner: Elks Rodeo. Not the largest rodeo, but townspeople make it one of the best; (605) 842-2141.

■ A U G U S T

Aberdeen: Dacotah Stampede Rodeo; (605) 662-7110.

Canton: Scandinavian Folk Festival. Lutefisk and big socks; (605) 987-5728.

Deadwood: Days of '76. Wild West rodeo performances, parades, and genuine blackjack, poker, slots; (605) 578-1876.

Fort Pierre: Turkey Races. Friendly wagers on fast gobblers; (605) 223-2402.

Huron: South Dakota State Fair. Week-long rodeo and nightly entertainment; (605) 352-1431.

Madison: Prairie Village Threshing Jamboree. Weaving looms, belching steam engines, and old-time hand-made everything; (605) 256-3644.

Pine Ridge: Oglala Nation Rodeo; (605) 867-5821.

Rapid City: Central States Fair. Top-name entertainers, rodeo and stock car action combined with one of the ten best fairs in the United States; (605) 342-8325.

Scotland: Scottie Stampede Rodeo; (605) 387-2398.

Sioux Falls: Sioux Empire Fair. A large fair with distinctly agrarian slant; (605) 339-7178.

Sturgis: Black Hills Threshing Bee. Old-time machinery and friendly folk who'll tell you how it used to be done; (605) 347-2556.

Sturgis: Sturgis Rally and Races. The largest motorcycle rally in the world. Rock bands, hill climbs, and drag races; (605) 347-6570.

Watertown: Pro Bowl Rodeo; (605) 886-4370.

Yankton: Riverboat Days PRCA Rodeo; (605) 665-9231.

Yankton: Yankton Riverboat Days. Celebrating the era when everything came by water; (605) 665-7378.

■ S E P T E M B E R

Crazy Horse Memorial: Crazy Horse Memorial Night Blast. An opportunity to witness history in the making and an impressive dynamite explosion; (605) 673-4681.

Deadwood: Deadwood Jam. Classic entertainment from high-caliber bands; (605) 578-1876.

Eureka: German Schmeckfest. Hearty fare and beer steins; (605) 284-2130.

Sioux Falls: Northern Plains Tribal Arts. Annual show displays works by more than 100 artists from tribes throughout the Midwest and West. Two-day affair is enlivened by Indian dance, music, and storytelling; (605) 334-4060.

Spearfish: Yellow Jacket Stampede Rodeo; (605) 642-6434.

Powwows

Yankton: Great Plains Fiddlers Contest. Pickers and grinners rosin up the bow; (605) 665-3636.

■ OCTOBER

Custer State Park: Buffalo Roundup. The roar of 6,000 hooves pounding the prairie in one of the largest buffalo roundups in the world; (605) 255-4515.

Sioux Falls: SDRA Championship Finals Rodeo; (605) 775-2621.

■ NOVEMBER

Custer State Park: Buffalo Auction. Buy a buffalo for less; (605) 255-4515.

Pierre: Capitol Christmas. Decorated trees from throughout South Dakota adorn the capitol rotunda; (605) 224-2048.

■ DECEMBER

Oakwood Lakes State Park: Frozen Foot Rendezvous. Hardy souls re-create a winter encampment. "Mountain men" don leather and furs, and dwell in tents and tepees; (605) 693-4589.

■ POWWOWS

Be sure to call ahead to find out dates and locations. Keep in mind that starting and ending hours for special dances are rarely precise, since performance times depend upon dancers' and musicians' readiness, not the hour on the clock.

■ BLACK HILLS

Black Hills Powwow and Indian Art Market. Rapid City; (605) 341-0925.

■ CENTRAL

Cherry Creek Powwow. Cherry Creek; (605) 964-4000.

Iron Lightning Powwow. Iron Lightning; (605) 964-4000.

Lower Brule Powwow & Rodeo. Lower Brule; (605) 473-5561.

Labor Day Powwow. Winner; (605) 842-1875.

■ NORTHEAST

Flandreau Santee Sioux Powwow. Flandreau; (605) 997-3891.

Mother's Day Powwow. Aberdeen; (605) 226-7527.

Sisseton-Wahpeton Agency Village. Several throughout the year; (605) 698-3911.

■ NORTHWEST

Eagle Butte Fair & Powwow. Eagle Butte; (605) 964-4000.

Takini School Wacipi. Howes; (605) 538-4399.

■ SOUTH-CENTRAL

Oglala Lakota College Wacipi. Kyle; (605) 455-2321.

Oglala Nation Powwow. Pine Ridge; (605) 867-5821.

Wakpamni Lake Fourth of July Powwow. Batesland; (605) 288-1873.

■ SOUTHEAST

Dakota Wesleyan Wacipi. Mitchell; (605) 995-2637.

Great Plains Powwow. Sioux Falls; (605) 339-7039.

Winter Recreation/Volksmarches

■ WINTER RECREATION

■ BLACK HILLS

Deer Mountain Ski Area. 3 miles (5 km) south of Lead on U.S. 85, P.O. Box 622, Deadwood, 57732-0622; (605) 584-3230 or (605) 584-3709, fax (605) 578-2200.

Latchstring Winter Sports Center. Spearfish Canyon, U.S. 14A, P.O. Box 798, Spearfish, 57783-0798; (605) 584-2207.

Mount Meadow Resort. Deerfield Lake, 16 miles (26 km) northwest of Hill City. HCR 87, Box 25A, Hill City, 57745; (605) 574-2636.

Sunset Motel/Dr. Fun Snowmobile Tours. 525 Crook St., Custer; (605) 673-2821.

Terry Peak Ski Area. P.O. Box 774, Lead, 57754-0774; (605) 584-2165, snow conditions (800) 456-0524.

Trailshead Lodge. Snowmobile rentals. 21 miles (34 km) southwest of Lead on U.S. 85 South. P.O. Box 873, Lead, 57754-0873; (605) 584-3464.

■ NORTHEAST

Doug's Rentals (Interlakes Sports Center). 702 S.W. 10th St., Madison, 57042; (605) 256-3556

Pleasant Valley Lodge & Ski Area. 12 miles (19 km) east of Clear Lake on S.D. 22. R.R. 1, Box 256, Gary, 57237; (605) 272-5614.

■ SOUTHEAST

Great Bear Ski Area. 2 miles (3 km) east of Sioux Falls on I-29 at Rice St. 5901 Rice St., Sioux Falls, 57103; (605) 367-4309.

■ VOLKSMARCHES

On certain Saturdays and Sundays in the warm summer months, some South Dakotans band together in large groups and embark on day-long hikes known as "volksmarches." Following are some of the more popular ones:

■ BLACK HILLS

Bear Butte Seasonal Volksmarch. (605) 347-5240.

Crazy Horse Memorial Volksmarch. (605) 673-4681.

Custer State Park Seasonal Volksmarch. (605) 255-4515.

Spearfish Volksmarch. (605) 642-3232.

■ CENTRAL

West Whitlock Volksmarch. (605) 765-9410.

■ NORTHEAST

Lake Herman Seasonal Volksmarch. (605) 256-3613.

Sica Hollow Volksmarch. (605) 448-5701.

■ AERIAL TOURS

■ BADLANDS

Badger Helicopters, Inc. Badlands from the air. East entrance to Badlands National Park, I-90, Exit 130. Open mid-May to mid-September. Write: Route 7, Highway 51 S., Janesville, WI, 53546; (605) 433-5322, or (608) 752-4001.

■ BLACK HILLS

Black Hills Balloons. Hot air balloon flights over various regions in Black Hills area, plus Badlands and Devils Tower. Year-round. Write: P.O. Box 210, Custer, 57730-0210; (605) 673-2520, fax (605) 673-5075.

Dave McPherson. 1313 Evergreen Dr., Sturgis, 57785; (605) 347-3301.

Rushmore Helicopters, Inc. Three tours from mid-May to mid-September. Write: P.O. Box 133, Keystone, 57751-0133; (605) 666-4461, fax (605) 666-4461.

Terry Peak Chairlift. Summer chairlift rides open Memorial Day through Labor Day. Outside Lead/Deadwood. Write: P.O. Box 774, Lead, 57754-0774; (605) 584-2165 or (605) 584-2167; (800) 456-0524.

■ MOTORCOACH TOURS

In addition to those taking passengers in and out of the state, a number of motorcoaches take visitors on historic tours through specific regions of the state. Following is a list of motorcoach tour companies which operate in South Dakota:

Affordable Adventures. P.O. Box 546, Rapid City, 57709-0546; (605) 342-7691, fax (605) 342-3417.

Alkali Ike Tours. P.O. Box 594, Deadwood, 57732-0594; (605) 578-3583 (summer) and (605) 578-2510 (winter).

America Tours West. P.O. Box 167, Keystone, 57751-0167; (605) 666-4545, fax (605) 666-4996.

Dakota Bus Service, Inc. P.O. Box 609, Spearfish, 57783-0609; (605) 642-2353, fax (605) 642-7707.

Golden Circle Tours. 40 N. Fifth St., Custer, 57730; (605) 673-4349.

Gray Line of the Black Hills. P.O. Box 1106, Rapid City, 57709-1106; (605) 342-4461 or (800) 456-4461.

Jack Rabbit Tours. 3405 S. Cliff Ave., Sioux Falls, 57105; (605) 335-2290 or (800) 759-8687, fax (605) 335-6252.

Old West Tours. 701 Fairway Dr., Gillette, WY 82716. Write P.O. Box 2437, Gillette, WY 82717-2437; (307) 682-6820, fax (307) 686-1201.

Original Deadwood Tour. P.O. Box 363, Deadwood, 57732-0363; (605) 578-1546 or (605) 578-2408.

Aerial Tours/Motorcoach Tours

Black Hills Caves

Potato Creek Tours. 409 Summit, Lead, 57754; (605) 642-4473; nights and weekends: (605) 584-2255.

Rocky Mountain Holiday Tours. P.O. Box 8411, Ft. Collins, CO 80525-8411; (303) 482-5813 or (800) 237-7211, fax (303) 482-5815.

Shebby Lee Tours, Inc. P.O. Box 1032, Rapid City, 57709-1032; (605) 343-4852, fax 347-7558.

Stagecoach West Bus Service. P.O. Box 264, Rapid City, 57709-0264; (605) 343-3113, fax (605) 342-6990.

TP Consultants/Black Hills Sightseeing. P.O. Box 3709, Rapid City, 57709-3709; (605) 341-3436, fax (605) 341-1402.

■ BLACK HILLS CAVES

Some of the largest caves in the world have formed in the limestone formations beneath the Black Hills. Walking tours take visitors on less-strenuous routes, while spelunking tours put cavers on their bellies, pinching through the darkness. Although the pre-eminent caves—Wind and Jewel—have been explored in the book's text, private cave attractions are listed below.

Beautiful Rushmore Cave. Half-mile (.6 km) guided tour of limestone cavern featuring the largest number and variety of cave formations. Six miles (9.6 km) east of Keystone on S.D. 40. Open May through October. HCR 89, Box 123, Keystone, 57751; (605) 255-4467 or 4634, fax (605) 341-4614.

Black Hills Caverns. A variety of tour options. Museum features specimens of cave and geological formations. Four miles (6.4 km) west of Rapid City on S.D. 44. Open May to October. R.R. 8, Box 570, Rapid City, 57702; (605) 343-0542, fax (605) 342-8224.

Jewel Cave National Monument. R.R. 1, Box 60AA, Custer, 57730; (605) 673-2288.

Sitting Bull Crystal Caverns. Guided tours offered. S.D. 16. Open May to October. P.O. Box 1760, Rapid City, 57709-1760; (605) 342-2777, fax (605) 342-7305.

Stagebarn Crystal Cave. Guided tours available. 10 miles (16 km) north of Rapid City on I-90, Exit 48. Open May to Labor Day. HC80, Box 442, Piedmont, 57769; (605) 787-4505.Wind Cave National Park, R.R. 1, Box 190, Hot Springs, 57747; (605) 745-4600.

Wonderland Cave. Two-level living cavern 300 million years old. Open May 1 to Nov. 1. P.O. Box 83, Nemo, 57759-0083; (605) 578-1728, fax (605) 342-8984.

■ ARCHAEOLOGY AND PALEONTOLOGY

■ B A D L A N D S

Badlands National Park. Fossils 37 to 23 millions years old erode out of buttes and gullies while pronghorns, bison, and bighorn sheep drift across old homesteads and hunting grounds of the Sioux Indians. The park has marked trails and is open to hiking. Park rangers conduct interpretive programs and give special presentations in summer. Open year round, though hours vary. P.O. Box 6, Interior, 57750-0006; (605) 433-5361.

■ B L A C K   H I L L S

Mammoth Site. Huge Columbian and woolly mammoths came here to drink, but they got trapped in this prehistoric sinkhole and perished. This is where the big boys are buried. The fossils of more than 40 mammoths have been discovered so far, and digging continues. One block north of U.S. 18 Bypass, Hot Springs. Open year-round. P.O. Box 606, Hot Springs, 57747-0606; (605) 745-6016.

■ S O U T H E A S T

Prehistoric Indian Village, Museum & Site. Only National Historical Archaeology Landmark open to the public in South Dakota. Guided tours, artifacts, walk-through lodge reproduction, audio-visual show, walking tour stations, complete buffalo skeleton, gift shop. Indian Village Road, on the shores of Lake Mitchell. Memorial Day to Labor Day. Box 621, Mitchell, 57301-0621; (605) 996-5473.

■ MOUNTAIN BIKING

With more than 6,000 miles (9,660 km) of fire trails, logging roads, and abandoned railroad grades, the Black Hills region is the top spot for pleasure biking in South Dakota. Trails criss-cross the backcountry and provide exciting opportunities for mountain biking. In addition, many cities and parks throughout South Dakota have bike trails and paths, especially Sioux Falls and Rapid City.

Golden Circle Tours/Black Hills Mountain Bike Tours. Visit the backcountry of the Black Hills on a mountain bike tour or self-guided trip with current maps and trail descriptions. Open year-round. 40 N. Fifth St, Custer, 57730; (605) 673-4349; fax (605) 673-2141.

Natural History and Cultural Center. Unguided mountain bike rentals during spring, summer, and fall months in beautiful Spearfish Canyon, a National Scenic Byway. Open year-round. P.O. Box 798, Spearfish, 57783-0798; (605) 584-2207.

Trail Rides

■ TRAIL RIDES

Ballinger Ranch. P.O. Box 186, R.R. 1, Canton, 57013; (605) 987-2629 or (605) 338-6772.

Blue Bell Lodge and Resort. S.D. 87 South, Custer State Park. HC 83, Box 63, Custer, 57730; (605) 255-4531, fax (605) 255-4706.

Canyon Ranch. Near Veblen. R.R. 1, Box 86, Veblen, 57270; (605) 738-2480.

Dakota Badland Outfitters. P.O. Box 85, Custer, 57730-0085; (605) 673-5363.

Deadwood Stables. At Deadwood Gulch Resort; U.S. 85 South, Deadwood, 57732; (605) 578-2523.

Gunsel Horse Adventures. P.O. Box 1575, Rapid City, 57709-1575; (605) 343-7608, fax (605) 642-8443.

Hart Ranch Arena and Trailrides. Upper Spring Creek Rd., Rapid City, 57709. P.O. Box 6500, Rapid City, 57709-6500; (605) 341-5702 or (800) 782-2267, fax (605) 341-1671.

Millers JR Bar Ranch Trail Rides. At "The Fort" 3 miles (5 km) north of Custer on U.S. 385. HCR 83, Box 97, Custer, 57730; (605) 673-2199 or 673-2772.

Nemo Guest Ranch. Nemo Rd., 16 miles (26 km) northwest of Rapid City. P.O. Box 77, Nemo, 57759-0077; (605) 578-2708, fax (605) 343-1916.

Smitty's Trail Rides, Inc. Palmer Gulch, 5 miles (8 km) west of Mount Rushmore on S.D. 244. P.O. Box 295, Hill City, 57745-0295; (605) 574-2525 or (800) 233-4331, fax (605) 574-2574.

■ WATER SPORTS OUTFITTERS

Far West River Boat. Riverside Park, Yankton. P.O. Box 22, Yankton, 57078-0022; (605) 665-9760.

Missouri River Outfitters, Inc. 124 Court St., Vermillion, 57069; (605) 624-4823.

Oahe Windsurfing. 1909 Kennedy Dr., off U.S. 12 west of Mobridge, P.O. Box 310, Mobridge, 57601; (605) 845-7921.

Pactola Pines Marina. Box 3125, Keystone Rt., Rapid City, 57701; (605) 343-4283.

Sea Gull's Sailboards. R.R. 3, Box 209, Brookings, 57006; (605) 693-4441.

■ ROCK CLIMBING

Reach for the Sky Mountaineering. P.O. Box 655, Rapid City, 57709-0655; (605) 343-2344.

Sylvan Rocks Climbing Lessons & Adventures. *Two locations:*

Sylvan Lake, Custer State Park. P.O. Box 725, Custer, 57730-0725

Box 600, Hill City, 57745; (605) 574-2425, fax (605) 342-1487 c/o Sylvan Rocks.

■ NATIONAL FORESTS, PARKS, GRASSLANDS, MONUMENTS, AND MEMORIALS

Badlands National Park. P.O. Box 6, Interior, 57750; (605) 433-5361.

Black Hills National Forest. R.R. 2, Box 200, Custer, 57730; (605) 673-2251.

Buffalo Gap National Grassland. P.O. Box 425, Wall, 57790-0425; (605) 279-2125.

Custer National Forest. P.O. Box 2556, Billings, MT 59103; (406) 657-6361.

Fort Pierre National Grassland. P.O. Box 417, Pierre, 57501-0417; (605) 224-5517.

Grand River National Grassland. P.O. Box 390, Lemmon, 57638-0390; (605) 347-3592.

Jewel Cave National Monument. R.R. 1, Box 60AA, Custer, 57730; (605) 673-2288.

Mount Rushmore National Memorial. P.O. Box 268, Keystone, 57751; (605) 574-2523.

Wind Cave National Park. R.R. 1, Box 190, Hot Springs, 57747; (605) 745-4600.

■ IMPORTANT ADDRESSES

■ STATE AGENCIES

Department of Game, Fish and Parks. 523 E. Capitol Ave., Pierre, 57501-3182; Hunting & Fishing (605) 773-3485, Parks (605) 773-3391.

Department of Transportation. 700 E. Broadway Ave., Pierre, 57501-2586; (605) 773-3265.

Governor's Office of Economic Development. 711 E. Wells Ave., Pierre, 57501-3369; (605) 773-5032.

Office of Indian Affairs. 118 W. Capitol Ave., Pierre, 57501-2017; (605) 773-3415.

State Historical Society. 900 Governors Dr., Pierre, 57501-2217; (605) 773-3458.

South Dakota Arts Council. 230 S. Phillips Ave., Suite 204, Sioux Falls, 57102; (605) 339-6646.

South Dakota Tourism. 711 E. Wells Ave., Pierre, 57501-3369; (605) 773-3301, fax (605) 773-3256.

■ REGIONAL TOURISM

Black Hills, Badlands & Lakes Association. 900 Jackson Blvd., Rapid City, 57702-2583; (605) 341-1462.

Dakota Heritage & Lakes Association. 618 E. 41st St., Sioux Falls, 57101-6028; (605) 336-2602.

Glacial Lakes & Prairies Tourism Association. P.O. Box 244, U.S. 212 West and Third St. SW, Watertown, 57201-0244; (605) 886-7305.

Great Lakes of South Dakota Association. P.O. Box 786, 121 Grand Ave., Pierre, 57501-0786; (605) 224-4617.

National Forests/Important Addresses

RECOMMENDED READING

■ HISTORY

Ballantine, Betty and Ian, eds. *The Native Americans: An Illustrated History.* Atlanta: Turner Publishing, 1993. A large-format, highly illustrated history of America's indigenous peoples. Beautiful archival photographs and paintings.

Crow Dog, Mary, with Richard Erdoes. *Lakota Woman.* New York: Grove Weidenfeld, 1990. An irreverent, lively account of the American Indian Movement in the 1970's as told by a feisty Sioux resident of the Rosebud Reservation.

Frazier, Ian. *Great Plains.* New York: Penguin, 1989. A journey through the Great Plains with accounts of the famous (and infamous) folks who've visited there.

Huseboe, Arthur R. *An Illustrated History of South Dakota.* Sioux Falls: Center for Western Studies, 1991. Nearly 400 pages of highly illustrated text, with coverage of Hamlin Garland, Oscar Howe, Laura Ingalls Wilder, Gutyon Borglum, and, yes, Lawrence Welk.

Hunt, N. Jane. *South Dakota Historical Markers.* Sioux Falls: Brevet Press, 1974. Everything you wanted to know about roadside stops but were afraid to ask.

Lazarus, Edward. *Black Hills, White Justice.* New York: HarperCollins, 1991. A history of the Sioux Nation from 1775 to the present, focusing on its interactions and conflicts with the United States.

Lewis and Clark. *Original Journals of the Lewis and Clark Expedition.* New York: Arno Press, 1969. The Corps of Discovery in the explorers' own words.

Mandat-Grancey, Edmond Baron de. *Cow-boys and Colonels.* Lincoln: University of Nebraska Press, 1984. First published in London, 1887. Entertaining diary of a nineteenth-century French aristocrat's travels through Dakota territory, with hilarious descriptions of the miners and cowboys he meets along the way.

Milton, John. *South Dakota.* Nashville: Norton & Co. Inc., 1977. A historian retraces the state's past.

Petsch & McGregor. *South Dakota's Rock History.* Vermillion, South Dakota: Science Center University. The geology of the state.

Progulske, Donald. *Yellow Ore, Yellow Hair, Yellow Pine.* Brookings, South Dakota: South Dakota State University, Bulletin No. 616, July 1974. The impact of gold and the Custer Expedition on settlement of the Black Hills.

Sandoz, Mari. *Crazy Horse: The Strange Man of the Oglalas.* Lincoln: University of Nebraska Press, 1961. A vivid portrayal of one of the legendary Sioux leaders.

Smith, Rex Alan. *The Carving of Mount Rushmore.* New York: Abbeville Press, 1985. Definitive history of the carving of the world's largest work of art. *Moon of Popping Trees.* New York: Abbeville Press, 1975. The plight of the Sioux tribes leading up to the tragedy at Wounded Knee and the hardships that followed.

Tallent, Annie. *The Black Hills or the Last Hunting Grounds of the Dakotahs.* Sioux Falls: Brevet Press, 1974. The first white woman to settle in the Black Hills revisits the early days and the search for gold.

■ LITERATURE

Brown, Dee. *Bury My Heart at Wounded Knee.* New York: Holt, Rinehart, Winston, 1970. The story of the last massacre of Native Americans.

Cecil, Chuck. *Stubble Mulch.* Flandreau, South Dakota: Prairie Publications Inc., 1992. Humorous essays that set South Dakota apart from the nation.

Clark, Badger. *Sun and Saddle Leather.* Boston: The Gorham Press, 1915. South Dakota's poet laureate writes of pines and prairies and the settler's way of life.

Dexter, Pete. *Deadwood.* New York: Random House, 1986. A look at the colorful characters and wild and woolly past of a Black Hills gold mining town.

Enright, Gary. *The Last Wolf: The Legend of Three Toes.* Parker, CO: Insight Publishing, 1992. The story of the killer wolf who plagued northwestern South Dakota—as told from the perspective of the wolf.

Erdoes, Richard. *Tales from the American Frontier.* New York: Pantheon, 1991. Legends and sagas of the American West, of settlers, trappers, Indian warriors, and outlaws.

Erdoes, Richard, and Alfonso Ortiz, eds. *American Indian Myths and Legends.* New York: Pantheon, 1984. A master storyteller and an eminent anthropologist's collection of 160 American Indian myths from 80 tribal groups.

Garland, Hamlin. *A Son of the Middle Border.* Lincoln: University of Nebraska Press, 1979. Frontier and pioneer life from a Pulitzer Prize winner.

Kohl, Edith Eudora. *Land of the Burnt Thigh.* St. Paul: Minnesota Historical Society Press, 1986. Two sisters battle the elements to "prove up" their South Dakota homestead.

Mills, Billy. *Wokini.* New York: Crown, 1994. A self-help guide written within the context of traditional Plains Indian mythology. The Sioux author is an Olympic gold medalist.

Neihardt, John. *The Song of Hugh Glass.* New York: MacMillan, 1915. An incredible tale of courage and tragedy told in prose.

Neihardt, John. *Black Elk Speaks.* New York: Pocket Books, 1959. The powerful recollections of a Lakota holy man.

Neuharth, Allen H. *Confessions of an S.O.B.* New York: Doubleday, 1989. After picking up cowpies on the Dakota plains, this multi-millionaire headed one of the largest media chains in the world.

Rölvaag, Ole Edvart. *Giants in the Earth.* New York: Harper & Row, 1929. A nineteenth-century immigrant family strives to eke out a living on the prairie.

Wilder, Laura Ingalls. *Little House on the Prairie* series, including *Little Town on the Prairie, On the Shores of Silver Lake, The First Four Years.* New York: Harper & Row, 1971. A young girl recounts growing up on the prairie.

■ GUIDES

Eagle/Walking Turtle. *Indian America.* Santa Fe: John Muir Publications, 1993. A comprehensive guide to the calendar of events and addresses of Indian reservations in the United States. Brief histories of the major tribes.

Pettingill & Whitney. *Birds of the Black Hills.* Ithaca, New York: Cornell Laboratory of Ornithology, 1965. A guide to winged species in western South Dakota.

Smithsonian Guide to Historic America: The Plains States. New York: Stewart, Tabori & Chang, 1990. Guide to the historic sites of the Great Plains states with photographs of significant landmarks.

I N D E X

COMPASS
AMERICAN
GUIDES

Available at your local bookstore, or call (800) 733-3000 to order.

COMPASS AMERICAN GUIDES are available at special discounts for bulk purchases for sales promotions or premiums. Special editions, including personalized covers and corporate imprints, can be created in large quantities for special needs. For more information, call Special Markets at Fodor's Travel Publications, (800) 800-3246.

Arizona (4th Edition)
0-679-03388-2
$18.95 ($26.50 Can)

Chicago (2nd Edition)
1-878-86780-6
$18.95 ($26.50 Can)

Colorado (3rd Edition)
1-878-86781-4
$18.95 ($26.50 Can)

Hawaii (3rd Edition)
1-878-86791-1
$18.95 ($26.50 Can)

Wine Country (1st Edition)
1-878-86784-9
$18.95 ($26.50 Can)

Montana (3rd Edition)
1-878-86797-0
$18.95 ($26.50 Can)

Oregon (2nd Edition)
1-878-86788-1
$18.95 ($26.50 Can)

New Orleans (3rd Edition)
0-679-03597-4
$18.95 ($26.50 Can)

South Dakota (2nd Edition)
1-878-86747-4
$18.95 ($26,50 Can)

Southwest (2nd Edition)
0-679-00035-6
$18.95 ($26.50 Can)

Texas (2nd Edition)
1-878-86798-9
$18.95 ($26.50 Can)

Utah (4th Edition)
0-679-00030-5
$18.95 ($26.50 Can)

Boston (1st Edition)
1-878-86776-8
$18.95 ($26.50 Can)

Pacific Northwest (1st Edition)
1-878-86785-7
$19.95 ($27.95 Can)

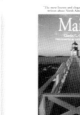

Alaska (1st Edition)
1-878-86777-6
$18.95 ($26.50 Can)

Minnesota (1st Edition)
1-878-86748-2
$18.95 ($26.50 Can)

Idaho (1st Edition)
1-878-86778-4
$18.95 ($26.50 Can)

New Mexico (2nd Edition)
1-878-86783-0
$18.95 ($26.50 Can)

Maine (2nd Edition)
1-878-86796-2
$18.95 ($26.50 Can)

Manhattan (2nd Edition)
1-878-86794-6
$18.95 ($26.50 Can)

Las Vegas (5th Edition)
0-679-00015-1
$18.95 ($26.50 Can)

San Francisco (4th Edition)
1-878-86792-X
$18.95 ($26.50 Can)

Santa Fe (2nd Edition)
0-679-03389-0
$18.95 ($26.50 Can)

South Carolina (2nd Edition)
0-679-03599-0
$18.95 ($26.50 Can)

Virginia (2nd Edition)
1-878-86795-4
$18.95 ($26.50 Can)

Washington (1st Edition)
1-878-86758-X
$17.95 ($25.00 Can)

Wisconsin (2nd Edition)
1-878-86749-0
$18.95 ($26.50 Can)

Wyoming (3rd Edition)
0-679-00034-8
$18.95 ($26.50 Can)

■ ABOUT THE AUTHOR

A fourth-generation South Dakotan, Tom Griffith brings to this guide a native's first-hand perspective of the state. An award-winning journalist and photographer, Griffith attended the University of London and graduated from the University of Wisconsin before pursuing a career in the newspaper business that took him to Montana and Arizona. He is former Director of Communications for the Mount Rushmore Preservation Fund and is author of three books about the memorial: *America's Shrine of Democracy*, *The Four Faces of Freedom*, and *A Sculptor's Son*, as well as dozens of history- and travel-related magazine articles. Griffith runs his own Rapid City–based advertising, marketing and public relations firm. When he's not reading or writing, Griffith enjoys mountain biking and hiking in the Black Hills and teaching his two children the intricacies of trout fishing.

■ ABOUT THE PHOTOGRAPHER

Paul Horsted's roots in South Dakota began in the late 1800s, when his great grandparents homesteaded in the east-central part of the state. Horsted worked for three years as chief photographer for the state tourism department in Pierre, logging thousands of miles to cover events, people, and places all over South Dakota. His photographs have appeared in several books about Mount Rushmore, the Black Hills, and the Badlands, as well as in magazines such as *LIFE*, *Travel-Holiday*, and National Geographic publications. When not traveling, he and his wife reside in Custer, South Dakota.